I0564866

The Vibrant Table

The Vibrant Table

RECIPES FROM MY ALWAYS VEGETARIAN, MOSTLY VEGAN, AND SOMETIMES RAW KITCHEN

ANYA KASSOFF

with photographs by Masha Davydova

ROOST BOOKS

Boston & London

2014

Roost Books
An imprint of Shambhala Publications, Inc.
Horticultural Hall
300 Massachusetts Avenue
Boston, Massachusetts 02115
roostbooks.com

9 8 7 6 5 4 3 2

Printed in United States of America

⊗ This edition is printed on acid-free paper that meets the American National Standards Institute Z39.48 Standard.
♻ Shambhala Publications makes every effort to print on recycled paper. For more information please visit www.shambhala.com.

Distributed in the United States by Penguin Random House LLC and in Canada by Random House of Canada Ltd

Designed by Katrina Noble

Library of Congress Cataloging-in-Publication Data

Kassoff, Anya.
The vibrant table: recipes from my always vegetarian, mostly vegan, and sometimes raw kitchen/Anya Kassoff, with photographs by Masha Davydova.—First edition.
Pages cm
Includes index.
ISBN 978-1-61180-097-5 (hardcover: alk. paper)
1. Vegan cooking. 2. Vegetarian cooking. 3. Natural foods. 4. Food habits—Russia (Federation)—Anecdotes. I. Title. II. Title: Recipes from my always vegetarian, mostly vegan, and sometimes raw kitchen.
TX837.K257 2014
641.5'636—dc23
2013020556

To the memory of my father Nikolai, whose endless talents still inspire me and give me strength; and to my maternal grandmother, Nina, who taught me so much of what makes me who I am today.

CONTENTS

RECIPE LIST

Basic Recipes and Techniques

1: Breakfast & Snacks

2: Savories

SALADS AND SIDES

SOUPS

MAINS

3: Teatime & Sweets

4: Playtime

INTRODUCTION

As far back as I can remember, my dreams were about food. Don't get me wrong, I was never exactly starving. True, I had a hunger, but not just for any meal to simply feed my belly. My hunger was for color and variety served right in the middle of my dinner plate—a trying urge while growing up in a Soviet state of culinary blandness. As a child, my most persistent and vivid dream was of huckleberry ice cream. I don't remember having ever tried a huckleberry. Yet night after night, before falling asleep, I imagined how the black of a huckleberry would blend with milky white ice cream to make the most otherworldly purple swirls.

I was raised in the Northern Caucasus, a region of Russia (back then, the USSR) cradled between the Black and Caspian seas, where the steppe slowly transitions into mountains. My mother says she surely spent half of her life waiting in lines, to buy one thing or another to feed the family. I do not have her impressive waiting record, as the food deficit slowly dwindled during my youth, though I still remember how standing in winding, bustling queues went hand in hand with buying almost anything during my childhood and into early adulthood. It seemed almost natural; most of the time there was no way around it. I remember the butter line particularly well; it always stretched the longest and buzzed the loudest, around a couple of blocks, to make for a full-day affair. We felt a sense of accomplishment when we walked away after finally procuring a few paper-wrapped bricks of butter, like victory after a long, tiring battle, with the promise of a flavorful dinner ahead. If nothing else, all that waiting brought up a few generations of truly patient people.

Looking back, I realize that as many great pleasures as the Iron Curtain blocked us from (think denim, Western music, chewing gum), it also managed to shelter us from some of the flaws of the advanced world. For one, we had no knowledge of TV dinners or fast food. The kind of farm-to-table movement that is slowly taking over in the United States was our way of life—the only difference being that it was not by choice. Import was virtually nonexistent; therefore all the available produce was local and seasonal. Granted, I tasted my first banana at the age of sixteen, but we were lucky to eat only the freshest fruits and vegetables, many of which we grew ourselves. Resourcefulness was the key to survival, and to this day remains one of the essential traits of the Russian people. The majority of our summer crop was canned and preserved for the winter, and I don't remember a single family that didn't prepare this way for the off-season. Finding a fresh tomato in January was unheard of, but a can of plump and juicy preserved summer tomatoes was only as far away as the cellar. Our meals lacked variety, especially during the harsh winters, but necessity truly is the mother of invention, and it is those simple meals I remember most fondly.

Growing up, I was surrounded by home cooks of all sorts. Eating out was rarely an option, and every Soviet woman had to cook all her family's meals every day. My mother was different, though; she not only cooked but created in the kitchen. Never mind limitations—she found ways to overcome them with cooking that was innovative for her time. I hardly realized that as a child, spoiled by the fact that her dishes were always the tastiest and most beautiful ones. Our home was always lively with visitors, and the whole party often ended up around the kitchen table, where much laughter and conversation happened over her delicacies. My mother was born at the beginning of World War II, and her whole generation suffered severe hardship and hunger. Reflecting on it now, it makes sense that she wanted to feed us in the most gourmet way possible. It was her compensation for years of near starvation.

My mother was also very protective of her cooking world and seldom let me intrude. By the time I moved out, I could hardly peel a potato. But when I got married and became the owner of my first kitchen, she gave me the most priceless gift of all: a thick notebook full of her handwritten recipes, which would become my bible for years to come. The kitchen soon became my favorite place. I grew just as adventurous with my cooking and even prepared dishes my mother hadn't tried or conquered. Of course, a lot of those experiments ended up in the trash during the first year or two. Soon enough, I became the one whose kitchen was the most frequented by friends, just as my mother's had been.

While spending night after night cooking, I managed to get two degrees, one in engineering back in Russia and another in dentistry in the United States. Both unrelated to food or even to each other, those occupations did not keep my interest for very long. I always found myself back in the kitchen, finding comfort in chopping, sautéing, and baking. Many friends read into this passion of mine much deeper than I did, encouraging me to pursue a career in food, but for many years I was convinced that cooking should stay a hobby. It took some time for me to realize that doing what I love most is where I should be putting all of my best energy.

As for my dream, I finally had the chance to try huckleberry ice cream many years later, on my first trip to Utah. It was as magical as I had imagined, proof that dreams sometimes do come true.

Becoming Health Conscious

I come from a culture where meat is eaten for breakfast, lunch, and dinner, and a meal is not a real meal without some kind of meat. Vegetarians are seen as alien creatures and vegetarianism as a sort of illness that one will eventually overcome. After my move to the United States, I was awed by the overwhelming variety of produce available year-round. Being naturally curious about new ingredients, I began exploring vegetarian cooking and found that a dish without meat could be just as satisfying and more interesting than meat-centered dishes in many ways. Though I could live without labels like *vegetarian, vegan,* and *raw,* I like to embrace those culinary challenges, especially since they are better for the health of my family and the planet.

Raw food holds a special place in my heart. It helped me heal after I had unexpected health issues after the birth of my second daughter, Paloma. My older daughter, Masha, encouraged me to start a food blog for documenting

my raw food escapades. *Golubka*, the blog, quickly developed into a passion, with a wonderful worldwide readership that grows every day. Masha and I work as a photographer-cook team; she generally takes care of the visuals while I come up with recipes, although the roles are sometimes interchangeable. The blog has evolved as my food interests have changed—I've shifted my focus from sharing all-raw recipes to recipes that utilize the most nourishing ingredients in the tastiest ways possible, raw or not. I still like to incorporate the techniques and ideas of raw cuisine into our everyday meals, without feeling confined or making too many rules.

Some recipes in this book provide instructions for both raw and cooked preparation of a dish. Depending on what you feel like and how much time you have, you will have a choice in the matter.

All the recipes in this book are representative of my approach to my family's diet. I've always believed that taste develops in early childhood, and

that our children will grow to like most of the foods we offer them, as long as the introduction happens from the very beginning. I will never forget the gratitude with which Paloma slurped down her first green smoothie, even though the dandelion greens I used made it impossibly bitter. For three and a half years now, she drinks several glasses of this green goodness daily. I hope to raise her to have a healthy relationship with eating and appreciation for natural, wholesome ingredients. I'm grateful for my husband, Ernie, who is open-minded about food and fully supports my efforts, embracing a healthier way of eating just as he once liked to embrace a Philly cheesesteak.

When it comes to ingredients, I honor their taste and freshness by cooking according to season. I always try to choose the most nourishing ingredients possible, but flavor remains a priority. It is important to me that desserts are not too sweet and savories are not too salty but rather full of flavor. I take care not to overcook ingredients, letting the cooking process enhance rather than conceal flavor. For me, a feeling of lightness after a meal is important—I consider it part of the experience.

My Russian background influences my desire to make everything from scratch and my craving for unprocessed ingredients. I am always looking for novelty in the kitchen, seeking out new ingredients, and taking inspiration from traveling. We live on the Gulf Coast of central Florida now, and our growing season is in the winter. We enjoy fresh strawberries from the farmers' market when snow covers the ground up north. During the summer, we like to travel away from the stifling heat and find inspiration from beautiful summer markets around the world.

With a few exceptions, the recipes in this book are vegan and gluten-free, as a creative challenge to myself and to appeal to a wider audience. No one in my family has been diagnosed with gluten intolerance, but I have noticed I feel my best when I avoid wheat products. I find myself preferring the taste of egg- and dairy-free crusts and cremes to those containing animal products. Creating vegan recipes is as much a culinary choice as it is a choice for health.

Mostly I love the process of cooking and never look at it as a chore. There are few things in life that I would rather be doing than preparing wholesome meals and feeding people. Some of these recipes are simple, and some take a little more time, but all of them take love, and I hope that it shows.

How to Use This Book

There are a few things you should consider when cooking from this book. The most essential one is to use the freshest seasonal fruit and vegetables. The quality of your produce can make or break a recipe when it comes to this type of unencumbered cooking, where the fruit and vegetables are the focus and should be at their most flavorful state. There is a world of difference between a sweet, ruby red summer strawberry and the tasteless, greenhouse-grown berries in supermarkets during the winter. The integrity of other elements is important to the taste of these dishes as well, especially when it comes to the freshness of nuts, spices, sweeteners, and cocoa products, the quality of cheese, and the origin of eggs.

Some of the ingredients in these recipes might be new to you, but they are not meant to be intimidating. Stocking a whole-food pantry takes time—I built up an extensive collection of ingredients gradually, over a few years. All my friends know I would rather be gifted a pouch of saffron or a fancy salt than just about anything else. I include lesser known ingredients because I want them to become well-known and beneficial to more people. If you are new to vegan and gluten-free cooking, especially baking, you might notice a longer list of ingredients than you are used to. In gluten-free baking, it is essential to blend a variety of flours to develop the best taste and texture. Once your pantry is stocked and your kitchen has adapted, I promise that working with these ingredients will become second nature.

Some recipes call for salt and black pepper *to taste*. In my opinion, this kind of seasoning is often too personal of a preference to list an exact amount. It is all up to your palate and what you are accustomed to. I like to moderately salt my food with good sea salt, while my husband likes his meals barely salted, using lots of freshly ground black pepper instead. I leave these decisions up to you where appropriate.

Sweetness is another matter of preference. In our family, we tend to like our desserts modestly sweetened and prefer subtly flavored sweeteners. To me, even the best of desserts can be ruined with too much sugar. As much as I've tried to work it out somewhere in the middle, incorporating feedback from our many recipe testers, the recipes are still sweetened to my general taste. I invite you to be flexible, taste as you go, and adjust accordingly. In many recipes, the type of sweetener recommended greatly contributes to the flavor of the dish, so substitute with caution.

Keep in mind that the fresh herbs, spices, and citrus are the epicenters of flavor for many dishes in this book. Take them away and the dish may lose its zest and unique flavor. If you don't like tarragon, for instance, you may want to substitute another aromatic and distinctive herb in the Tarragon Millet and Pear Stuffed Squash (page 150) instead of just leaving it out. If cardamom is not what you crave, you may want to move on from the Citrus Broccolini with Cardamom Tofu (page 158). Be open-minded: you may like the taste of a specific herb or spice when cooking with it from scratch much more than you remember it from a previous dish. This has happened to me a few times with many of the spices I now use all the time.

I have yet to find the perfect cookbook, in which every single recipe turns out exactly to my liking and looks just like the beautiful photo in the book. There are many variables in home cooking, and the end result will differ from kitchen to kitchen (and cook to cook). No two mangoes are exactly alike, even from the same tree, not to mention the difference between species, regions, seasons, and weather conditions. Kale from California tastes different from kale grown in Florida; arugula is not nearly as spicy in Italy as it is in the United States; figs are much sweeter where the sun shines brighter, and so on. When comparing ingredients from different continents, we'll inevitably discover oceans of differences. It took me ages to adjust to the food in the United States when I moved here from Russia. I had to reconsider and readjust many of the flavors, textures, and cooking times I knew from previous experiences. Even on a local scale, different brands of flour can change the outcome of and require a correction to a recipe that was tested many times before. Same goes for equipment; not all ovens are created equal and every pan sizzles differently.

I've tried my best to make the recipes flexible and forgiving. If you see that your gluten-free dough is too dry or wet, add more liquid or flour until it feels right, and most likely the recipe will turn out just fine. If you know there is no way your oven will cook the winter squash in the twenty minutes indicated in the recipe, adjust the cooking time accordingly. Trust your intuition and experience, adjust, experiment and substitute, and let our recipes stir up your own new ideas. I hope this book will inspire you to feel open-minded and free in your kitchen.

My Ingredients

PRODUCE

Fresh fruit and vegetables occupy most of the space in my shopping bags. The produce section of our local health food stores and greenmarket is where I spend most of my time when I shop. It is important to me to use seasonal, organic, and/or local produce whenever possible. Putting all other reasons aside, seasonal and organic fruit and vegetables simply taste so much better than those grown with pesticides. I often hear the opinion that organic doesn't make a difference in flavor, but my taste buds tell me otherwise. Organic and local produce stays fresh longer. And last, I try not to invest in nonorganic farming practices for the obvious health and ecological reasons.

HERBS AND SPICES

I deliberately place herbs and spices second in this list, as they are an essential part in my cooking. I don't use artificial flavorings, cream, or butter, and cheese and eggs come into play once in a blue moon, so it is up to fresh herbs

and spices to develop flavor in my dishes. Many are extremely nutritious and even therapeutic. Growing herbs yourself saves money while providing you with the freshest taste. I have a small herb garden on my balcony. As for the spices, most often I prefer to buy them in the bulk section, whole and in small quantities, grinding them by hand just before they go into a dish.

Everyday Herbs

Cilantro (coriander)

Parsley

Basil

Dill

Other Herbs

Thyme

Mint

Tarragon

Lemongrass

Oregano

Lemon verbena

Lemon balm

Everyday Spices

Black peppercorns

Ginger (fresh or ground)

Cumin

Coriander

Cardamom

Cinnamon

Nutmeg

Turmeric

Red chile flakes and chili powder

Vanilla beans

Other Spices

Pink peppercorns

Paprika

Garam masala

Mustard seeds

Fenugreek seeds

Curry blends

Cloves

Allspice

FLOURS

With the exception of spelt flour, all flours that I use in this book are gluten-free and all are organic.

Brown rice flour may be the most versatile gluten-free flour because of its mild taste. It has a grainier texture than wheat flour and is best used in combination with other flours. If you can find superfine brown rice flour, it will offer a much smoother texture. Because superfine brown rice flour is not the easiest to find and more expensive, all my recipes use regular brown rice flour.

Similar to brown rice flour in texture, **white rice flour** can be used in place of brown rice flour for a lighter-color finished product.

Buckwheat flour is my favorite flour to work with. It has a smooth texture and a slightly nutty, mild flavor, plus a high nutritional value. Buckwheat is not a true grain, but the seed of a plant related to rhubarb. I love it in most baked goods, from crepes to cakes, and even pasta. It is commonly combined with chocolate. Keep in mind that if you grind your own buckwheat flour at home like I do (see page 11), it yields a much more neutral, lighter-colored flour than the darker, more rustic store-bought variety.

Almond flour is a versatile and mild-tasting flour produced by grinding raw, blanched almonds. It works great in cookies, cakes, and other baked goods, as it is naturally moist and contains healthy monounsaturated fats and protein. I sometimes use it interchangeably with **almond meal,** which is simply almond flour made from unblanched almonds. You can make almond meal at home by soaking almonds overnight, rinsing them well, drying them completely, and grinding them into flour in a food processor (see page 11). You can skip soaking and drying and grind the raw almonds as you buy them. If you decide to make your own almond flour or meal, grind the almonds in small quantities and watch the process carefully, making sure the almonds don't turn into butter.

Quinoa flour has a distinct taste, and I mostly use it in small amounts mixed with other flours.

Quinoa flakes are not exactly flour, but I enjoy mixing them with other flours in many recipes, especially for muffins and pancake batter. They are made by steamrolling quinoa, just like how rolled oats are produced from steamrolled oat groats. The flakes add lightness and absorb liquids very well.

Oat flour is one of my favorite flours, with a very mild and pleasant taste. Although naturally gluten-free, the majority of oats grown in the United States are cross-contaminated with gluten. Look for oats labeled gluten-free if you are sensitive to gluten. To make oat flour, grind rolled oats using a high-speed blender or food processor. You can also make it by grinding oat groats, but only if you use a high-speed blender that can break them down.

Coconut flour is great for adding flavor to baked goods and for its ability to absorb water and thicken batter, which is valuable in gluten-free and vegan baking. It is also high in protein and fiber and adds tenderness to the resulting dough.

Tapioca flour (or tapioca starch) is a thickener that helps with the binding of ingredients, especially in tart crusts.

Millet flour is a bright yellow flour that is nutritious and easy to digest.

Hazelnut flour is a sweet and nutty-tasting flour made from finely ground hazelnuts. Most of the time I make it myself by grinding hazelnuts in a food processor.

Amaranth flour is another pseudo-grain flour that is high in many minerals and vitamins, protein, and fiber. It is known for its distinct, nutty, malt flavor. I like to mix it with other gluten-free flours. It is an especially good substitute for quinoa flour and vice versa.

Arrowroot powder is natural starch with a neutral taste, used as a thickener.

SPROUTED FLOURS

Although it is not necessary to use sprouted flours for the recipes in this book, I recommend using them whenever you can. I've made a habit of first soaking and then sprouting (see page 36) most of the grains I bring home. Once sprouted or even just soaked in purified water overnight, grains become much more nutritious and easier to digest. The sprouting process produces vitamin C and a number of enzymes and increases vitamins B_2, B_5, and B_6 and the carotene content. The protective outer coating of grains and nuts has inhibitors that prevent the absorption of many nutrients by our bodies. During the soaking stage, those inhibitors are neutralized as they are shed in the water. Another amazing fact is that our bodies recognize and digest sprouted grains as vegetables and no longer as starch.

Once grains are soaked, germinated, or sprouted (depending on the grain), I dry them in the dehydrator. After that, it takes seconds for my high-speed blender to grind them into a fine flour.

I usually have sprouted or germinated buckwheat, quinoa, oat, amaranth, and millet flours in tightly covered jars in my refrigerator. This approach to flours not only assures their absolute freshness but also contributes to significant money savings. You don't need to buy a whole bag of a special flour when you only need ¼ cup of it for a new recipe. Instead, you can grind just the needed amount of inexpensive bulk grains as you go.

If you don't have a dehydrator, you can simply spread your sprouted, germinated, or soaked grains on several layers of paper towels or clean kitchen towels and air-dry them before grinding them in a high-speed blender, coffee grinder, or mill. You can also buy sprouted flours online (see Resources) or in some health food stores.

Sprouted or whole spelt flour is the only gluten-containing flour that I use. It has a texture similar to whole wheat flour and a nutty, slightly sweet flavor. Its gluten breaks down and digests easier than the gluten in regular wheat. Some people with gluten sensitivity are able to tolerate spelt, especially sprouted spelt, as sprouting greatly reduces the gluten content.

NUTS AND SEEDS

I always keep a few bags of assorted nuts on hand, using them for a quick nut milk, butter, or cream, or chopped in baked goods or salads. The nuts I use most often are almonds, walnuts, pecans, pistachios, hazelnuts, Brazil nuts, and cashews. Pumpkin, sunflower, and sesame seeds also play a big part in my cooking.

As with grains, I soak and dehydrate most nuts and seeds prior to using them, to neutralize the enzyme inhibitors that prevent nutrients from being absorbed. The exceptions are hazelnuts and Brazil nuts, as they don't contain enzyme inhibitors. I also don't soak pistachio and macadamia nuts because of a personal taste preference. I like to keep my nuts refrigerated for freshness.

Chia seeds, some of my best friends in the kitchen, are an increasingly popular superfood with unique health benefits. Along with flaxseeds, they are widely used in vegan baking to replace eggs. Chia seeds turn into a gel when mixed with liquids, becoming a great binder and thickener. I love them not only for their thickening ability but also for their neutral taste and versatility. I prefer chia seeds over flaxseeds, as they do not interfere with the taste of other ingredients. Chia seeds have an impressive nutritional record and the optimum omega-3 to omega-6 ratio. At our house, we go through bags of chia quickly, using the seeds to make chia pudding (page 67), fruit mousses (page 267), smoothies, and baked goods. I like using them whole or grinding them into a meal in a coffee grinder or a high-speed blender (1 cup of chia seeds = $1\frac{1}{3}$ cups chia meal). Chia meal is also available in health food stores. Unlike most nuts and seeds, chia seeds stay stable and store very well at room temperature without becoming rancid.

With a few exceptions (like the Key Lime Pie Breakfast Parfait on page 67 and Peach and Raspberry Tartlets on page 267), you can substitute flaxseeds for chia if you prefer.

GRAINS AND LEGUMES

Quinoa is quick and easy to cook, and great in salads and on its own. I like to mix three types of quinoa—black, red, and white—for a nice presentation and a more interesting taste. For a simple meal, serve it warm with ghee or olive oil, mixed with a handful of chopped fresh salad greens or herbs.

Quinoa is also very easy to sprout (see page 37), after which it becomes even more nutritious and great for salads, stuffings, and so on.

Heirloom forbidden black rice used to be the grain of Chinese emperors, and it may be my favorite type of rice. It's delicious in salads, side dishes, or on its own. Forbidden rice turns purple when cooked and has a very high nutritional content, including important amino acids, minerals, and vitamins.

Buckwheat is the grain of my childhood; I grew up eating buckwheat porridge on a near daily basis and love its nutty, comforting taste. Buckwheat is also great for cereals and raw buckwheat crispies (page 34). Use toasted (not raw) buckwheat for making porridge.

Rolled oats are incredibly versatile and useful in everything from savory crusts to desserts. Look for gluten-free rolled oats if you are gluten sensitive.

Amaranth is not a true grain but the seed of a plant, just like buckwheat, millet, and quinoa. It makes a very light and nutritious porridge, and has a nice texture with a little crunch, similar to biting into a poppy seed.

Millet is a nutritious ancient seed, originally cultivated in Africa and China. It is highly alkaline, which makes it easy to digest and soothing to the stomach. Millet combines well with vegetables and makes for great stuffing.

Beans and legumes are essentials of vegetarian cooking and very versatile. I keep a supply of all kinds of dried and canned beans and legumes in my pantry for all occasions. As you will see throughout the book, I don't use beans only in savory dishes; I also like to include them in nourishing desserts for children.

SALT

I like to experiment with different salts for seasoning. Some of my favorite fancy salts include pink Himalayan, gray, and smoked. My all-purpose salt is finely ground Celtic sea salt.

OILS AND BUTTERS

Olive oil is the most common oil in my kitchen and useful for nearly any occasion. The type of olive oil to use is truly a matter of personal preference. I like olive oil from Spain, but the best kind I've ever had was pressed on a friend's farm in Greece.

Ghee (**clarified butter**) is my number one choice for baking; it is also great for frying and happens to be absolutely delicious. Ghee is a type of clarified butter, a staple in Indian cuisine, and believed to have medicinal qualities in Ayurvedic medicine. I didn't know about the Indian roots of ghee until several years ago but grew up eating it and watching my mother make clarified butter back in Russia. To make ghee, butter is heated and cooked slowly at very low heat, which separates the pure fat (ghee) from milk solids and water. The last two are disposed of, making the butter less diluted and giving it a higher smoking point, which is great for cooking. By removing the milk solids, you also get rid of carbohydrates (lactose) and casein, the protein that many people are sensitive to.

The difference between ghee and clarified butter is determined by certain traditions and the length of time the butter is cooked. To make clarified butter, it is enough to heat it until it separates into three layers: the upper, foamy layer and the milk solids at the bottom are discarded, and the middle golden layer is the clarified butter. This takes 15 to 20 minutes. To make ghee, the butter must be cooked longer, until the milk solids are caramelized, the moisture is greatly decreased, and the flavor is deepened. Depending on the amount of butter, this may take several hours. Some sources also state that real ghee must come from butter made from cultured (sour) milk.

Ghee can be found in nonrefrigerated sections of many health food or Indian stores. It doesn't take much effort to make ghee, and it keeps fresh for months. There are different ways of making it—on the stove top, in a double boiler, or in the oven. I prefer to make ghee in a double boiler; this technique assures that the butter won't burn and lets me safely cook it longer, until the milk solids are caramelized.

Grapeseed oil is made by cold-pressing grape seeds and is ideal for sautéing, baking, and frying because of its high smoking point. Grapeseed oil is rich in nutrients and has a light and clean taste, and it can be used in place of olive oil in salads.

Coconut oil is an important ingredient for making dairy-free creams and soufflés; it also can replace butter in baking. Not all coconut oils are the same; some have a very strong coconut taste and can overwhelm other flavors easily. I prefer Nutiva's extra-virgin organic coconut oil for its mild flavor.

I grew up with **sunflower oil** as the most common all-purpose plant oil. I still like it a lot for its pleasant sunflower-like taste and beautiful color, and use it interchangeably with olive oil for sautéing and in salads.

Nut and seed butters are easy to make at home and are widely available at health food stores. All you need to make nut butter at home are nuts, a food processor, and, in some cases, vegetable or nut oil. Aside from peanut butter, which I do not use, the most common and versatile butter is made of almonds. The other kind I always have on hand is sesame tahini. I also like to make pecan, pistachio, and hazelnut butters occasionally. Any of those are great as a nutritional snack and very useful in dressings, sauces, and baking, especially in vegan baking.

You can use raw or toasted nuts and seeds; it's a matter of personal preference, but raw nut butter will be more nutritious.

If you have a dehydrator, the best thing to do is soak the nuts and seeds overnight, then rinse them well and dry them completely in a dehydrator. It makes them easier to digest (see page 12) and contributes to better taste and texture of the butter. From my experience, hazelnut butter is best made of roasted hazelnuts, while pistachios and macadamia nuts don't need to be soaked or roasted before being ground into butter.

NUT AND SEED OILS

I like to use various nut oils in salads and savory dishes, as well as for infusion in desserts. A couple of drops of sesame oil, for instance, can quickly turn a bland dish into a flavorful one. My favorite nut oils are walnut, hazelnut, and almond, although I experiment with pistachio, pumpkin seed, avocado, and macadamia oils as well. I recommend buying nut oils in small bottles and keeping them refrigerated to prevent rancidity.

VEGETABLE BROTH, STOCK, OR BOUILLON

I prefer to make my own vegetable broth, although I know many good cooks who use bouillon cubes with great success. If you have a preferred brand of cubes or canned or boxed broth, feel free to use it in these recipes, just as long as you like its flavor. See page 28 for my favorite recipe, plus general tips on creating your own delicious variations.

SWEETENERS

I use **coconut sugar** almost exclusively, unless a liquid sweetener is needed or if coconut sugar will interfere with the color of the dish. Coconut sugar is made of pure coconut palm tree sap and is full of amino acids, minerals, vitamin C, and B vitamins. Coconut sugar is also low glycemic, inulin rich, and almost neutral on the pH scale. Most important, I love its caramel taste, which doesn't have the slightest note of coconut in it.

Honey is my second sweetener of choice. I use local raw honey for its exceptional flavor.

I use **agave syrup** when a recipe needs a light-colored liquid sweetener with a neutral taste. It is produced from several species of the agave plant and is a good option for those allergic to honey. Agave syrup is known to have a much lower glycemic index than table sugar. I like to use raw light agave syrup.

Dates are a great natural sweetener, which also thicken custards and creams. I recommend buying Medjool dates with pits, as they stay moist and fresh longer. I buy dates in bulk at the local health food store or online (see Resources, page 319).

I use **maple syrup** occasionally, when its distinct roasted caramel flavor is appropriate and as long as it's 100 percent pure. Replace it with other liquid sweeteners if you prefer.

OTHER SWEET OPTIONS: YACÓN SYRUP
AND JERUSALEM ARTICHOKE SYRUP

I did not include yacón syrup or Jerusalem artichoke syrup in any of the recipes in this book only because they are not easy to find and can be expensive. However, if you have or can find these sweeteners, I recommend them wholeheartedly. Yacón and Jerusalem artichokes are crisp, sweet-tasting tuberous roots. Both syrups are low-glycemic and nutritious as far as sweeteners go. Yacón syrup is much less sweet than agave, and it has a delicious caramel flavor that can add character to your desserts. Jerusalem artichoke syrup contains a large amount of inulin and fiber, can aid digestion, and is truly heart healthy. The taste reminds me of rosehip syrup, which is a very popular health remedy back home in Russia.

Homemade coconut milk is a real treat and easy to prepare. You need a fresh young Thai coconut (not the mature, hairy kind you see in most supermarkets). Open the coconut with a cleaver and hammer—*carefully*—and pour all the coconut water into the blender. Scoop out the meat from the inside of the coconut and blend it with the water until smooth. You will get a delicious coconut milk that you can drink straight from the blender or use in recipes. Young Thai coconuts can be found at Asian markets and some health food stores.

CHOCOLATE

When I have my choice, I prefer homemade raw chocolate (see page 32). I love its pleasant bitterness and powdery texture. When buying chocolate, I go for the kinds that don't have dairy, soy lecithin, and other additives, just cocoa and a sweetener. Such chocolate is almost always dark, on the bitter side, tends to be more expensive, and is meant to be savored one small piece at a time. For cooking and baking, I use dairy- and soy-free organic chocolate chips or buy blocks of dark baking chocolate and chop or shave portions from it as needed.

Bittersweet chocolate lends an intense chocolate flavor to desserts.

I like to keep a bag of **raw cacao powder** on hand for use in any recipe that calls for cocoa. Natural **unsweetened cocoa powder** can be used, especially for baking.

Raw, food-grade **cocoa butter** can be found in some health food stores and through multiple online suppliers. I use it in making raw chocolate, raw cookies, and other desserts, often in place of coconut oil.

Cacao nibs are raw, unprocessed, crushed cacao beans that have all the benefits of the best chocolate, minus the sugar and other additives. They are an interesting alternative to chocolate chips, with a nice crunchy texture, delicious bitterness, and a real cocoa flavor. I love them in cookies, breakfast cereals, and snacks. Find them in health food stores or online.

White chocolate appears twice in this book, even though we hardly ever eat it. (This assures you that these two recipes must really let it shine.) The sweetness and milkiness of white chocolate pair so well with the tartness of lemons in the Lemon Bars (page 227), and it perfectly contrasts with dark chocolate in the Black and White Chocolate Cups (page 267).

My latest discovery, vegan white chocolate chips, can be found in some health food stores and online (see Resources, page 319).

NUT MILKS

Nowadays you can buy milk made of almost any nuts or seeds, but the most common and useful in my kitchen is **almond milk.** Almonds have a mild, neutral taste, making almond milk very versatile. Drink it on its own, pour over cereal, or use instead of dairy milk in cooking and baking. Making nut milk at home is easy: all you need are nuts, purified water, a good blender, and a nut milk bag or cheesecloth.

I use unsweetened, full-fat canned **coconut milk** for the recipes in this book. It is a great substitute for dairy in baked goods, soups, and creams.

ON EGGS AND DAIRY

Many recipes in this book that would traditionally call for eggs use alternative ingredients instead. I do not have an aversion to eggs; quite the opposite—

I cherish the eggs we buy from a friend's family farm a couple of times a month. I know how much work, dedication, and love goes into those gorgeous, sunny yolks and would never want to waste, overuse, or overcook them. I would rather soft-boil them and enjoy them with good salt and a sliced tomato, or make a tender omelet with loads of fresh greens, than use the eggs in dishes or baked goods that are perfectly delicious without them. On the other hand, I don't want to compromise the success of any dish, so when eggs are necessary for texture, I often use just one. One egg works as well as three in many dishes.

I use the same approach with cheese. Good-quality cheese is full of flavor and a very small amount goes a long way, enough to bring complexity or saltiness to a dish. Quality cheeses are expensive but worth every penny and meant to be savored in small quantities. To me it's better to add just a touch of good-quality cheese to a dish than to drown it in the rubbery, low-quality stuff. Most often I prefer unpasteurized goat's and sheep's milk cheeses. Not only are they full of fresh, rustic flavor, they don't contain casein (a protein in cow's milk that many people have a sensitivity to) and are not altered by the process of pasteurization, so they are easier to digest.

I almost completely stopped using cow's milk and cream years ago, for many reasons. For one, modern farming and production methods seriously concern me. Pasteurization destroys vitamins and certain enzymes and interferes with your body's calcium absorption from milk. Homogenized milk allows unwanted digestive enzymes right into the bloodstream, possibly

damaging blood vessels and resulting in plaque accumulation. Casein, the protein in cow's milk, is hard to digest, and I don't miss it a bit. Last, as my palate has grown to love almond milk and other nut and grain milks, I no longer like the taste of cow's milk.

Occasionally we buy fresh raw goat's milk from a friend's farm for making ricotta cheese (page 26) or kefir. I also buy organic butter to make ghee or clarified butter (pages 14 and 27).

THICKENERS

In recipes in which the liquid component needs a thickener, **Irish moss** is always my first choice. Five dessert recipes and a gelatin call for Irish moss in this book. Still a fairly unknown ingredient, Irish moss is a tasteless raw seaweed and an excellent natural thickener that's full of nutrients. The more cooks discover it, the more popular it will become, I hope. It is easy to buy online and fairly inexpensive, keeping in mind that one pound will last a long time and holds up well in the refrigerator. Choose whole-leaf, wild-crafted Irish moss (see Resources, page 319). You will need a reliable digital kitchen scale to work with Irish moss.

If you decide that Irish moss is not for you, you can substitute it with **gelatin**—there are instructions for working with both ingredients in the aforementioned recipes. I use vegan gelatin; regular gelatin is derived from animal skin and bones and is not considered part of a vegetarian lifestyle. You can buy vegan gelatin in some health food stores or online (see Resources, page 319).

POWDERS, SEAWEEDS, AND OTHER SUPERFOODS

As a health-conscious and curious cook, I like to keep a wide array of natural powders and superfoods in my pantry.

I use vanilla-flavored **pea protein powder** in smoothies, especially when I aim for a very light, low-sugar smoothie using ripe kiwis or pears instead of banana. Pea protein is a great source of plant-derived protein and improves the flavor and texture of such drinks. **Hemp protein powder** is useful for shakes and smoothies as well. Hemp is a rich source of protein, essential fatty acids, and iron, while being cholesterol-free and low in saturated fat.

I like to add **hemp hearts** (shelled hemp nuts) to breakfast cereal, sprinkle them on fruit and salads, and use them in snacks and desserts.

Ever since I learned how to make raw chocolate (page 32), I have been a big fan of **mesquite** and **maca** powders. Mesquite powder is ground from the pod of the mesquite plant, and its sweet and nutty taste makes it ideal for desserts. We love it in raw chocolate and smoothies and as a flavorful addition to baked goods. Mesquite is high in protein, has a low glycemic index, and is a good source of fiber, calcium, iron, manganese, lysine, zinc, and potassium. Maca is a very mild sweetener and has a unique flavor that I've become very attached to. Maca root comes from Peru, where it has been known for its nutritional and medicinal value for centuries. Among many other amazing properties, maca is said to be able to improve the function of the endocrine system by supporting the health of the adrenal and pituitary glands. I like to add both mesquite and maca powders to smoothies, desserts, and healthy sweet snacks.

Occasionally I add freeze-dried powders of various berries and vegetables as a nutritious coloring ingredient to a dessert, smoothie, or fun food project with Paloma.

Paloma has been snacking on **goji berries** (or *chiki-berries* as she calls them) since she was very little. Goji are considered a superfood berry, along with açaí, noni, mulberry, and sea buckthorn. Goji berries are rich in vitamin A and other antioxidants and can be used in snacks and baked goods in place of raisins.

My appreciation for seaweed doesn't end with Irish moss. **Sea vegetables** are known for their overwhelming health benefits and are among the healthiest foods on the planet. I always have a package or two of untoasted nori in the fridge for a quick snack and a bag of dulse flakes to sprinkle on salads or soups. Nori are the seaweed sheets used in sushi rolls. Dulse is a raw seaweed that is commonly used in place of salt in the raw food diet. I also like experimenting with other seaweeds like kombu, wakame, kelp, and arame, adding them to soups and salads.

WATER

I believe it's important for the water we consume to be filtered or purified. As we drink a lot of water throughout the day and use water to brew tea, soak nuts and grains, and cook with all the time, we installed a reverse osmosis filter for our drinking water years ago. As expensive as it seemed at the time, it has paid for itself many times over. Reverse osmosis is the best filtration system you can have, but there are many others available, including inexpensive pitcher-style filters and filters that attach to your kitchen faucet.

Tools and Equipment

KNIVES

Sharp, good-quality knives are essential to a safe and productive time in the kitchen. The knife I use most of the time is a 6-inch chef's knife with a scalloped edge, which is not very common in combination. I prefer this size and style for convenience and ease of control during preparation. The knife

is manufactured by Dexter-Russell, a commercial cutlery brand, and can be found in restaurant supply stores. Other knives I like to use are a 5-inch scalloped-edge fruit knife, paring knives, a Chinese chef's knife, and straight blade knives of various sizes.

POTS AND PANS

I have a Zepter brand, Swiss-made set of pots and pans that has been with me for nearly twenty years. Ernie and I brought back the whole heavy set all the way from Russia, which was difficult at the time, but so worth it in the end. They are heavy-bottomed and made of a very good-quality stainless alloy steel, which is amazing for cooking. I also own a cast-iron Dutch oven and a couple of cast-iron sauté pans. I use nonstick skillets for gluten-free crepes and pancakes. My favorite ones are a 5-inch (13 cm) pan for crepes and a tiny 4-inch (10 cm) omelet pan for pancakes. The 5-inch is an unusual size for crepes, but I like a smaller diameter for easier flipping and handling of fragile gluten-free crepes.

You'll notice how much I use my 9 × 9-inch (23 cm) square **baking pan** throughout the book. It seems to be the universal size for whatever goods I have in mind. I also use **ceramic baking dishes** of different sizes and shapes for baking vegetables and savory dishes. I have both rimmed and unrimmed **baking sheets**; both types are useful in different situations. Mostly I use unrimmed baking sheets for cookies and chips and rimmed for everything else.

My favorite **tart molds** are a round, 9-inch (23 cm) nonstick tart pan with a removable bottom and a set of six 4-inch (10 cm) tartlet pans. For a more interesting presentation I use an 8 × 8-inch (20 cm) square mold and a 4½ × 13½-inch (11 × 35 cm) elongated, rectangular pan.

I own several mini (4-inch [10 cm]) **Bundt cake pans**, which make a pretty presentation.

The set of ten **ice pop molds** really comes in handy in summer heat, when seasonal fruit easily becomes a refreshing frozen treat.

I love my collection of **ramekins** and use them often for crumbles, puddings, and soufflés.

I can never have enough **cookie cutters** and love to browse specialty bakery and vintage shops for interesting new ones. Fun shapes enhance presentation and are especially useful when baking with children.

Although most of the recipes in this book are very forgiving and you can get by measuring the ingredients by volume (in cups), a **kitchen scale** is a convenient tool to have. Weighing ingredients (flours in particular) on a reliable digital scale can ease and speed up the cooking/baking process and make for better, more precise results.

A **food processor** is useful for mixing and grinding ingredients. The brand is not crucial, as there are many good-quality food processors on the market.

One of my most loved kitchen tools is a **high-speed blender.** I burned through many low-horsepower blenders before allowing myself to buy a high-speed Blendtec. My only regret is that I didn't do it earlier, as it has endlessly improved my time in the kitchen. The two most well-known and comparable brands of high-speed blenders are Blendtec and Vitamix, and both take blending to a different level. Most recipes in this book can be made with a regular blender, unless noted otherwise.

A high-speed blender will break down any tough leaves in your green smoothie and make it feel like the smoothest of milkshakes. Nut and seed milks come out rich and take just minutes to make, and the possibilities for blending soups, puddings, creams, and mousses are endless. A high-speed model also allows dry ingredients to be ground into flour in seconds, which opens up a new world of fresh baking. This freedom to make flours at home will save you a few dollars, as bulk grains are generally less expensive than ready-made flour.

My **coffee grinder** is devoted to the grinding of spices, small amounts of seeds and grains, and to powdering coarse coconut sugar. I don't drink coffee (unless I am in Europe, where I find the whole experience and flavors much more appealing). If you grind coffee at home, keep a separate grinder for anything other than coffee if you do not want to contaminate flavors.

When not pressed for time, and when grinding very small amounts of spices, I use a marble **mortar and pestle**. It is also useful for crushing garlic and fresh herbs.

The **mandoline slicer** is especially useful for thin slicing fruits and vegetables. Most have several different blade attachments and all can be used to achieve slices of different thicknesses.

Since I use citrus so often in my cooking, a good **zester** (such as a Microplane) is an essential tool. It can also be used for shaving nutmeg, chocolate, and cheese.

I have been using my twin-gear masticating **juicer** almost daily for years. Compared with a centrifugal juicer, which is the most common and usually less expensive type that spins at high speeds, a masticating juicer is much quieter and extracts the juice more slowly, without overheating and damaging the vitamins and enzymes. The volume of the juice produced is greater, and it stays fresh longer. A masticating juicer is also very effective with leafy vegetables, herbs, and wheatgrass, unlike the centrifugal kind.

If you like ice cream and sorbet and experimenting with flavors of frozen treats, a home **ice cream maker** is for you. I have an uncomplicated Cuisinart model; it is fairly inexpensive, consists of only a chilling chamber and mixer base, and is very easy to use. This device has brought us lots of joy, especially during hot summers, and I recommend it wholeheartedly.

A **food dehydrator** is a versatile addition to any kitchen, especially when exploring raw food. There are some recipes in which an oven is not a substitute; my recipe for Kale Chips (page 310) is an example. I dry soaked and sprouted grains and nuts in the dehydrator and make raw crackers, cookies, fruit leathers, raisins, and other dried fruit, as well as many more healthy and fun foods. My 9-tray Excalibur has served me well for several years. Nonstick Teflex sheets are very useful for lining your dehydrator trays and work much better than parchment paper.

Nylon nut milk bags are useful for making nut milk and sprouting grains. They are inexpensive and easy to find online or in the produce section of some health food stores.

It is very important for me to have reliable **food storage ware** that preserves freshness as long as possible. I cook often and prepare a variety of dishes simultaneously, so proper storing of ingredients and finished products is essential to the success of my dishes. In my opinion, **glass** is far superior to plastic, and I own sets of Pyrex glass containers, as well as all sizes of mason jars for the most convenient storage system.

Basic Recipes and Techniques

Here are some very useful and basic recipes and techniques that are a great contribution to the arsenal of any home cook. Many of my recipes refer back to these basic components.

HOMEMADE RICOTTA CHEESE
Makes about 1 cup

4 cups (1 liter) whole goat's or cow's milk
½ teaspoon sea salt (optional)
3 to 4 tablespoons freshly squeezed lemon juice

1. Pour the milk into a large stainless steel or ceramic saucepan; add salt if preferred. Begin to heat over medium-low heat, stirring periodically to prevent the milk from sticking to the bottom of the pan. Watch closely; you don't want your milk to boil over. If it begins boiling, remove from the heat immediately.

2. Right before the milk begins to boil, remove it from the heat and add the lemon juice, 1 tablespoon at a time. Stir occasionally and watch closely for signs of separation. Very soon you will start seeing the whey, greenish in color, separating from the ricotta curds. As soon as you see that, stop adding lemon juice. Leave the liquid undisturbed for 5 to 10 minutes to let the cheese curds form and separate from the whey.

3. Line a large bowl with several layers of cheesecloth. The cheesecloth should be large enough for its ends to drape over the sides of the bowl. Pour the ricotta mixture into the bowl, making sure the corners of the cheesecloth stay outside the bowl. Draw the corners of the cheesecloth together over the bowl and tie them together, or secure the corners with string or a rubber band, creating a sack. Hang the sack over a bowl by suspending it from your faucet or the knob of your kitchen cabinet.

4. The amount of time you leave your ricotta hanging depends on how dry and dense you want it to be. For the Cherry Ricotta Bake (page 48) or Squash Blossom Quiche (page 143) recipes, you want the ricotta to be drier. For dry ricotta, drain it for 2 to 4 hours. If you intend to eat the ricotta on its own and prefer it moist and spreadable, it's ready almost right away, within 15 minutes to 1 hour.

The ricotta can also be drained further and pressed until it becomes a dense and rich paneer cheese, a popular ingredient in Indian cuisine.

Tightly cover the ricotta and store in the refrigerator for up to 3 days, if not using it right away.

Note: The leftover whey is a high-quality, protein-rich product and can be used in numerous ways. Use it in place of water or milk in smoothies, soups, stews, breads, pancakes, crepes, and other baked goods. Boil rice, quinoa, and other grains in whey, or even water your plants with it for a nutritional boost.

GHEE (CLARIFIED BUTTER)

2 pounds (8 sticks [908 g]) butter yields about
3¼ cups (27 oz [800 ml]) ghee

1. Cut each stick of butter into 6 or 7 pieces. Place the butter into a medium-sized heatproof bowl. The volume of the container should be approximately twice as large as the volume of the butter. Prepare a large heavy-bottomed pan or saucepan that can accommodate the bowl of butter within. Half-fill the large saucepan with water and place the bowl inside the saucepan. Make sure the bowl is stable and not floating. The water in the saucepan should be approximately level with the butter and shouldn't be near the top of the bowl. Bring the water to a boil over medium heat.

2. Immediately lower the heat until the water is gently simmering. The butter will melt and separate into three layers. Continue to cook, undisturbed, until the upper, foamy layer turns a light golden color, about 2 hours or longer. Keep an eye on the water level in the saucepan and add more hot water if it gets low.

3. Once ready, remove the butter from heat and let cool slightly. Skim the foam with a slotted spoon and discard it. Strain the golden ghee into a clean, dry jar through a cheesecloth-lined fine-mesh sieve. Pour carefully, trying to keep the milk solids on the bottom of the saucepan from sliding into the sieve. Discard the milk solids once you have poured off all the clarified butter.

4. The finished product should be clear and golden in color. Keep the jar tightly covered. You do not need to refrigerate the ghee, but you can if you prefer. The ghee will become solid but soft at room temperature and will harden in the refrigerator. Ghee stays fresh for months.

Note: Make sure to use good-quality unsalted butter.

VEGETABLE BROTH
Makes about 9 cups (2.2 liters)

2 tablespoons ghee (page 27) or olive oil
7 black peppercorns
2 teaspoons coriander seeds
2 teaspoons fennel seeds
1 teaspoon dried thyme or 3 to 5 fresh thyme sprigs
1 large yellow onion, peeled and roughly chopped
4 garlic cloves, peeled and roughly chopped
1 leek, white and tender green parts only, diced
3 medium carrots, peeled and diced
1 large fennel bulb, coarsely chopped
3 parsnips, peeled and diced
3 celery stalks, diced
1 medium celery root, peeled and coarsely chopped
5 bay leaves
1½ teaspoons salt
10 cups (2.4 liters) purified water
Handful (about ¼ cup) fresh flat-leaf parsley leaves
Handful (about ¼ cup) fresh dill, chopped
½ lemon (optional)

1. Heat the ghee in a large stockpot over medium heat. Add the peppercorns, coriander seeds, fennel seeds, and thyme and cook for about 1 minute, until fragrant. Add the onion and garlic and sauté for 2 to 3 more minutes, stirring every minute or so.

2. Add the leek, carrot, fennel, parsnips, celery, celery root, bay leaves, and salt and sauté for 10 minutes, stirring occasionally. Add the water, raise the heat to high, and bring to a boil. Lower the heat, partially cover, and simmer for 20 minutes, or until all the vegetables are soft.

3. Remove the pot from the heat, then add the parsley and dill. Squeeze fresh lemon juice over the broth, if using. Cover the pot and let it sit for several hours or overnight in the refrigerator. This resting time will help the broth develop a full flavor. Strain the broth and use as needed, refrigerate for up to 3 days, or freeze it for future use. The broth will keep frozen for at least 1 month.

TIPS FOR HOMEMADE VEGETABLE BROTH

For homemade vegetable broth, it is really not necessary to follow a precise recipe. If you don't have exactly the same ingredients listed in my recipe, you can still cook up a tasty broth.

For a very simple broth, cover any vegetables you have on hand with water and bring to a boil. Add salt, a few peppercorns, and bay leaves, then lower the heat and simmer until all the vegetables are soft. Add more salt to taste, and add herbs and lemon juice if you like. Let sit for a few hours or overnight before straining. You even can make a simple aromatic broth by infusing boiling water with lemongrass and ginger (see Vegetable Miso Soup, page 281).

Here are some tips for making delicious veggie broth:

- Roughly chop the vegetables to increase their surface area of contact with water for an easier flavor infusion.

- For a more complex flavor, sauté the vegetables, especially onions, garlic, carrots, and celery, for a few minutes in the stockpot prior to adding the water.

- Save tough asparagus ends, stems of broccoli, cauliflower, kale, and other leafy vegetables and herbs, and use them in your broth. (The extra bits can be stored in the refrigerator for up to a week.)

- Add mushrooms if you want your broth to have deep umami flavors.

- Add 5 to 7 dates or prunes for a fuller-bodied broth.

- If you do not need a neutral-colored stock, add tomatoes as a savory flavor enhancer.

- Make sure you begin with cold water and cook the broth gently at a steady simmer so the vegetables can release their flavor gradually.

ALMOND MILK

This is the most basic recipe for almond milk, with just almonds and water, no additional ingredients. This recipe can be modified by adding a sweetener, such as pitted dates or honey, and/or spices, such as cinnamon, cardamom, nutmeg, or even turmeric. This same technique can also be used with most other nuts and seeds. Some nuts, like macadamias, and seeds, like hemp hearts, don't need to be soaked and their milk doesn't need to be strained. Do a little research ahead of time, or just experiment. You can purchase nylon nut milk bags online or at many health food stores. Cheesecloth can also be used as a strainer, though it will most likely be messier.

Makes about 2½ cups (600 ml)

1 cup (140 g) almonds, soaked overnight in purified water
3 cups (720 ml) purified water

Drain and rinse the soaked almonds. Put the almonds in a blender (preferably a high-speed model) with the fresh water and blend until completely smooth. Strain the mixture through a nut milk bag or cheesecloth. Discard the pulp, or save it for another recipe. The milk will stay fresh in the refrigerator for up to 2 days.

Note: Nut and seed pulp can be saved and used in recipes for cookies, granola, cakes, and even hummus.

ALMOND BUTTER

Makes about 1¼ cups

2 cups (280 g) almonds, preferably soaked and dehydrated or toasted (see page 36)

Place the almonds in a food processor and grind into fine crumbs. Continue grinding the almonds until you see the ground almonds become oily, then forming a ball. You may need to stop the machine and scrape the sides and bottom of the bowl to get all of the nuts into the grinding vortex. Stop grinding when you achieve a soft and smooth butter. Almond butter can be kept refrigerated for up to 1 month.

Note: This technique can be used with most nuts. Nuts usually don't need additional oil to be ground into butter, but you may run into unusually dry nuts. If the ground nuts refuse to release oil and form a ball, add a little bit of olive oil or any nut oil, a tablespoon at a time, to help the process.

SESAME TAHINI

Makes about 2 cups

2 cups (280 g) sesame seeds, raw (soaked and dried if preferred) or toasted
  (see page 12)
¼ to ½ cup (60 to 120 ml) olive oil

Grind the sesame seeds in a food processor, adding the oil gradually, ¼ cup
(60 ml) at a time. If ¼ cup (60 ml) is enough to make the mixture smooth,
don't add any more; if it is still dry and isn't grinding well, add another ¼ cup
(60 ml) oil and keep processing until smooth. Keep refrigerated for up to 1
month.

RAW CHOCOLATE

By definition, raw food is food that has never been heated above 118°F (48°C),
which is beneficial because it preserves heat-sensitive enzymes and vitamins. If you love chocolate and consider it an indulgence, this delicious and
nourishing raw chocolate is for you. Begin with raw cacao products, which are
made by separating the cacao bean into cocoa powder and butter. To make my
raw chocolate, the two are combined once again by gently melting the cocoa
butter and stirring in the powder, along with other nutritious ingredients.
Raw cacao is considered a superfood for its abundance of important vitamins,
minerals, and enzymes.

Makes about 9 ounces (250 g)

1 cup packed (100 g) shredded raw cocoa butter
½ cup (45 g) raw cacao powder
¼ cup (40 g) mesquite powder
2 tablespoons maca powder
2 tablespoons agave syrup

1. Place the shaved cocoa butter in a medium heatproof bowl, then nest the
bowl in a heavy-bottomed pan or shallow saucepan filled with water. The
water level should not be so high that the bowl is floating, and the water level
should be nowhere near the top of the bowl. Heat the water gently over low
heat so the cocoa butter can melt slowly without overheating.

2. Once the cocoa butter is melted, remove the bowl from the water and turn
off the heat. Sift the cacao powder, mesquite powder, and maca powder into
the cocoa butter, add the agave, and mix thoroughly. Pour the chocolate into

molds and freeze until it is firm throughout, 5 to 10 minutes. Remove the chocolate from the molds and store in the refrigerator for up to 2 to 3 weeks.

Note: Technically you don't have to keep this chocolate in the refrigerator, but I prefer the texture of it so much better when chilled. Since this chocolate is not tempered, it will not be glossy and snappy when at room temperature.

Simple silicone or plastic chocolate molds are very handy tools for making your own chocolate. They are usually inexpensive and can be found at specialty baking shops or online. If you don't have any, you can still make the chocolate by spreading it on a parchment paper–covered baking sheet or cutting board to approximately ¼ inch (½ cm) thick. Refrigerate the chocolate until firm and then break or cut into pieces.

BUCKWHEAT CRISPIES

Makes 1 heaping cup (about 190 g)

1 cup (200 g) raw buckwheat groats

1. Place the buckwheat in a medium bowl (or into a nut milk bag and then a bowl) and cover with purified water, with the water level 1 to 2 inches (2½ to 5 cm) above the grains. Let soak for at least 1 hour or overnight.

2. Pour the grains into a colander and rinse very well (or if you used a nut milk bag, rinse through the bag) to remove the sliminess that raw buckwheat produces when soaked. This may take longer than rinsing other grains, but it is very important for maintaining its taste and texture.

3. Spread the rinsed, soaked groats on a clean kitchen towel and let air-dry completely for about 24 hours, depending on the temperature and humidity in your kitchen. If you have a dehydrator, spread the soaked groats on a Teflex-lined dehydrator tray and dehydrate at 115°F (43°C) overnight, or until completely dry. If you are keeping your groats in the nut milk bag, place the bag full of grains on a mesh screen–covered dehydrating tray, flatten the bag to spread the groats within the bag as much as you can, and dehydrate just like that.

4. Once completely dry, store the crispies in an airtight glass container in the refrigerator for up to 1 month. You can use them for the recipes in this book, add to your morning cereal, sprinkle on salads or desserts, or grind into flour.

Note: Soaked groats can be sprouted then dehydrated for added nutrition. Soaked and dried groats will increase slightly in size but decrease in weight. Depending on the soaking time and the way you dry them, 1 cup of buckwheat crispies will vary in weight, losing almost one-quarter of its weight. Further sprouting will change the weight and volume of buckwheat even more (see page 39).

BLANCHING VEGETABLES

Blanching is one of my favorite ways to cook many vegetables, especially summer ones. It is easy and quick, and leaves vegetables cooked only slightly, staying somewhat crunchy and retaining their fresh taste.

Every vegetable has a recommended blanching time, and I specify these particular times in each recipe. However, there are some general tips for successful blanching to help preserve the color and prevent overcooking of vegetables:

- Using a large amount of water for blanching minimizes the time needed for the water to resume boiling after you submerge the vegetables into it, which in turn minimizes the cooking time and preserves color.

- Salting your water well helps to season the vegetables evenly as well as maintain the chlorophyll brightness (about 2 tablespoons of sea salt per 1 quart/1 liter of water should be enough).

- Cool the vegetables as quickly as you can after removing them from the boiling water to stop the cooking process. Shock them in an ice-water bath or run them under very cold tap water in a colander.

1. Bring a large pot of well-salted water to a rolling boil. Drop the vegetables in and time the blanching from this moment, even though the water will not resume boiling right away. Boil them for the required amount of time recommended in the recipe.

2. If you are blanching only one type of vegetable, drain the vegetables by pouring out the whole contents of the pot into a colander over the sink. If you are blanching several types of vegetables that require different blanching times, use a large slotted spoon to remove them from the boiling water, reserving the water for the next vegetable. In either case, quickly drop your blanched vegetables into an ice-water bath (a large bowl with icy-cold water) immediately after removing them from the boiling water. You can also use

a colander that fits inside the pot for easy and quick removal. The colander must allow the vegetables to be immersed in the water.

3. Once the vegetables are completely cooled, drain them over a colander. Prepare and use according to the recipe.

SOAKING, GERMINATING, AND SPROUTING

See page 12 to learn about the benefits of sprouting. I soak, germinate, and/or sprout most of my grains, nuts, and seeds prior to using them or grinding them into flours.

Soaking

1. To soak, germinate, or sprout an ingredient, the ingredient should be raw (untoasted) and will usually be labeled as such. Rinse and drain the desired amount of raw grains, beans, nuts, or seeds and place into a clean bowl at least three times bigger than the amount of the dry ingredient. Cover with purified water, making sure the water level is 2 inches (5 cm) above the dry ingredient. Alternatively, you can place the grains/beans/nuts into a nut milk bag, then place the bag into a bowl and cover with water. Using a nut milk bag is especially helpful when working with small grains such as amaranth and quinoa.

2. Soak quinoa, oats, buckwheat, amaranth, millet, beans, and almonds overnight. For softer nuts and seeds like pecans, walnuts, and cashews and sunflower, pumpkin, and sesame seeds, 2 to 4 hours is usually enough. Buckwheat can be soaked for as little as 1 hour to make it soft and perfectly edible.

3. Drain and rinse the grains/beans/nuts very well. If using a nut milk bag, leave the grains in the bag when rinsing, sprouting, and even drying (providing you are using a dehydrator for drying and your grains are not tightly packed). When the soaked ingredient is thoroughly rinsed and drained, it is ready for drying, germinating, sprouting, cooking with, or using in snacks, creams, or salads. It all depends on the ingredient or recipe you are working with.

Notes: I often sprout quinoa, oats, amaranth, and chickpeas. Other than chickpeas, I don't sprout other beans for cooking. Soaked almonds, pecans, walnuts, and sunflower seeds are great for snacking on and in salads (make sure to keep them refrigerated). Otherwise, I dehydrate them until dry and use them for making nut butters, milk, or flour. Soak cashews for creams and dehydrate pumpkin and sesame seeds for future use. Buckwheat can either be dehydrated for use in breakfast cereals, snacks, or flour, or sprouted and then dehydrated for the same purpose.

Buckwheat groats require a bit more attention, as after soaking in water for just an hour, they become very slimy. It is important to rinse the groats very thoroughly at the end of soaking to completely wash away the sliminess. A full rinse assures proper germination and/or sprouting, and the right taste of the end product.

Germinating and Sprouting

1. The process between soaking and sprouting of a grain/bean/nut is called germination. As long as you start with a raw product, germination will be as beneficial for the composition of the grain as sprouting. Biologically, there is no difference between those two processes and both dramatically increase the bioavailability of a raw grain/bean/nut.

2. After soaking and rinsing very well, place the grains/beans/nuts back into a bowl and cover it with a clean, damp kitchen towel or several layers of damp paper towels. The ingredients will germinate and sprout at room temperature.

3. Rinse and drain the ingredients every 8 hours. The grains, seeds, or beans should begin to show sprouts after 24 to 48 hours.

4. When you are satisfied with the size of the sprouts, rinse them one last time and drain them well. At this point, you can use the sprouts fresh, or dry

them for use in flours, granola, and so on. Fresh sprouts should be kept refrigerated and will stay fresh for up to 3 days.

5. To dry the sprouts, spread them on Teflex-covered dehydrator trays or place the nut milk bag full of sprouts into the dehydrator. I dry my sprouts at 115°F (46°C). The drying time varies from grain to grain and also depends on the quantity. Sometimes overnight is all the time needed for the product to be completely dry; other times it takes 24 hours or more. Check the sprouts every few hours to monitor the dryness. Note: Certain grains, such as quinoa, buckwheat, and amaranth, will continue to sprout for some time while drying in the dehydrator. Some will even sprout without any germination time if placed in the dehydrator right after soaking.

If you don't have a dehydrator and are looking to make sprouted flours, don't wait for the sprouts to become too apparent. Germinate the grains for 6 to 8 hours, then rinse and drain well. Spread them on a clean kitchen towel or several layers of paper towels until they are completely dry. They will most likely sprout during this time. To shorten the drying time, change the towel after a few hours.

6. After your sprouted, germinated, or soaked grains/nuts/beans are completely dry, they can be ground into flour or left whole. Use a high-speed blender, grain mill, food processor (for nuts), or coffee grinder (for grinding in small batches) to make flour. Keep the sprouted dry grains or flours refrigerated in an airtight glass container for up to 2 months.

Note: Many grains, nuts, and seeds that are labeled "raw" still encounter high heat in processing and packaging. Nuts like almonds and cashews can only be sprouted if they are truly raw. In the United States, most almonds available in stores are pasteurized, and cashews are harvested with a high-temperature technique, so they will not sprout even if labeled raw. Some small farms and companies sell untreated almonds and cashews online. Make sure the package indicates that they are unpasteurized and/or sproutable. Most oat groats sold in the United States are steam-treated to prevent rancidity; sproutable oat groats are usually labeled as such.

SEED-TO-SPROUT YIELDS

1 cup (200 g) raw dried buckwheat groats results in about 3 cups fresh sprouts, 1½ cup dried sprouts, and 1¼ cups (175 g) sprouted flour

1 cup (200 g) dried quinoa results in about 2½ cups fresh sprouts, 1⅓ cups dried sprouts, and 1½ cups (210 g) sprouted flour

1 cup (200 g) dried chickpeas results in about 2½ cups fresh sprouts, 1½ cups dried sprouts, and 1½ cups (180 g) sprouted flour

1

Breakfast & Snacks

IT IS HARD FOR ME TO IMAGINE LIFE WITHOUT BREAKFAST, no doubt the most loved meal in our family. Perhaps this love has to do with the optimism of morning time, a new beginning when the whole day is ahead and anything seems possible. I grew up in a household where breakfast was mandatory—no one ever considered leaving the house without a nice bite to eat and a warm cup of tea. Unsurprisingly, I brought that habit to my own family, and even though weekend mornings offer more time than weekdays, breakfast remains a very important and enjoyable daily ritual. I go to bed excited for the next morning, mulling over ideas for the ingredients I have on hand while falling asleep. Many of the dishes I make for breakfast conveniently double as snacks, which often make their way into Paloma's school lunch box.

More often than not I begin my morning with a glass of water with a generous squeeze of lemon, chased by some green juice. I make the juice with plenty of ginger, which gives it a nice spicy kick that wakes me right up. Paloma starts her day with a green smoothie, although she occasionally becomes curious about the juice and asks for a taste. After that, the most loved breakfast in our house is a bowl of raw cacao–buckwheat granola with seasonal fruit, cacao nibs, and homemade nut milk. It never gets old, as the flavors of the fruit, which change monthly, keep it interesting. Whenever we switch from, say, mango to strawberries, from cherries to figs, or from grapes to persimmons, our breakfast becomes new and exciting once again.

Savoring this seasonal variety leads me to the world of smoothies, one filled with endless possibilities. Some smoothies are so hearty that they can be lunch-worthy, especially if time is in short supply on that particular day. On weekends, I like to make more elaborate breakfasts that involve baking or another longer process.

Although we have some established favorites, the idea of the perfect breakfast is ever-changing in our kitchen. Whether it is a baked ricotta pie, chia pudding, or crepes, I always aim for a nourishing morning meal to start us off right for the day ahead.

Greens for Breakfast

No matter what kind of day is ahead, we hardly ever begin it without some variation on these green drinks. Most often it will be a juice for the adults and a smoothie for Paloma, although it is never set in stone. Green drinks are said to be an acquired taste, but I loved them on my first sip. Greens are extremely nutritionally concentrated, and having them first thing in the morning is energizing.

At home I make green juices and smoothies according to what I have on hand that day. Florida's growing season stretches out between the months of October and April. I take full advantage of our farmers' market, where I stock up on fresh greens from a local organic farm to last us for the week. For the rest of the year, I rely on health food stores and produce from other states with a milder summer.

The recipes here are just a general guideline; feel free to experiment and find your own favorite medleys and ratios. We like plenty of ginger and herbs in our juice, but if you are new to juicing, start with more neutral flavors like apple, cucumber, and kale. Same goes for the smoothies—include more fruit and less leafy greens at first, experimenting with zingier ingredients as your palate adjusts to the flavor.

Paloma was introduced to green drinks very early in life, when she was ten months old, and has grown up loving them. I know, however, that the green color may prevent some children (or adults!) from wanting to try them. There are a couple of smoothie recipes in this book (Chocolate Milkshake, page 302, and Matcha Kiwi Smoothie, page 71) that show you how to successfully hide the leafy color and taste while still enjoying their benefits.

Green Smoothie

Serves 4 to 5

1. Remove any hard stems from your greens, especially if using mature leaves of plants such as kale, Swiss chard, or collard greens. Tear the leaves into pieces. I like to use a variety of greens, especially ones that are in season.

2. Place a handful of leaves, all of the fruit, and the water into the blender and blend until liquefied. Continue by adding more greens, a handful at a time, stopping the blender in between the additions and then blending as you go. These steps will allow you to fit in as many greens as possible. When the greens are all in, blend until completely smooth. The consistency should be creamy and resembling a milkshake. If the shake seems too watery, add more greens or fruit. If it is too thick, add water, a few tablespoons at a time. It may take a few rounds of making smoothies with different combinations of greens and fruit to find the perfect consistency.

Note: If you are using a high-speed blender such as Blendtec or Vitamix, your shake may become slightly warm toward the end of blending. You can simply blend in some ice if you are drinking it right away or make the shake in advance and chill it in the refrigerator before drinking. If you don't have a high-speed blender, using more tender greens like spinach and Swiss chard rather than kale and collard greens will give you the best results. The green smoothie will stay fresh in the refrigerator for up to 5 days—just make sure to mix it well before drinking.

1 bunch any green leafy vegetable, such as Swiss chard, spinach, kale, romaine lettuce, or bok choy, or a combination of several different types
1 to 2 ripe bananas
½ cup frozen berries and/or other fruits, such as strawberries, blueberries, and peaches
½ ripe mango or other fruit (optional)
2 cups purified water

Substitute ripe kiwi or pears for the bananas for fewer calories and less sugar. Add half an avocado or 1 to 2 tablespoons naturally flavored vegetable protein powder (such as pea protein powder) to give your shake more flavor and creaminess.

Green Juice

Serves 4 to 5

1 bunch celery
2 to 3 large cucumbers, cut into chunks
2 to 3 green apples, cut into chunks, or 1 grapefruit, segmented
2 to 3 kale leaves or other leafy greens
½ bunch parsley
½ bunch cilantro
½ bunch dill
2-inch piece fresh ginger, or to taste
Any other herbs and/or green vegetables, such as fennel fronds, mint, sugar snap peas, or broccoli (optional)
Squeeze of lemon or lime (optional)

Run all the ingredients through a juicer. Serve immediately or keep refrigerated for 2 to 3 days in an airtight glass bottle or jar. The juice may separate after a few hours in the refrigerator, so shake well before drinking.

Cherry Ricotta Bake

1 large or 2 small apples,
peeled, cored, and cut
into small cubes (1 to 1¼
cups)

Juice of ½ lemon

⅓ cup (85 ml) unsweetened
almond milk

1½ tablespoons ground
chia seeds

4 tablespoons coconut
sugar, divided

Seeds of 1 vanilla bean or 1
tablespoon vanilla extract

1 tablespoon coconut oil,
melted, plus more for
oiling the baking dish

15 ounces (426 g) ricotta
cheese

3 tablespoons raisins

3 tablespoons rolled oats

Zest of 1 lemon

½ teaspoon ground
cinnamon

Pinch of sea salt

1½ cups (about 210 g)
Rainier cherries, pitted
or left whole, divided

I make this breakfast on
Sundays, after our trip to
the farmers' market to
buy raw goat's milk from
a friend's farm. I make my
own goat's milk ricotta
(page 26) for this recipe,
but any ricotta will work. If
using store-bought ricotta,
it is a good idea to drain
it of any extra liquid (see
Note) to thicken the ricotta
and improve the texture of
the finished dish.

Serves 4 to 6

This recipe is a variation on a nostalgic dish most Russians are familiar with, *zapekanka*, a kind of cheese soufflé. Farmer cheese is mixed with eggs and sugar, some semolina or flour, with an occasional splash of vanilla or handful of raisins, then poured into a ceramic dish and baked until browned. Every family has their own recipe and idea about how to make it best. It is usually served in slices, like a pie. My version is lighter but still packed with flavor. Cherries are optional; any other fruit can be used, though Rainier cherries baked whole into the pie make a particularly stunning presentation.

1. Preheat the oven to 400°F (200°C). Lightly oil a medium (about 10 × 6 inches [25 × 15 cm]) glass or ceramic baking dish with coconut oil.

2. Place the cubed apples into a colander and squeeze the lemon juice over them (this will prevent the apples from turning brown). Set the apples aside while you prepare the rest of the ingredients.

3. In a blender, mix together the almond milk, ground chia seeds, ½ tablespoon of the coconut sugar, and the vanilla. Add the coconut oil, blend, and set aside. You can also whisk the ingredients by hand until thoroughly combined.

4. In a large bowl, combine the ricotta, 3 tablespoons of the remaining coconut sugar, the raisins, oats, lemon zest, cinnamon, and salt. Fold in the chia mixture. Gently stir in the apple cubes and 1 cup of the cherries, reserving the rest for the top.

5. Spoon the mixture into the lightly oiled baking dish and smooth the batter with the back of a spoon. Arrange the reserved ½ cup cherries on top, lightly pressing them halfway into the batter. Sprinkle the remaining ½ tablespoon coconut sugar on top.

6. Bake for 30 minutes, or until golden on top. Let cool slightly before serving. Divide among plates or bowls and serve with your morning tea or coffee. If you leave the cherries whole, don't forget about the pits and take care not to bite into them.

Note: To drain ricotta for use in baking, line a sieve with two layers of cheesecloth and place it over a bowl that is deeper than the sieve. There must be space between the bottom of the sieve and the inside of the bowl. Spoon the desired amount of ricotta into the sieve and tie the corners of the cheesecloth loosely around the cheese. Cover the wrapped cheese with plastic wrap and refrigerate it overnight or up to 24 hours. The excess liquid will drain and collect in the bowl. Discard the liquid and unwrap the ricotta when you're ready to use it.

Brazil Nut Oat Yogurt

Makes about 4 cups (1 liter)

I love almost any kind of yogurt, but most of all I love the tangy, unsweetened variety. When I discovered the possibility of vegan homemade yogurt, I was thrilled. Since then I've made it with fresh coconut and nuts, but the one I was most impressed with is oat yogurt. It is easy to prepare and varies in flavor and texture every time you make it, depending on the fermentation time and the temperature of your kitchen. Unlike dairy yogurt, no starter is needed to make oat yogurt, as beneficial *Lactobacillus* microorganisms occur naturally in the air and thrive on starch, water, and fiber. They produce lactic acid, which suppresses the growth of fungi, yeast, and unwanted bacteria, making fermented foods beneficial for the digestive system and body (also see Chunky Beet Sauerkraut, page 105 for another fermented food recipe).

Note: Brazil nuts are not only full of rich, earthy flavor; they also contain lots of selenium, and eating even a few of them replenishes the deficit of selenium found in most people's diet. If you prefer fruity yogurt, add your fruit of choice into the blender with the yogurt—frozen berries work especially well here. Add a tablespoon or so of cacao nibs before blending the yogurt to give some crunch and many important minerals to breakfast. Add a little honey for a sweeter yogurt or some nut or oat milk for a drinkable yogurt.

Requires a high-speed blender

1 cup (200 g) oat groats, preferably raw
1 cup (120 g) rolled oats
½ cup (80 g) Brazil nuts

1. Rinse and drain the oat groats. In a large glass or ceramic bowl, combine the oat groats and rolled oats and cover with purified water, making sure the water level is about ½ inch (1 cm) above the oats. Soak for 8 hours or overnight.

2. In a high-speed blender, blend the soaked oats with the soaking water until smooth. You may need to add more water, 2 tablespoons at a time, to achieve the ideal thickness of the yogurt. (The fermentation process does not thicken the yogurt.) Pour the mixture into a large glass bowl.

3. In a food processor, pulse the Brazil nuts into tiny pieces until they are the texture of very coarse flour, taking care to not overprocess, as the chunks of nuts in the yogurt add flavor and texture.

4. Fold the ground nuts into the oat mixture. (If you prefer a smooth yogurt, process the Brazil nuts in the blender together with the oats, adding more water as needed.)

5. Loosely cover the bowl with a lid or several layers of cheesecloth and let the mixture sit at room temperature for 1 to 3 days. Stir the yogurt with a wooden spoon every 8 hours. Taste the yogurt every time you mix it; you will recognize a telltale yogurt-like taste when fermentation has started. The length of fermentation depends on the kitchen's temperature and how tangy you like your yogurt. I prefer it sour, so I let it ferment longer. If your house is chilly, especially in the winter, consider wrapping the bowl with towels and placing it near a stove or another warm place. Once the yogurt is sour enough to your liking, it can be kept refrigerated for up to 1 week.

Metal can interfere with the fermentation process, so always use a wooden spoon and glass/ceramic ware when making yogurt.

TO MAKE AN OAT YOGURT STARTER

Although you don't need a starter to make oat yogurt, reserving about ¼ cup of the oat yogurt as a starter for the next batch can be helpful. Using a starter will help speed up the fermentation process the next time you're making this recipe. Keep the starter refrigerated in a container covered with several layers of cheesecloth. Remember that the lactobacilli in your starter are living organisms and they need food, so you must make a new batch of yogurt every 1 to 2 weeks to introduce more starch and fiber into the culture. Otherwise they will eat all the available food and will no longer be active and healthy.

Cacao Buckwheat Granola

Makes 2½ cups (about 475 g)

When I was in junior high, I visited my paternal grandparents, Anya and Aleksey, every Friday after class to help out with house chores and grocery shopping. They lived in a historic neighborhood, and theirs was the very first stone house built in our town, dating all the way back to the eighteenth century. My namesake, Anya was always waiting for me with a table piled with simple, rustic dishes to share. Often it was soup with *galushki* (a homemade pasta), dumplings stuffed with country-style cheese, chicken, and *kisel* (a traditional fresh fruit pudding). Always on her table was buckwheat porridge served cold with milk. And my grandmother would serve some of the best stories alongside those late lunches. Ever since, the taste of buckwheat brings back images of cozy meals and priceless memories.

Until a few years ago, I only used roasted buckwheat in porridge, or *kasha* in Russian. These days, raw buckwheat plays a big role in my family cooking. I've provided both the baked and raw (requiring a dehydrator) method of preparation—both are delicious and simple. You can use the baked granola recipe as a base and experiment with adding different nuts, seeds, dried fruits, rice, or quinoa puffs.

TO MAKE THE BAKED GRANOLA

1. Preheat the oven to 260°F (130°C).

2. In a large bowl, combine all the ingredients. Spread the mixture on a parchment paper–lined baking sheet and bake for 1 hour.

3. Let the granola cool completely on the baking sheet before breaking it into pieces. Store it in an airtight glass jar in the refrigerator for up to 1 week. Serve with seasonal fruit and a splash of nut milk (page 18).

TO MAKE THE RAW GRANOLA

1. Drain and place the soaked buckwheat groats into a colander or leave in a nut milk bag and rinse thoroughly under running water. Buckwheat becomes slimy after soaking, and it is very important to rinse it out completely to achieve the proper taste and texture. In a food processor, pulse all the ingredients until they are well combined.

2. Spread the buckwheat mixture on two Teflex-lined dehydrator trays. Dehydrate at 115°F (45°C) for 6 to 8 hours or overnight. Break the granola into pieces and keep refrigerated in an airtight container for up to 1 month.

For the baked granola

2 cups (varies from 310 to 340 g) buckwheat crispies (page 34) or 2 cups (400 g) raw buckwheat groats

½ cup (70 g) cacao nibs

¼ cup (65 ml) maple syrup or other liquid sweetener of your choice

3 tablespoons coconut oil, melted

For the raw granola

2 cups (400 g) raw buckwheat groats, soaked in purified water for 2 to 8 hours

½ cup (70 g) cacao nibs

½ cup (70 g) coconut sugar

¼ cup (60 ml) water

Seeds of 1 vanilla bean or ½ tablespoon vanilla extract (optional)

If you have the time to prepare them, buckwheat crispies make the best base for the baked granola. The crispies are made by soaking raw buckwheat groats for at least 1 hour and then drying them into crisps (see page 34). Unsoaked buckwheat, although still delicious, will be somewhat harder and will not absorb the flavors as much.

Apple and Carrot Breakfast Salad

For the dressing

6 tablespoons almond butter

6 tablespoons water

4 tablespoons honey, plus more to taste

½ teaspoon bee pollen

1 teaspoon ground cinnamon

Dash of freshly grated nutmeg

For the salad

3 medium firm apples, such as Honeycrisp, Fuji, Gala, peeled, cored, and shredded (about 2 cups)

3 small to medium carrots, peeled and shredded (about 2 cups)

½ cup (60 g) raisins, soaked overnight, then drained (soaking optional)

Serves 4

My maternal grandmother, Nina, to whom I was very close, influenced me in many areas of life. Nina went through true hardship during and after World War II, surviving alone with five small children, which made her very reserved and ascetic in her lifestyle, including her cooking.

We spent nearly every summer of my childhood in her wooden house in a small town on the shore of the Volga River, swimming, fishing, gardening, building stick houses, and interacting with nature. There was nothing that Nina couldn't do. She was somehow able to fit an impossible amount of tasks into one day, sewing and knitting for us, fixing things around the house, working as a nurse, cooking, at the same time being able to carry a conversation on almost any subject, and impossible to beat in a game of chess. My grandmother was the one I always ran to for advice, even into my adult years.

She liked to cook light, and this was her go-to healthy breakfast whenever she felt like we kids needed a vitamin boost. The salad could not be simpler in preparation—just finely shredded carrots and apples dressed up with a bit of sugar or farm-fresh sour cream—but the combination becomes special for its unique simplicity. During berry season, we would often add fresh-picked wild blueberries to the salad. I substitute raisins whenever blueberries are not available, especially the plump, juicy raisins I've made myself from the abundance of grapes harvested in the fall.

1. Combine all the dressing ingredients in a blender and blend until smooth.

2. In a large bowl, combine the salad ingredients and pour the dressing over, mixing well. Distribute the salad among bowls and serve.

Note: I use a mandoline with the shredding attachment for making this salad. It is very sharp and shreds apples into long pieces without making them mushy. If you are using a box grater, use the side with the largest holes and make sure the apples are firm; otherwise, they will turn to mush.

Chestnut and Buckwheat Crepes with Leeks and Mushrooms

Makes about six 8-inch (20 cm) or eighteen
5-inch (12 cm) diameter crepes

Crepes were the ultimate breakfast treat in our household when I was growing up. Transparent and thin, bubbly and golden, served with sour cream or jam—that's how I remember them in my mother's kitchen. For a heartier meal, she would stuff them with ground beef, farmer cheese, or wild mushrooms. The latter was my favorite, and mastering my own mushroom filling was a big goal of mine for my own family.

These crepes are very different from those of my childhood; they are lighter and more nutritious. There are no eggs, wheat, dairy, or butter—the usual suspects in traditional crepes—but I bet my mother would never know it if she tasted them herself.

1. In a small saucepan over low heat, warm 1 cup of the almond milk to about 105°F (40°C).

2. In a medium bowl, combine the flours with baking soda and salt. Pour in the warm almond milk and whisk until a smooth batter forms. Let sit for 30 minutes.

3. Briefly wash the shiitakes to remove any remaining dirt, squeezing out excess water with your fingers. Slice the mushrooms. In a large sauté pan, heat the ghee over medium heat. Add the leeks and sauté for about 8 minutes, stirring often, until softened. Add the shiitakes, season with salt and pepper, and sauté for another 3 to 4 minutes, until the shiitakes are softened. Add the coconut milk and herbs, if using, and sauté for another couple of minutes, or until the milk is absorbed into the vegetables. Season with salt and pepper again. Turn off the heat, cover, and set aside.

4. In a small saucepan, bring the remaining ½ cup almond milk to a boil. Add to the crepe batter in a continuous stream, stirring constantly until the texture is smooth and even. Add the grapeseed oil and stir to combine.

5. Heat a nonstick sauté pan or skillet over medium heat, then add about 1 teaspoon of oil for a 5-inch (12 cm) pan or about 2 teaspoons for an 8-inch (20 cm) pan. Start cooking the crepes by adding 2 tablespoons of batter at a time to a 5-inch pan or about ⅓ cup to an 8-inch pan. Turn the pan as you pour, letting the batter flow over the entire surface. Don't worry if the first crepe is not perfect or if it sticks to the pan a little—the first one is usually the test one.

For the crepes
1½ cups (375 ml) unsweetened almond milk, divided

½ cup (70 g) buckwheat flour

¼ cup (25 g) chestnut flour or additional ¼ cup (35 g) buckwheat flour

½ teaspoon baking soda

Pinch of salt

1 tablespoon grapeseed oil, plus more for cooking if needed

For the leek and shiitake mushroom filling
About 14 ounces (397 g) shiitake mushrooms, stems removed

1 tablespoon ghee (page 27) or grapeseed oil

2 medium leeks, white and tender green parts only, thinly sliced

Sea salt and freshly ground black pepper

4 tablespoons unsweetened full-fat canned coconut milk

1½ teaspoons minced fresh thyme (optional)

1½ teaspoons minced fresh rosemary (optional)

1½ teaspoons minced fresh sage (optional)

6. Cook the crepe for about 1 minute, until the surface is bubbly and the edges begin to turn a golden brown color. Using a thin spatula, separate the edges and then the entire crepe from the pan, making sure the batter is cooked enough to be able to hold its shape during flipping. If not, let it cook a little longer. Flip the crepe and cook the other side for about 1 minute. Continue in the same fashion until all batter is used up. I rarely add more oil as I make more crepes, but if you feel that it is necessary to avoid sticking, add 1 to 2 teaspoons at a time. The less batter you use, the thinner your crepes will be. If the batter seems too thick, add more hot milk to the batter, 2 tablespoons at a time, and mix well.

7. To serve, add about 2 tablespoons of leek and shiitake filling to each crepe and roll them up as you go; you can also serve the crepes with the filling on the side.

Notes: A good nonstick skillet is essential to the success of any pancakes or crepes. Because I use all gluten-free flours, no eggs, and fresh vegetables in my crepe recipes, the batters are particularly delicate and require a reliable good-quality nonstick frying surface. For the same reasons I like to use a smaller, 5-inch (13 cm) pan for such crepes. The smaller diameter of the pancake makes it easier to flip over.

To make sturdier, less tender crepes, whisk 1 egg with the warm milk and flour at step 2. This may also be helpful if you are new to making crepes.

Strawberry Oat Milk Smoothie

Requires a high-speed blender

For the oat milk

1 cup (200 g) oat groats, soaked overnight in purified water

2½ cups (600 ml) purified water

For the oat layer

1 cup (240 ml) oat milk

1 tablespoon honey

Seeds of ½ vanilla bean

A few ice cubes

For the strawberry layer

About 2½ cups (14 oz [400 g]) fresh strawberries

½ cup (110 ml) oat milk

2 tablespoons honey or other sweetener of choice

Seeds of ½ vanilla bean

1 tablespoon cacao nibs

1 cup ice cubes

Serves 3 to 4

This is a perfect breakfast smoothie—soothing, nutritious, and full of oats. The thick oat milk makes it substantial enough for a light meal or satisfying snack, while vanilla seeds and cacao nibs give it a decadent note. In my experience, strawberries combine best with the softness of oat milk, but other fruits and berries can be used as well. Aside from making it look pretty, arranging the smoothie in layers makes for a more interesting taste.

TO MAKE THE OAT MILK

Drain and rinse the oat groats. In a high-speed blender, combine the oats with the purified water and blend until smooth. The oat milk will keep refrigerated for up to 3 days. Shake or stir well before drinking.

TO MAKE THE OAT LAYER

Combine all the oat layer ingredients in a high-speed blender and blend until smooth. Set the mixture aside while you make the strawberry layer. It is not necessary to wash the blender before the next step.

TO MAKE THE STRAWBERRY LAYER

Combine all the strawberry layer ingredients in a high-speed blender and blend until smooth.

TO ASSEMBLE

Starting with the oat layer, pour in enough to fill about one-third of the glass. Continue with the strawberry layer, filling the glass at about three-quarters full. Then add a little bit more of the oat layer to finish the assembly. In order to prevent the layers from mixing too soon, pour each layer over the back of a teaspoon.

Note: I buy vanilla beans in packages of 20 to 30 beans online. Not only are they ten times less expensive than those sold in supermarkets; they are also much fresher and more plump. I store vanilla beans in a tightly covered jar at room temperature and never throw away the pod after removing the seeds for a recipe. Here are a few of my favorite ideas to make use of vanilla pods:

- *Slip the empty pods into jars and fill them with nuts or coconut sugar to infuse with flavor.*
- *Toss them into the blender when making smoothies or nut milk.*
- *Place the pods in a saucepan when heating nut milk for custard.*
- *Grind them with sugar when making powdered sugar.*

Amaranth Pumpkin Porridge
with cranberries and cardamom

Serves 6 to 8

Pumpkin porridge is a traditional Russian dish that reminds me so much of autumn mornings in my mother's kitchen. Traditionally this dish is made with millet, rice, or corn and a generous amount of butter. This is a much lighter version made with the highly nutritious amaranth. The flavors of vanilla bean, cardamom, coconut sugar, and cranberries combine to make a very warming meal, perfect for chilly mornings in fall and winter.

I recommend soaking the amaranth for at least eight hours to neutralize the inhibitors that prevent the digestion of nutrients in grains and nuts.

1. In a large saucepan, combine the almond milk, pumpkin, coconut sugar, cardamom, and salt. Slice open the vanilla bean lengthwise, scrape out the seeds, and add the seeds and pod to the saucepan. Bring to a gentle boil, then lower the heat and simmer, partially covered, for 15 minutes.

2. Drain and rinse the amaranth in a very-fine-mesh strainer. Add the amaranth to the saucepan and bring the mixture up to a simmer, then let it simmer for 15 minutes. Meanwhile, preheat the oven to 350°F (180°C).

3. Stir the cranberries and ghee into the porridge. Transfer the mixture to a lightly oiled medium glass or ceramic baking dish and bake uncovered for 15 to 20 minutes, until the porridge becomes bubbly on top. Remove from the oven and let cool slightly before serving. Divide among bowls and enjoy as is or top with more almond milk to make it creamier.

3 cups (750 ml) unsweetened almond milk

1 pound (454 g) pumpkin, kuri, or other winter squash, peeled, seeded, and cut into bite-size cubes

3 tablespoons coconut sugar

½ teaspoon freshly ground cardamom

½ teaspoon sea salt

1 vanilla bean

1 cup amaranth (245 g), soaked for 8 to 12 hours in purified water

½ cup dried or fresh cranberries

1 tablespoon ghee (page 27) or any oil of choice, plus more for oiling the baking dish

Key Lime Pie Breakfast Parfait

Serves 4

I am not exaggerating when I say that the Key Lime Pie smoothie from Sarma Melngailis's *Living Raw Food* cookbook is Paloma's favorite meal, not just drink, of all time. Otherwise, she changes her food preferences weekly like any four-year-old. Sarma's blend of banana, avocado, apple, and lime juice works its magic every time—it is a perfect balance of rich, sweet, and tangy. Inspired, I deconstructed Sarma's recipe to include chia seed pudding, another energizing breakfast option, in a breakfast parfait. Chia pudding is most often made with vanilla or chocolate nut milk with the same ratio as the seeds to apple juice in this recipe; you can substitute this in place of the apple version. I used white chia seeds for better presentation, but the more common black chia will work just as well.

TO MAKE THE APPLE-CHIA PUDDING

1. Juice 2 of the apples. You should end up with about ¾ cup (180 ml) of apple juice. Pour it into a blender, add ½ banana, ½ tablespoon of the lime juice, and ½ tablespoon of the honey, and blend until smooth.

2. Pour the mixture into a jar that has a tight lid and add the chia seeds. Secure the lid and shake the contents until everything is thoroughly blended. Let the mixture sit for 15 minutes to thicken, shaking the jar periodically until you have a pudding-like texture. (You can also whisk it together in a bowl instead of shaking it in a jar, stirring the mixture periodically.)

3. Cut the remaining ½ apple into small cubes and place into a small bowl. Drizzle ½ tablespoon of the remaining lime juice over it to prevent discoloration and set aside.

TO MAKE THE AVOCADO LAYER

In a blender, puree the avocado with the remaining lime juice, ½ banana, 2 tablespoons honey, and 2 tablespoons water until smooth. Add more water if needed to achieve the desired creaminess.

TO ASSEMBLE

Cube the remaining ½ banana. Arrange the parfait layers in any way you like, alternating the apple-chia pudding, apple and banana cubes, and avocado puree. Drizzle honey on top and serve immediately or chill the parfaits in the refrigerator for a couple of hours first. The parfait will still be very good the next day, although the surface of the avocado creme may discolor a little.

2½ small to medium firm green apples, divided

1½ ripe bananas, divided

Juice of 1 lime (about ¼ cup or 60 ml), divided

2½ tablespoons honey or agave syrup, divided, plus more for drizzling on top

¼ cup (45 g) chia seeds

1 ripe but firm Hass avocado

2 tablespoons purified water, plus more if needed

Note: If you don't have a juicer, you can use ¾ cup good-quality store-bought apple juice to make the apple-chia pudding.

Zucchini, Chocolate, and Blueberry Pancakes

Makes ten to fourteen 4-inch (10 cm) diameter pancakes

1 cup (240 ml) unsweetened full-fat canned coconut milk

1 tablespoon ground chia seeds or flaxseeds

⅓ cup (40 g) millet flour

⅓ cup (60 g) white rice flour

⅓ cup (40 g) quinoa flakes

Handful (about ¼ cup or 25 g) oat bran (optional)

Large pinch of sea salt

⅓ cup (60 g) good-quality chopped dark chocolate or chocolate chips

1 large egg

2 tablespoons coconut sugar

1 tablespoon grapeseed oil, plus more for the pan

1 medium zucchini (about 6 oz [170 g], to make about 1 cup finely shredded zucchini)

1 cup (150 g) fresh or frozen blueberries

If you ask Paloma what her favorite pancakes are, the answer will always be Mom's chocolate pancakes! No surprise there—chocolate is a food made of magic. In reality, these pancakes are more zucchini than they are chocolate, but your child doesn't have to know that. Despite the generous amount of shredded zucchini in the recipe, you can't see or taste it much when the pancakes are cooked. Plus, zucchini brings lightness, fluffiness, and added nutrients to these pancakes. I use semisweet dairy- and soy-free mini chocolate chips, which can be found in most health food stores. You can also use chopped raw chocolate or any other chocolate of choice. If you prefer a less sweet pancake, eliminate the chocolate and/or the blueberries from the recipe.

1. In a small bowl, combine the coconut milk and ground chia seeds. Mix thoroughly and set aside.

2. In a large bowl, combine the flours, quinoa flakes, oat bran, salt, and chocolate chips.

3. In a medium bowl, beat the egg with coconut sugar with a hand mixer until foamy, creamy, and doubled in volume. Pour the milk and chia mixture into the egg mixture, add the grapeseed oil, and mix well to combine.

4. Pour the liquid ingredients into the bowl with the dry ingredients and mix well to incorporate. Fold in the shredded zucchini.

5. Heat up a nonstick skillet over medium heat. Pour a small amount of grapeseed oil into the pan, then ladle ¼ cup of the batter into the pan for each pancake. The batter will be thick. Use a spatula to spread the batter evenly in the pan, forming pancakes 4 inches (10 cm) in diameter. It is easier to use a small omelet pan that holds one pancake at a time so you can make them more uniform. Otherwise, cook as many pancakes as your pan can hold at one time.

6. Scatter several blueberries on top of each pancake and gently press them into the batter with the spatula. Cook the batter until it becomes bubbly throughout, about 1 minute. Flip the pancakes very carefully with a thin spatula and cook the other side for about 1 minute, until golden.

7. Serve the pancakes immediately, topped with maple syrup, honey, yogurt, and/or more berries.

Matcha Kiwi Smoothie

Serves 2

Matcha tea powder is a product unique to Japan, made of a high-quality green tea plant. It takes a particular climate and special growing and processing techniques to produce the brilliant green powder. Matcha is delicious simply mixed with hot water for a flavorful tea or added to baked goods, ice cream, or smoothies to lend its subtle but complex taste. The powder contains L-Theanine, which is known to increase mental clarity, and is also rich in chlorophyll, antioxidants, and many nutrients.

Making this smoothie is an opportunity to add green leafy vegetables to your morning meal without even tasting them. It is important for the flavor to drink it cold, so have your ingredients chilled or add more ice to the blender. I prefer this smoothie slightly less sweet, but you could try adding honey, a couple of dates, stevia, or agave syrup if you'd like.

Penni, one of our recipe testers, suggested blending a large sprig of fresh mint with this smoothie.

In a high-speed blender, combine all the ingredients and blend until smooth. Adjust the sweetness and/or temperature of the smoothie to taste by adding sweetener or ice if needed. Pour into glasses and serve immediately.

Note: Vanilla-flavored pea protein has a pleasant taste, light color, and creamy texture. It's great in smoothies, especially when you are aiming for a lower-calorie drink.

Requires a high-speed blender

1 teaspoon matcha powder

1 large or 2 small ripe sweet kiwis, peeled and chopped

1 large ripe frozen banana, broken into pieces

1 cup (240 ml) almond milk (page 30)

Flesh of ½ avocado

3 Swiss chard leaves or other green leafy vegetable, tough stems removed

1 tablespoon pea protein powder (optional)

4 to 6 ice cubes, if needed

Carrot Orange Muffins

Makes 10 muffins

I didn't grow up eating muffins. After a few years of living in the United States—and finding Nigella Lawson's almond and orange muffin recipe—I came around. Hers were the first muffins I ever baked, and I became a convert right there. This light but hearty recipe is a tribute to that first batch of muffins. Their aroma rising out of the oven is a sure way to gather everyone in the kitchen.

In the fall, I often make these muffins with 1 cup of shredded butternut squash and 1 small shredded apple instead of carrots. Try using apple juice instead of orange juice in that variation or simply substitute coconut milk for all the liquids. Add fresh or dried cranberries or raisins, maybe even some chopped nuts, along with the shredded vegetables.

Note: I also make a vegan version of these muffins, which my husband prefers to the original, and he insists that I share it below.

1. Preheat the oven to 375°F (190°C). Lightly grease 10 holes of a muffin pan or line the pan with silicone or paper liners (silicone liners will work best; if you are using paper, oil with nonstick cooking spray). In a medium bowl, combine the flours, oats, orange zest, baking powder, baking soda, spices, and salt and set aside.

2. In a large bowl, beat the egg with the coconut sugar using a hand mixer until the mixture is foamy, creamy, and doubled in size. Add the orange juice, almond milk, almond butter, coconut oil, and vanilla. Mix until smooth using a hand mixer.

3. Add the dry ingredient mixture to the wet ingredients, stirring to combine. Do not overmix. Add the carrots, working them in gently without overmixing.

4. Distribute the batter evenly among 10 muffin cups. Sprinkle the remaining oats on top. Bake the muffins for 25 to 30 minutes, until a toothpick comes out dry and the tops are browned. Remove from the pan and let cool on a rack before serving. Store in an airtight container in refrigerator for up to 3 days.

For my husband's favorite vegan muffins, exclude the egg and combine the coconut sugar with the dry ingredients. Add 1 tablespoon ground chia seeds to the coconut milk, mix well, and let the mixture sit for 10 to 15 minutes while you prepare the other ingredients. Then mash 1 very ripe banana into the chia mixture with a fork.

⅔ cup (80 g) millet flour

⅓ cup (40 g) quinoa flour

⅔ cup (80 g) rolled oats, plus more for sprinkling on top

Zest of 1 orange

1 teaspoon baking powder

½ teaspoon baking soda

½ teaspoon ground cinnamon

¼ teaspoon freshly grated nutmeg

⅛ teaspoon freshly ground cardamom (optional)

Pinch of sea salt

1 large egg

¼ cup (35 g) coconut sugar

⅓ cup plus 1 tablespoon (100 ml) freshly squeezed orange juice, from about 1 orange

⅓ cup (80 ml) unsweetened almond milk

3 tablespoons almond butter

3 tablespoons coconut oil, melted

1 teaspoon vanilla extract or seeds of ½ vanilla bean

1 cup finely shredded carrots, from about 2 medium carrots

Turmeric Ginger Tea

1 to 2 lemons, juiced or in
slices
2- to 4-inch (5 to 10 cm)
piece fresh turmeric
root, peeled and
grated or sliced, or 1½
teaspoons turmeric
powder
2- to 4-inch (5 to 10 cm)
piece fresh ginger,
peeled and grated or
sliced, or 1½ teaspoon
ginger powder
Honey to taste (optional)
6 cups (1½ liters) boiling
water

Serves 6

This is an easy, sunny drink, perfect for any morning—it wakes up your body gently with the aroma of fresh spices and alkalizing lemon juice. Drink it hot to curb the winter chill or pour it over ice to cool off in the warmer months.

Turmeric is known as the king of spices and has traditionally been used to cure many ailments, from skin problems to blood clots. It is also a powerful anti-inflammatory agent. Fresh turmeric root can be found at Asian markets or organic grocery stores in the late summer, when it's in season, but turmeric powder works well too. Turmeric's vibrant color is so much fun to work with in the kitchen, but be careful—it dyes *everything* brilliant yellow. You will quickly understand why it is used as a natural fabric dye.

Every ingredient in this recipe can be adjusted to your taste, adding some honey if you prefer a sweeter drink.

1. In a large heatproof saucepan or bowl, combine the lemon, turmeric, ginger, and honey. Pour the boiling water over the ingredients and stir well. Cover the pan or bowl and let the tea steep for about 10 minutes.

2. Ladle and strain the tea into mugs and enjoy it warm, or let the tea cool completely, then store in a glass jar or bottle in the refrigerator. Leave in the pieces of lemon, ginger, and turmeric for further infusion. Strain the tea before serving.

Fig Bars

1½ cups (300 g) dried figs,
   soaked overnight in
   purified water
¼ cup (70 g) honey or other
   sweetener of choice
Juice and zest of 1 lemon
1½ cups (150 g) oat flour
1 cup (100 g) almond flour
½ cup (90 g) brown rice
   flour
1 teaspoon baking powder
½ teaspoon baking soda
¼ teaspoon sea salt
½ cup (125 g) unsweetened
   almond milk
⅓ cup (80 g) almond butter
4 tablespoons coconut
   sugar, plus more for
   sprinkling
1 tablespoon vanilla extract
Rolled oats for sprinkling
   on top (optional)

Makes 8 large or 16 small bars

A few years ago, I shared a raw fig bar recipe on *Golubka* that was very popular with readers, though it was a bit complex and required some hard-to-find ingredients. It inspired me to develop this baked version, which is simpler and more accessible yet just as nutritious and comforting—perfect to pack in a lunch box or as a quick breakfast.

1. Drain the figs, reserving the soaking liquid. In a food processor, blend the soaked figs with the honey and half of the lemon juice. If your food processor needs more liquid to puree the figs, add some of the soaking liquid, 1 tablespoon at a time. Take care not to make the fig puree too liquidy—aim for a thicker puree, as it needs to hold its shape. You can store the fig puree in the refrigerator for up to 3 days, until ready to use.

2. Preheat the oven to 400°F (200°C).

3. Meanwhile, combine the flours, baking powder, baking soda, lemon zest, and salt in a large bowl. Mix well.

4. In a medium bowl, combine the almond milk, almond butter, coconut sugar, and vanilla. Whisk to incorporate. Mix in the rest of the lemon juice. Pour the liquid ingredients into the dry mixture and knead into a soft dough. Divide the dough in half.

5. Line a 9 × 9 × 2-inch (23 × 23 × 5 cm) baking dish with parchment paper, extending it up the sides of the dish. Evenly distribute half of the dough in the dish by lightly pressing it into the bottom of the pan. Spoon in the fig puree and spread over the dough in an even layer.

6. Crumble the remaining half of the dough on top of the fig layer, a small amount at a time. Lightly press down on the dough so the crumbles stick together as much as possible without disturbing the fig layer.

7. Sprinkle the top layer of dough with coconut sugar and rolled oats. Bake for 20 to 25 minutes. If you want your bars to have a golden brown top, turn on the broiler for the last minute or two of baking, but watch closely so the top does not burn. Remove the pan from the oven and let cool completely.

8. Lift the fig bars from the pan with the parchment paper and place on a cutting board. Cut into 8 large or 16 small bars with a sharp knife. The bars will be soft and may be a little crumbly on top, but they are nevertheless delicious.

Kale and Mustard Muffins

Makes 12 muffins

Ever since I added muffins to my repertoire, the savory kinds have kept me most intrigued. They are the perfect opportunity to pack some nutritious vegetables into a tasty snack, such as kale. I love how the spice of the mustard and smokiness of Worcestershire sauce combine with buckwheat flour and greens. These muffins are slightly denser than traditional ones, but the flavor is so rich that the texture doesn't interfere.

1. Preheat the oven to 400°F (200°C). Lightly grease a 12-hole muffin tin or line it with silicone or paper liners. (Silicone liners work best; if you are using paper liners, oil the insides with nonstick cooking spray.) In a food processor, grind 1 cup of the pumpkin seeds into a coarse flour. Lightly toast the remaining ¼ cup pumpkin seeds on a dry skillet over medium heat for 3 to 4 minutes, shaking the pan frequently.

2. In a large bowl, combine the ground and toasted pumpkin seeds, the flours, cheese, baking powder, baking soda, mustard powder, and salt. Aerate with a fork.

3. In a medium bowl, whisk together the coconut milk, grapeseed oil, mustard, and Worcestershire sauce. Add the liquid ingredients to the dry ingredients and mix lightly with a fork, incorporating the chopped kale while you are mixing. Take care not to overmix—the batter should be lumpy, and the ingredients should be no more than barely combined.

4. Spoon the muffin batter evenly among 12 muffin cups, then sprinkle the tops with the pumpkin seeds. Bake for 20 to 25 minutes, until the tops are golden brown and a toothpick inserted in the center comes out clean. Remove the muffins from the oven and immediately sprinkle the tops with a little cheese and Worcestershire sauce. Put the muffins back in the oven and bake for another 5 minutes, then remove the muffins from the oven.

5. Let the muffins cool slightly in the pan, just enough for you to be able to handle them. Remove the muffins and place them on a wire rack to cool before serving. Store in an airtight container in refrigerator for up to 3 days.

Note: Make sure to buy anchovy-free Worcestershire sauce if you are vegetarian or vegan.

1¼ cups (200 g) pumpkin seeds, plus more for sprinkling on top

¾ cup (105 g) buckwheat flour

½ cup (90 g) brown rice flour

½ cup (50 g) almond flour

⅓ cup (30 g) shredded Manchego cheese, plus more for sprinkling on top

1 teaspoon baking powder

½ teaspoon baking soda

1 teaspoon English mustard powder (optional)

¼ teaspoon sea salt

1¼ cups (310 ml) unsweetened full-fat canned coconut milk

¼ cup (60 ml) grapeseed oil or other vegetable oil of choice, plus more for greasing the muffin pan if not using liners

2 tablespoons Dijon mustard

2 tablespoons Worcestershire sauce (see Note), plus more for drizzling

2 cups loosely packed finely chopped kale, from about 3 to 5 leaves, stems removed

Chocolate Hemp Bars
with prune caramel

1 cup (170 g) prunes,
soaked in purified water
overnight
9 ounces (250 g) raw
chocolate, good-quality
dark chocolate, or
chocolate chips
1 cup (150 g) hemp hearts
1 cup quinoa puffs (70 g) or
1 cup (155 g) buckwheat
crispies (page 34)

Makes 16 bars

Hemp hearts are shelled hemp seeds and are a rich source of protein, essential fatty acids, and iron, while cholesterol-free and low in saturated fat. I love them sprinkled on fruit in the morning, in salads throughout the day, or added to crackers or cookies.

In a way, these bars are like a very healthy candy bar; the combination of chocolate and caramel with the nutty hemp hearts and crispy quinoa puffs sounds right at home in the supermarket checkout aisle. But these are a thousand times better for you. Enjoy these bars as a snack, dessert, or even for breakfast, particularly if you are using raw chocolate. I make the caramel with prunes, but you can experiment with dried apricots or a combination of apricots and prunes instead.

1. Drain the prunes and reserve the soaking water. Place them into the bowl of a food processor and puree until smooth, adding small amounts of the soaking water as needed. The puree should be as thick as possible, so use the least amount of water needed for the food processor to blend the prunes into a smooth puree. Set aside.

2. In a large bowl, make the raw chocolate according to the instructions on page 32 or melt the dark chocolate or chocolate chips in a double boiler. Fold the hemp hearts and quinoa puffs into the melted chocolate until evenly incorporated. The mixture will be thick. (If you are using raw chocolate and like your treats on the sweet side, you may want to add 1 to 2 additional table-spoons of agave syrup or another sweetener into the mixture. Raw chocolate is less sweet than store-bought chocolate.)

3. Line a 9 × 9 × 2-inch (23 × 23 × 5 cm) baking pan with parchment paper. Spoon half of the melted chocolate mixture into the pan. Spread the mixture evenly, making sure to fill the corners of the pan.

4. Spoon the prune caramel on top of the chocolate layer and level it with the back of a spoon.

Note: You can buy quinoa puffs online (see Resources, page 319) and in some health food stores.

5. Spread the remaining half of the hemp-chocolate mixture evenly on top of the prune caramel, working with small portions of the mixture at a time to create an even layer. Take care to not press too hard and disturb the prune layer. With a sharp knife, carefully score the bars: 3 horizontal lines and 3 vertical lines, creating 16 bars. Cut the bars all the way through (after you freeze the bars, you will break them apart). Place the pan in the freezer until the surface of the bars is firm, about 30 minutes or longer.

6. Carefully remove the bars from the pan and break them apart into individual squares. The bars will keep refrigerated in an airtight container for up to 1 week. Serve cold.

2

Savories

WHEN THINKING ABOUT SAVORY FLAVORS, MY MEMORIES take me back to a small, remote campground high up in the Caucasus Mountains. My parents made the four-hour journey there every year in the late summer and stayed for a month of mushroom and berry picking. My father was an avid nature lover and an expert on wild mushrooms, and this was his kingdom. To be fair, he was successful in anything he tried, being a specialist in engineering, writing, several sports, and business, all the while managing to be the best husband and father. The campground consisted of five wooden houses, a large public kitchen, and a Russian sauna (*banya*), situated on a mountain riverbank. The beauty of that place was, quite literally, breathtaking. The small valley was surrounded by young, high mountains, and the snow peaks seemed within reach. The air was crisp and sweet, the roaring sound of the river was almost musical, and the water was crystal clear and delicious. At night the stars shined so bright and in such abundance that there wasn't any room left for the dark sky.

Every year five families came to the campground to enjoy their time mushroom and berry picking. The men usually left right after breakfast and went their separate ways to places kept secret from everybody else in order to protect their mushroom crop. It was a foragers' competition, although a very friendly one. The women looked for berries, which included blueberries, woodland strawberries, raspberries, and stone bramble berries. By late afternoon, everyone reunited in the valley and showed off their lucky finds. The rest of the day was spent sorting, cleaning, salting, and marinating the mushrooms, and every meal thereafter involved them in its preparation. I remember eating the most delicious mushroom dumplings and mushroom borscht, along with pilaf, ragout, crepes, and even mushroom-topped deviled eggs. Each kind had its own deep, earthy flavor, and nothing could substitute or replicate the taste of their freshness. After a month in mushroom heaven, we had enough dried and preserved crop to last us through the next year.

Watching the women exercise their creativity in preparing wholesome savory dishes from what was foraged in wild nature fascinated me to no end, and those memories have remained vivid in my mind.

With the exception of breakfast, I see little distinction between particular dishes for certain times of day. Any savory dish I cook can become a substantial lunch or a light dinner. Though I tend to eat more during the day and a very light dinner, dinner is considered the main meal in many families. I decided to group most of the savory dishes in this book into one chapter, letting you decide which ones best suit your idea of lunch, dinner, or snack.

My free approach to the definition of dinner turns quite serious when cooking for company. I love planning meals and feeding friends and family, always aiming to impress with dishes that are both nourishing and tasty. I share some of these entertaining ideas in this chapter too.

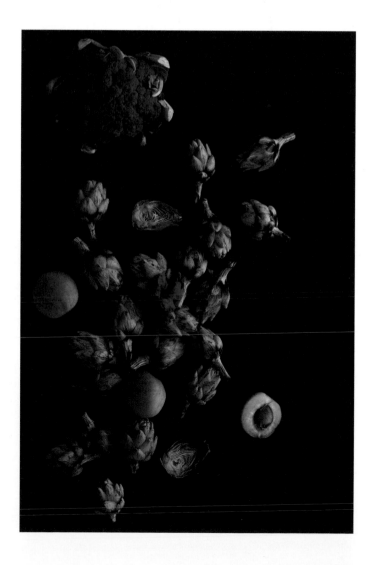

SALADS AND SIDES

Fava Bean, Quinoa, and Mint Salad

Serves 4

I await the spring arrival of fresh fava beans with little patience, cook with them all season long, and still cannot get enough. Aside from their flavor, the process of shelling and cooking with fava beans stimulates the senses. Their pods are soft inside, and the beans have a second, podlike jacket that reveals the most brilliant green bean when removed. The tender, buttery texture of fava beans is hard to replace, although fresh green peas come close.

   This salad is best in spring, when asparagus, fava beans, and peas are young and bursting with freshness. You can add or eliminate any of the vegetables, depending on what is available or to your taste.

1. Whisk together all the dressing ingredients in a small bowl until well combined and set aside.

2. In a medium saucepan, combine the quinoa with 2 cups water, add a generous pinch of salt, and bring to a boil. Lower the heat, cover, and simmer for 20 minutes. Remove from the heat and let cool.

3. Bring a large pot of well-salted water to a boil. Meanwhile, prepare a large bowl of ice water. Blanch the fava beans for 3 minutes, then remove the beans from the boiling water with a slotted spoon and transfer them to the ice-water bath to stop the cooking. When cooled completely, remove the fava beans from the ice-water bath and peel off the outer skin by gentle pressing against the sides of each bean with your fingers until the bean pops out.

4. Continue blanching the English peas, snow peas, sugar snap peas, and asparagus, boiling them for 2 minutes and shocking in the ice-water bath. Once cooled, drain the vegetables and place on paper towels or clean kitchen towels. Pat dry.

5. In a large bowl, combine the quinoa, blanched vegetables, cherry tomatoes, apricots, mint, and cilantro. Pour the dressing over the salad and grind some pepper on top. Mix gently and adjust the seasonings with salt and pepper. Serve at room temperature or refrigerate and serve cold within a day.

For the dressing

1 tablespoon maple syrup
1½ teaspoons Dijon mustard
2 tablespoons freshly squeezed lemon juice
2 tablespoons olive oil
Pinch of sea salt

For the salad

½ cup (100 g) white quinoa
½ cup (100 g) red or black quinoa
Sea salt
2 cups (300 g) fresh shelled fava beans, from about 2 pounds (907 g) fava bean pods
1 cup (145 g) fresh shelled peas, from about 9 ounces (255 g) English peas in the pod
Handful of snow peas, ends trimmed and strings removed
Handful of sugar snap peas, ends trimmed and strings removed
8 asparagus spears, tough ends removed, cut into 3 pieces each
Handful of cherry tomatoes, halved
5 fresh ripe or 10 dried apricots, soaked in purified water for 2 hours, chopped (optional)
About 20 fresh mint leaves, roughly chopped
Handful of fresh cilantro leaves (optional)
Freshly ground black pepper

Miso and Raspberry Forbidden Rice Salad

3 small golden beets

1 cup (215 g) heirloom forbidden black rice

½ cup (150 ml) olive oil

7 teaspoons miso paste

1 tablespoon honey

1½ tablespoons freshly squeezed lime juice

Freshly ground black pepper

1 bunch watercress (about 5 oz [140 g])

About 9 medium radishes, preferably Easter egg radishes, sliced

1 cup black raspberries or red raspberries

Handful of ground pistachio nuts for garnish (optional)

Serves 4

One summer I got my hands on the most beautiful black raspberries, and I developed this recipe to highlight their color. Combined with golden beets and black rice, it is stunning on the plate. If black raspberries are unavailable, feel free to use red raspberries. And if you can find Easter egg radishes, the salad becomes as pretty as a painting.

1. Cook beets in your preferred way—roast, boil, or steam them until cooked throughout (see Note). Let them cool.

2. While the beets are cooking, prepare rice according to the package instructions. Let cool.

3. Peel and slice the beets into about ¼-inch (½ cm) thick slices.

4. In a small jar with a tight-fitting lid, combine the olive oil, miso paste, honey, and lime juice; season with pepper and shake well to combine. Alternatively, whisk the dressing ingredients in a small bowl.

5. Arrange the watercress, rice, beets, radishes, and raspberries on serving plates and pour the dressing over the salad. Garnish with the ground pistachios.

Note: Roast beets wrapped in aluminum foil in a preheated 400°F (200°C) oven for 45 minutes to 1 hour, depending on their size, until tender throughout when pierced with a knife.

Boil or steam beets for 45 minutes to 1 hour, depending on their size, until tender throughout when pierced with a knife.

Strawberry Soba Salad

Serves 4

This recipe was inspired by a dish at Cha-Ya, a vegan Japanese restaurant in the Mission district of San Francisco. The salad combined soba noodles and strawberries with a fragrant ginger dressing. As it often happens when traveling, we went overboard with our food intake and at the end of the day craved the clean meals of Cha-Ya, each of which was amazingly flavorful and light.

Make this salad when the strawberries and peas are in season and enjoy all the bright flavors of spring and early summer.

TO MAKE THE DRESSING

In a small jar with a tight-fitting lid, combine all the dressing ingredients and shake well to combine. Alternatively, whisk the dressing ingredients in a small bowl.

TO MAKE THE SALAD

1. Cook the soba noodles in a saucepan of boiling water according to the package instructions, 5 to 7 minutes. Drain, and rinse with cold water.

2. Bring a large pot of well-salted water to a boil. Meanwhile, prepare a large bowl of ice water for shocking the vegetables. Blanch the snow peas, sugar snap peas, English peas, and edamame in the boiling water for 2 minutes. Quickly transfer them to an ice-water bath with a large slotted spoon. You can also pour all the blanched vegetables into a colander over the sink, then transfer them into the ice-water bath to stop the cooking.

3. Remove the vegetables from the ice water with a slotted spoon or drain through a colander, then gently dry with paper towels or a clean kitchen towel.

4. In a large bowl, combine the noodles, peas, edamame, carrot, bell pepper, cucumbers, seaweed, strawberries, and cilantro. Pour the dressing over the salad and stir gently to coat. Top with the sesame seeds and serve immediately.

For the dressing

1-inch (2½ cm) piece fresh ginger, peeled and grated

3 tablespoons sesame oil

1 tablespoon olive oil

1½ tablespoons nama shoyu or tamari

½ tablespoon honey

1 tablespoon freshly squeezed lime juice

For the salad

1 9-ounce package soba noodles

Sea salt

Small handful of snow peas, ends trimmed and strings removed

Small handful of sugar snap peas, ends trimmed and strings removed

1 cup (140 g) shelled fresh or frozen English peas

1 cup (140 g) shelled frozen edamame

1 medium carrot, thinly sliced or shaved with a vegetable peeler

1 medium red, orange, or yellow bell pepper (or the equivalent of 1 pepper in 2 or 3 colors), cored and thinly sliced

1 large or 2 small cucumbers, thinly sliced

2 pieces kombu seaweed or 1 nori sheet, cut into thin stripes

About 12 strawberries, hulled and sliced

½ bunch cilantro, leaves only

2 tablespoons sesame seeds, toasted

Summer Bounty Salad

Sea salt

About 10 ounces (285 g) young green beans or French beans, ends trimmed

About 6 ounces (170 g) fresh shelled green peas

1 small carrot, shaved with a vegetable peeler

1 small head radicchio, thinly sliced

About 10 radishes, thinly sliced

Zest and juice of 1 lemon

3 tablespoons chopped fresh parsley

3 tablespoons chopped fresh dill

2 teaspoons whole coriander seeds

1 teaspoon whole cumin seeds

1 teaspoon whole yellow mustard seeds

½ teaspoon whole fenugreek seeds (optional)

2 tablespoons olive oil

1 garlic clove, peeled and crushed with a knife

Handful of berries, such as cherries and raspberries (optional)

Serves 4 to 6

When I first made this salad, it was nothing more than an attempt to put together the produce I had on hand into one meal. It turned out so well that everyone who tried it declared it was one of the best salads they'd ever had. And I don't think anyone has changed their mind since.

1. Blanch the green beans in a pot of well-salted boiling water for about 4 minutes, until crisp-tender, then shock them in an ice-water bath. In the same water, blanch the peas for about 20 seconds, until crisp-tender, and shock them in the ice water. Remove the vegetables from the ice water when cool and gently dry them with a dishtowel or paper towels.

2. In a large bowl, combine the green beans, peas, carrot, radicchio, radishes, zest of the lemon, parsley, and dill.

3. In a mortar and pestle or coffee grinder, coarsely grind the coriander, cumin, mustard, and fenugreek seeds. Heat the olive oil in a small skillet over medium-low heat, add the crushed seeds and garlic, and cook for 2 to 3 minutes, until fragrant. Pour the hot oil over the salad, season with salt, and add a generous squeeze of lemon juice. Mix gently, add the berries, if using, and serve immediately.

Large Autumn Salad

Serves 4 to 6

This salad combines all the beauty of the autumn harvest in one bowl. It is colorful and nourishing, with a warming note of baked apple vinaigrette and bright bursts of fresh pomegranate. I prefer red kuri squash, also known as Hokkaido squash, for this dish. Its bright flesh has a sweet, creamy taste, and its skin is thin and edible when cooked, so you don't need to peel it—perfect for a salad. Other winter squashes such as kabocha or butternut will work great as well.

For the salad

1½ cups (about 150 g) Brussels sprouts

½ cup (60 g) pecan or walnut halves

3 to 5 and small or baby red beets, peeled and cut into 4 to 8 wedges, depending on the size of the beets

3 to 5 small or baby golden beets, peeled and cut into 4 to 8 wedges, depending on the size of the beets

2 tablespoons olive oil, divided

Sea salt and freshly ground black pepper

½ medium red kuri or other winter squash, seeds removed and sliced into wedges

½ teaspoon paprika

3 small or 2 large apples, cored and sliced

1 large ripe pear, stemmed, cored, and sliced

2 handfuls of fresh salad greens

1 ripe persimmon, sliced (optional)

Seeds of ½ pomegranate

For the baked apple vinaigrette

½ cup baked apple slices

2 tablespoons pomegranate molasses

1 tablespoon walnut or other nut oil

2 teaspoons apple cider vinegar

1 teaspoon Dijon mustard

¼ teaspoon sea salt

¼ cup (60 ml) olive oil

2 tablespoons purified water, plus more if needed

TO PREPARE THE SALAD

1. Preheat the oven to 350°F (180°C).

2. Wash the Brussels sprouts and remove the tough outer leaves and stems. Cut a cross through the stem of each sprout, place them in a large bowl, cover with water, and leave to soak for a couple of hours—this will leach away their bitterness.

3. Place the nuts on a baking sheet and toast them in the oven for 7 to 10 minutes. Remove from the oven and increase the oven temperature to 400°F (200°C).

4. Place the red and golden beets into 2 small separate baking dishes to prevent discoloration. Rub them with ½ tablespoon olive oil each and season with salt and pepper. Cover with foil and bake for 45 minutes, or until tender.

5. Drain the Brussels sprouts. Briefly dry with paper towels and cut each in half. Place them in a bowl with the squash slices, sprinkle with the remaining 1 tablespoon olive oil, salt to taste, and paprika and mix to coat.

6. Arrange the Brussels sprouts, squash, and apple slices on a baking sheet, alternating the ingredients. Bake for 20 minutes, or until the Brussels sprouts and squash are tender.

7. Reserve ½ cup of baked apple slices for the vinaigrette. In a large bowl, combine the beets, squash, the remaining apple slices, the Brussels sprouts, and pear.

TO MAKE THE VINAIGRETTE AND ASSEMBLE THE SALAD

1. In a blender, combine all the vinaigrette ingredients and blend until smooth. Pour over the salad and toss to coat.

2. Arrange the salad on a bed of fresh greens. Garnish with persimmon slices, pomegranate seeds, and toasted nuts before serving.

Note: If you are not a fan of Brussels sprouts, you can make this salad without them, and it will still be delicious.

Roasted Kala Chana Hummus

with crunchy tahini chickpeas

Serves 4 to 6

Kala chana is a variety of chickpeas (also known as garbanzo beans). They are dark brown, smaller, nuttier, and more nutritionally concentrated than tan chickpeas. I buy kala chana online; they come from India and are very inexpensive. If you want to add novelty to something as familiar as hummus, give kala chana a chance. Starting with canned chickpeas will give you a shorter preparation time.

This hummus can be made in one of two ways: using cooked or sprouted chickpeas. I like to sprout chickpeas, as I find them much easier to digest when sprouted. Both versions have a delicious spicy lemony flavor and can be used as a base for different additions, such as roasted garlic, tomatoes, bell peppers, or herbs. Mix the crunchy tahini chickpeas into the hummus for texture, eat as a snack, or sprinkle on salads.

DRIED OR CANNED CHICKPEAS

1. If using dried chickpeas, soak them for 8 hours or overnight in plenty of purified water. Drain and rinse thoroughly. Place the chickpeas in a large saucepan with 8 cups of purified water and bring to a boil. Lower the heat and simmer, uncovered, for 25 to 30 minutes, until tender (see Note). Add 1½ tablespoons salt during the last 10 minutes of cooking. Drain the chickpeas, reserving about ½ cup of cooking liquid for later. Set aside. If using canned chickpeas, drain them, reserving the liquid.

2. Preheat the oven to 400°F (200°C).

3. Cut the onion quarter into 3 or 4 wedges. Rub in ½ tablespoon olive oil, place on an aluminum foil–covered baking sheet, and roast for 20 to 25 minutes. Remove from the oven, let cool, then roughly chop and set aside. Keep the oven at 400°F (200°C).

4. Grind the cumin, coriander, mustard, cardamom seeds, and red pepper flakes in a designated coffee grinder or with a mortar and pestle. In a medium bowl, combine the spice mixture, tahini, the remaining 6 tablespoons olive oil, the lemon juice, coconut sugar, and the remaining 1 teaspoon salt. Mix well.

5. Divide the chickpeas into 2 equal portions, about 1¼ cups each. Set one portion aside for making the hummus. To make the crunchy chickpeas, place the other portion on a kitchen towel or several layers of paper towels and

1 cup (200 g) dried kala chana or tan chickpeas, or 2½ cups (390 g) canned chickpeas, drained

1½ tablespoons sea salt, for boiling the chickpeas, plus 1 teaspoon for the tahini mixture

¼ medium red onion

6½ tablespoons olive oil, divided, plus more for oiling the baking dish

1 tablespoon cumin seeds

½ tablespoon coriander seeds

1 teaspoon yellow mustard seeds

Seeds of 4 cardamom pods

¼ teaspoon red pepper flakes

6 tablespoons sesame tahini (page 32)

6 tablespoons freshly squeezed lemon juice

4 teaspoons coconut sugar

2 large garlic cloves, minced, divided

dry them well, removing the remaining skins. Place them in a medium bowl and add ¼ cup of the tahini mixture and about three-quarters of the minced garlic, tossing to coat. Spread the chickpeas on a baking sheet lined with parchment paper. Bake for 25 to 30 minutes, stirring every 10 minutes, until they are crisp and dark brown for kala chana or light brown for tan chickpeas. Watch them carefully toward the end, as every oven is slightly different and you may need a little less or more time for your chickpeas. Take care not to burn them.

Remove the baking sheet from the oven and let cool. The chickpeas will get crispier as they cool.

6. Combine the reserved portion with the remaining tahini mixture, the remaining garlic, and the roasted onion in a food processor. Blend until well combined and fairly smooth, scraping the sides of the bowl and adding the reserved cooking or canned liquid (if needed) to a desired consistency, 1 tablespoon at a time. Season with salt.

7. Serve with the crunchy chickpeas mixed in or on top of hummus, garnished with herbs, or on top of Quick Spelt Bread (page 315), fresh cucumber slices, or crackers/chips of your choice.

SPROUTED CHICKPEAS

1. Sprout chickpeas according to the instructions on page 36.

2. Follow steps 2, 3, and 4 from above.

3. Divide sprouted chickpeas into 2 equal portions, set one aside, and dry the other one on several layers of paper towels. In a medium bowl, combine the dried portion with ¼ cup of the tahini mixture and half of the minced garlic. Mix to coat and spread on a parchment paper–covered baking tray. Set aside. In the same bowl, combine ⅓ cup of tahini mixture, the remaining garlic, and the remaining chickpeas. Mix well, transfer to a small, shallow, lightly oiled baking dish, and cover with aluminum foil.

4. Place both the sheet and the baking dish into the oven and roast for 25 to 30 minutes, stirring the uncovered chickpeas (for crunchy chickpeas) every 10 minutes and the covered (for hummus) just once. Watch the uncovered chickpeas carefully; they should be crisp and dark brown for kala chana and light brown for tan chickpeas. Every oven is slightly different, and you may need a little less or more time for your chickpeas to be done. Take care not to burn them.

5. Remove both the sheet and the baking dish from the oven and let cool. Place the covered portion of the chickpeas in a food processor with the rest of the tahini sauce, garlic, and roasted onion. Blend until fairly smooth, adding water if needed to help with blending. Sprouted and roasted chickpeas are

When writing about hummus, I can't resist mentioning my husband, who will give just about anything for a hummus wrap, no matter what time of day it is. His dream afternoon is skiing some black diamond trails and snacking on a hummus wrap right on the slopes. This fixation is a subject of many jokes in our family and an incentive for me to always look for new hummus ideas.

slightly drier and harder than boiled chickpeas, so you will most likely use more liquid. Season with salt.

6. Serve with the crunchy chickpeas mixed in or on top of hummus, garnished with herbs, or on top of Quick Spelt Bread (page 315), fresh cucumber slices, or crackers or chips of your choice.

Note: The cooking time for chickpeas varies and is determined simply by how old they are. The longer they've been dry, the more time they need to cook. The chickpeas I buy in our local health food store never require more than 20 to 30 minutes of boiling time to be perfectly cooked. Most sources will tell you to boil chickpeas for 60 to 90 minutes after overnight soaking, but that amount of time would turn my chickpeas into a mushy mess. The best approach is to taste your chickpeas periodically and determine when they're done according to how tender they are.

Chunky Beet Sauerkraut

Makes one 10-liter or two 5-liter pots, or about 3 gallons capacity total (preferably ceramic crocks or food-grade buckets that are tolerant to high temperatures)

Cabbage and beets are staples in Russian cuisine, and there are as many ways to preserve them as there are households. Traditional sauerkraut is made in barrels and used in a simple potato-sauerkraut soup or as a condiment at meals. Good Russian sauerkraut should be crisp but not tough and is usually is made with shredded cabbage. This recipe is from my friend Elena's father, who makes it every winter in huge quantities, as his family is large and the sauerkraut is addictive. On top of being delicious, it's very good for you, as is anything made by way of natural fermentation.

2 medium cabbages, about 7 pounds (3 kg [200 g]) total
3 to 4 large beets
2 to 3 garlic heads, peeled
Red pepper flakes (optional)
½ gallon (2 liters) boiling water
2 tablespoons sea salt

1. Prepare a very large crock or plastic bucket, or split the amount of cabbage in two, depending on the size of the pots you have on hand. For the press, find a plate that fits inside your vessel and a heavy object, like a jar filled with water. Rinse the cabbage and remove the tough outer leaves. Cut the cabbage in half through the stem, then slice each half into 4 wedges, then cut them in half widthwise. You will have 16 pieces per cabbage. If you prefer, you may also cut or shred the cabbage however you'd like.

2. Peel the beets, then slice them into ¼-inch (½ cm) thick rounds. Arrange the vegetables on the bottom of the pot in layers. Begin with a single layer of cabbage, followed by beets and garlic, and some red pepper flakes, if using. Continue in the same order, pressing the vegetables snugly inside the pot to fill it almost completely.

3. Dissolve the salt in the boiling water to make a brine. Immediately pour the brine over the vegetables. Place a plate on top, followed by a heavy object to make a press. Cover. Let sit at room temperature, away from direct sunlight, for 3 days total.

4. Check the sauerkraut in 24 hours. The cabbage should have released its juices and the liquid should be covering the vegetables. If the brine doesn't cover the vegetables, boil more water and dissolve more salt (in the same ratio as the original brine) and pour it into the crock to cover the vegetables completely. You can also increase the weight of the press on top to further encourage the water to be released.

5. Taste the cabbage after 3 days. It should be pleasantly crunchy. Often the top layer of cabbage will be somewhat tough and chewy, but the cabbage from the middle of the pot should be at just the right crunchiness. The sauerkraut will keep in the refrigerator in an airtight container for months, providing that it is covered with brine completely, and the taste and texture will further improve after more time in the brine.

Cranberry Chutney

4 cups (400 g) fresh or
    frozen cranberries

2½ cups (350 g) light brown
    sugar

1 cup (240 ml) water

2 cinnamon sticks

4 to 6 whole cloves

1 tablespoon chopped fresh
    ginger

¼ teaspoon ground allspice

¼ teaspoon sea salt

2 medium Granny Smith
    apples

2 ripe but firm pears, such
    as Bosc or Anjou

1 small or ½ large yellow
    onion

1 cup golden raisins

⅓ cup (80 ml) apple cider
    vinegar

Makes about 8 cups

This chutney is a wonderful addition to any fall or winter menu, as it complements nearly any dish and is even good on its own. It can accompany a savory meal or be enjoyed as a dessert, thanks to the versatility of cranberries.

1. In a large saucepan, combine the cranberries, brown sugar, water, cinnamon, cloves, ginger, allspice, and salt. Bring to a boil over medium heat and cook for 10 to 12 minutes, stirring often, until the cranberries begin to pop open.

2. Peel and core the apples and pears and dice them into ½ inch (1¼ cm) cubes. Peel the onion and chop it into small pieces. Lower the heat to a simmer. Add the remaining ingredients to the cranberries and cook for about another 15 minutes, stirring frequently, until thickened.

3. Remove from the heat and cool to room temperature. Discard the cinnamon sticks and cloves. Serve immediately, or keep refrigerated for up to 10 days.

In the cellar of my childhood home, my mother kept dozens of jars of her homemade preserves, most of which were made from fruits and vegetables from her own garden. The cellar was a dark, cool, and mysterious place with a single dim lightbulb hanging from an uneven ceiling. I loved the musty smell and the mixed feelings of slight fear and excitement from venturing down there when my mother asked me to choose what I wanted to eat that day. The choices were myriad: pickled tomatoes, crunchy cucumbers with dill flowers, garlic and herb–stuffed bell peppers, eggplants mixed with herbs and spices. The fruit preserves and jams offered even more abundance: whole apricots in sweet syrup, black currants, sour cherries, strawberries, and golden quince.

Marinated Stuffed Poblano Chiles

with Jerusalem artichokes, grapes, olives, and pine nuts

Makes 6 stuffed chiles

These stuffed chiles remind me of my time in Spain and the fresh, vibrant food I tasted when I traveled to Catalonia. Although poblano chiles are more at home in Latin food cultures, the crunchy stuffing full of herbs is a nod to the Mediterranean. I use Jerusalem artichokes (also called sunchokes) in the stuffing, but you can substitute jicama or even ¾ cup cooked rice or quinoa.

Most poblano chiles give off a very mild, spicy fragrance when grilled, but occasionally they are quite hot. It is always a good idea to taste a tiny piece before grilling to make sure it's not an extremely fiery chile (it has happened to me before!). You can also substitute bell peppers for the poblanos.

For the chiles

6 large poblano chiles or bell peppers

2 to 3 garlic cloves, thinly sliced

2 tablespoons chopped fresh dill and/or other herbs

¼ cup (60 ml) olive oil

2 tablespoons apple cider vinegar

1 tablespoon red or white wine vinegar

For the filling

Zest and juice of 1 lemon

About 5 ounces (150 g) Jerusalem artichokes

½ cup (100 g) yellow heirloom cherry tomatoes or other tomatoes, cubed

½ small garlic clove, minced

6 assorted olives, such as Castelvetrano and black and green Cerignola, pitted and chopped

About ½ cup black or other grapes, chopped

¼ cup pine nuts, toasted (see page 12) if you like

3 tablespoons chopped fresh dill

3 tablespoons chopped fresh mint

3 tablespoons torn fresh opal or regular basil leaves

1½ teaspoons olive oil

Sea salt

TO MARINATE THE CHILES

1. Cut a slit down the side of each poblano. Carefully remove the seeds and membranes from the inside of each chile, taking care to keep it intact (you might want to wear gloves to protect your hands from burning). Turn on the broiler.

2. Place all the chiles on a foil-covered baking sheet and place under the broiler. Check every 2 minutes, turning the chiles as their skin blackens, until all sides are wrinkled and dark.

Remove the chiles from the oven, place in a bowl, cover with plastic, then let them cool. Once cooled, peel away the skin.

3. Arrange the chiles in a clean medium jar with a tight-fitting lid, placing the garlic slices and dill around them. Whisk the olive oil and vinegars in a separate bowl and pour the mixture over the poblanos. Tighten the lid and refrigerate overnight. This step can be done well in advance if you sterilize the jar before marinating. If you do this, the chiles will keep in the fridge for months and can be used in many different recipes, as an addition to salads, or a side dish.

TO MAKE THE STUFFING AND FILL THE CHILES

1. Fill a medium bowl two-thirds full with cold water and squeeze the juice from ½ lemon into it. Peel the Jerusalem artichokes and place them in the lemon water as you go to prevent discoloration.

2. Roughly chop the Jerusalem artichokes, then pulse them in a food processor until they are in rice grain–size pieces. (If using jicama instead of sunchokes, place the chopped pieces between several layers of paper towels to remove as much excess moisture as possible.)

3. In a medium bowl, combine the artichokes, the juice from the remaining ½ lemon, the lemon zest, tomatoes, garlic, olives, grapes, pine nuts, dill, mint, basil, olive oil, and a pinch of salt. Gently mix and place into a colander set over a bowl for 20 to 30 minutes to drain excess liquid.

4. Remove the poblanos from the marinade and gently squeeze them to remove excess marinade. Using a spoon, fill each chile with the drained stuffing. If you like, you can serve with more grapes on the side and garnish with basil.

Peach and Avocado Summer Rolls

Makes 15 rolls

These rolls are perfect for any outdoor summer party; they are quick and easy to make and impressive in appearance and flavor. I've witnessed the most dedicated meat eaters rave about these rolls, claiming that they are the best fare for cooling the summer heat. Just a warning: When you serve these rolls at a party, be prepared to give out this recipe many times over.

For the sauce

4 tablespoons smooth almond butter (page 30)
2 tablespoon tamarind paste
1 tablespoon maple syrup
1 tablespoon grated ginger
1 teaspoon nama shoyu or tamari

For the rolls

2 medium ripe, firm Hass avocados, peeled, pitted, and sliced
1 lime
¾ cup (120 g) pistachio nuts, chopped
1 tablespoon plus 1 teaspoon walnut or hazelnut oil
Generous pinch of Himalayan or good-quality sea salt
3 to 4 ounces (85 to 115 g) baby spinach leaves (about 3 cups loosely packed)
15 rice paper wrappers
3 medium peaches, pitted and thinly sliced
1 cup mixed fresh basil and mint leaves (optional)

Tamarind paste and rice paper wrappers can be found at any Asian market, and almost any sweet and sour Asian–flavored sauce, such as plum sauce, will work in place of the home-made sauce.

TO PREPARE THE SAUCE

In a bowl, whisk together all the ingredients until smooth.

TO MAKE THE ROLLS

1. Place the avocado slices in a shallow dish or on a plate and squeeze lime juice over them to prevent discoloration. In a small bowl, mix the pistachios with 1 teaspoon of the walnut oil and the salt and set aside. In a large bowl, combine the spinach leaves and the remaining 1 tablespoon walnut oil and mix gently with your hands to evenly dress the spinach.

2. Prepare a large bowl with slightly warm water for soaking the rice paper wrappers. Soak one wrapper at a time, turning it in the water and making sure the entire wrapper is submerged and becoming soft evenly. Keep in mind that wrappers will soften even more after you remove them from water, so don't soak them for too long to avoid tearing.

3. Working quickly, remove the wrapper from the water and lay it flat on a damp kitchen towel. Arrange 1 or 2 peach slices in the center, then top with 2 or 3 avocado slices, a handful of spinach leaves, several basil and mint leaves, and about ½ tablespoon pistachios, followed by 1 or 2 more peach slices. Fold in the bottom of the wrapper over the filling, then fold in the sides and roll tightly. Summer rolls are best when eaten right away; otherwise, keep them covered with damp paper towels in the refrigerator and serve within a day.

SOUPS

Black Lentil and Butternut Squash Chili

Serves 6 to 8

Back when I cooked with meat regularly, I deviated from my regular fare and tried a vegetarian chili recipe. I was surprised by how delicious it was. From then on, I made two small pots of chili at a time—one with meat and one without—but we always ran out of the vegetarian chili first. Since then, I've experimented with all kinds of vegetables in chili, and this somewhat unusual combination of winter squash, lentils, and a hint of cinnamon is one of my favorites. Uncooked, black lentils look like beautiful black pearls, and when mixed with the bright orange squash and red bell pepper make for a colorful pot of chili. Feel free to adjust the spices to your liking and make your chili as hot as you want.

1. In a large saucepan, heat the olive oil over medium heat. Add the leek, carrots, celery, jalapeño, and sliced garlic and sauté for 4 minutes, stirring periodically.

2. Add the squash, salt, chili powder, oregano, cumin, coriander, and cinnamon and sauté, stirring, for 2 to 3 minutes. Add the lentils, mushrooms, and bell pepper, stirring to coat.

3. Add the crushed tomatoes and broth and bring to a boil. Lower the heat, partially cover, and simmer for about 30 minutes, stirring periodically, until the lentils and vegetables are soft and cooked through. Add more broth or water toward the end of the cooking time if the chili is too thick. Adjust the salt and spices to taste.

4. Remove the chili from the heat and squeeze the juice of the lime into the pan. Stir ½ cup of the cilantro leaves and the minced garlic into the chili. Serve hot, with more lime or lemon juice if you like, and garnish with the remaining 1 cup cilantro. Another option is to top with good-quality grated cheese and/or a dollop of Greek yogurt.

2 tablespoons olive oil

1 medium leek, white and tender green parts only, thinly sliced

2 medium carrots, thinly sliced

2 celery stalks, thinly sliced

1 small or ½ large jalapeño, seeded and cut into small cubes

7 garlic cloves (4 thinly sliced, 3 minced)

1 medium butternut squash (about 1½ lb [680 g]), peeled, seeded, and cut into 1-inch (2½ cm) cubes

1 teaspoon sea salt, plus more to taste

2 teaspoons chili powder

½ teaspoon dried oregano

½ teaspoon ground cumin

½ teaspoon ground coriander

¼ teaspoon ground cinnamon

1 cup (200 g) black lentils, rinsed

2 medium portobello mushrooms, cut into 1-inch (2½ cm) cubes

1 small red bell pepper, cored, seeded, and cut into ¾-inch (2 cm) cubes

3 cups crushed canned tomatoes (27 oz [798 ml]), or about 4 medium tomatoes, shredded, to make 3 cups tomato puree

2½ cups (600 ml) vegetable broth (page 28) or purified water, plus more if needed

1 lime or lemon, plus more if needed

About 1½ cups fresh cilantro leaves

Avocado Cilantro Soup

3 large ripe but firm Hass
avocados, peeled and
pitted

Juice of 1 large lemon or
lime

1¾ cups (415 ml) vegetable
broth (page 28)

1 cup (240 ml) almond milk
(page 30)

2 generous tablespoons
thick yogurt of your
choice, such as oat
yogurt (page 50) or
Greek yogurt

1 teaspoon sea salt

⅛ teaspoon cayenne
pepper

⅓ cup finely chopped
yellow onion

½ cup chopped fresh
cilantro

Serves 6

There is no dish more comforting to me than a bowl of soup. With only a few exceptions, I was raised on hot, chunky, hearty soups, which we ate even in the warmer seasons. I discovered cold and creamy soups after I moved to the United States, and I am smitten. This soup is a delight; it takes minutes to prepare if you have vegetable broth on hand, but the flavor is surprisingly complex and refreshing. It is a perfect complement to other more involved dishes, and it is sure to be a crowd-pleaser.

1. Chill all the ingredients before making the soup.

2. In a bowl, mash the flesh of 2½ avocados with a potato masher or fork. Add the lemon juice, broth, almond milk, yogurt, salt, and cayenne and mix thoroughly.

3. Cube the remaining ½ avocado. Divide the cubed avocado among bowls along with the chopped onion and cilantro, reserving some for garnish. Ladle the soup into the chilled bowls and garnish with the reserved onion and cilantro.

Roasted Chestnut Soup

Serves 8

Every time I see fresh chestnuts at the Italian market, I can't resist buying a bagful. They are delicious in desserts and salads, and stunning in this creamy soup. You must take extra time to roast and peel them first, but if done properly, it doesn't take much effort and is completely worthwhile. Canned chestnuts can be used instead.

1. If using dried beans, rinse and soak them overnight in plenty of purified water.

2. Preheat the oven to 350°F (180°C).

3. Score a cross through the skin of each chestnut, place the chestnuts on a baking sheet, and roast for 15 minutes. Remove from the oven, let cool completely, and peel the skin from each chestnut. Roughly chop the chestnuts and set aside. There should be about 2½ cups chopped chestnuts.

4. Heat the ghee in a large saucepan over medium heat. Add the garlic, leek, onion, celery, chestnuts, and coriander and sauté for 3 to 4 minutes. If using dried beans, drain and rinse them in a colander, then add them to the pot. (Canned beans are added later.) Add 1 teaspoon of the salt and pepper to taste. Mix to coat.

5. Add the water to the pan and bring to a boil, then lower the heat and simmer for 30 minutes. Add the pear, coconut milk, and the remaining 1 teaspoon salt. If using canned beans, drain them and add them to the soup now. Simmer for another 15 minutes, or until the beans are thoroughly cooked (if using dried) and the chestnuts are soft.

6. Puree the soup in batches in a blender and adjust the salt and pepper to taste. Garnish with microgreens and pink peppercorns.

½ cup (95 g) dried or 1½ cups (340 g) canned white beans, such as cannellini

About 20 ounces (567 g) fresh chestnuts in the shell or 12½ ounces (345 g) canned chestnuts

2 tablespoons ghee (page 27) or olive oil

2 garlic cloves, minced

1 leek, white and tender green parts only, diced

½ medium yellow onion, diced

2 celery stalks, diced

1½ teaspoons ground coriander

2 teaspoons sea salt, divided

Freshly ground black pepper

6 cups purified water

1 large ripe pear, peeled, cored, and diced

⅓ cup (85 ml) unsweetened full-fat canned coconut milk

Microgreens for garnish

Pink peppercorns for garnish

Golden Gazpacho

Serves 8 to 10

The first gazpacho I tasted was a smooth tomato puree with pieces of the sweetest watermelon floating atop. The taste impressed me so much that since then I've been on a quest to develop the perfect gazpacho. This golden soup is the winner, beautiful in presentation and a great dish for cooling the summer heat. You can make it with red tomatoes, or even a good-quality store-bought tomato juice. As with any tomato dish, it is best prepared with heirloom tomatoes in season. Freshly picked basil is essential to this gazpacho—the fresher it is, the more flavorful it will be.

TO MAKE THE GOLDEN VEGETABLE JUICE

Chop all the vegetables into pieces that fit easily into the juicer and juice them. It should yield about 4 cups (1 liter) juice. A masticating juicer with a fruit attachment will work best for this type of juice. Refrigerate the juice until ready to use.

TO MAKE THE GAZPACHO

1. Reserve about 2 tablespoons of chopped bell pepper for garnish. In a large bowl or saucepan, combine all the ingredients except the yogurt, croutons, and basil for garnish. Mix well.

2. In a blender or food processor, puree 3½ cups of the soup, then return the puree back to the bowl.

3. Cover and refrigerate for 4 to 5 hours, until very well chilled.

4. Before serving, adjust the salt and pepper, ladle the gazpacho into chilled soup bowls, and garnish with Greek yogurt, if using, the reserved bell pepper pieces, croutons, if using, and basil leaves.

Note: To peel tomatoes, bring a large saucepan of water to a boil. Cut an X through the skin of the bottom of each tomato. Place the tomatoes into the boiling water for 30 seconds, then remove them with a slotted spoon and run cold water over them to stop the cooking. The skin should then peel away easily in your hands.

For the golden vegetable juice
4 medium yellow tomatoes

3 medium cucumbers, peeled

2½ large yellow bell peppers, cored and seeded

For the gazpacho
2 yellow bell peppers, cored, seeded, and finely chopped

9 medium yellow tomatoes (about 3 lb [1½ kg]), peeled (see Note), seeded, and finely chopped

3 or 4 small to medium (about 10½ oz [300 g]) cucumbers, peeled, seeded, and finely chopped

⅓ cup finely chopped yellow onion

3 garlic cloves, minced

⅓ cup packed fresh basil leaves, plus more for garnish

2 cups (500 ml) vegetable broth (page 28)

4 cups golden vegetable juice (see above)

2 tablespoons olive oil

2 tablespoons white wine vinegar

Sea salt and freshly ground black pepper

Greek yogurt (optional)

Garlic croutons (optional)

Pappa al Pomodoro

2½ pounds (1 kg 135 g) tomatoes in season, preferably heirloom

1¼ cups (300 ml) vegetable broth

1½ teaspoons coconut sugar

1 tablespoon olive oil

4 sprigs oregano (optional)

Handful of fresh basil leaves, plus more for garnish

Sea salt and freshly ground black pepper

4 slices bread of your choice

2 to 4 garlic cloves, peeled

Serves 4

Although these days we don't often eat bread, this simple tomato soup recipe so resembles a childhood snack that I couldn't resist sharing it. We didn't know much about Italian food while growing up, but one of the most delicious snacks of my childhood summers was toasted bread with fresh garlic from the garden rubbed onto it, paired with a thick slice of juicy tomato and salt.

1. Roughly chop the tomatoes and place them in a medium saucepan. Add the broth, coconut sugar, olive oil, oregano, and basil and season with salt and pepper. Bring to a gentle boil, then reduce the heat to low and simmer for 10 minutes.

2. Meanwhile, toast the bread in a toaster or on a grill. Rub the garlic all over each piece of bread and break it into bite-size pieces. Divide the bread among 4 soup bowls.

3. When the soup is ready, adjust the salt and pepper and ladle the soup over the bread. Let the soup bowls sit for a few minutes before serving so the bread can absorb the soup. Garnish with basil leaves.

Lazy Sweet Potato Dumplings in Vegetable Broth

Serves 6

Russian cuisine offers many varieties of dumplings, and most of them are time-consuming and labor-intensive to prepare. There is one kind of dumpling, however, invented especially for busy times. Instead of making pasta dough and a filling separately, all ingredients are mixed together—usually farmer cheese, eggs, and flour. Pieces of the dough are cooked in boiling water or broth and are called, literally, lazy dumplings. Here I adapted the same idea with sweet potatoes and buckwheat flour and eliminated the eggs. Served in flavorful homemade vegetable broth, these lazy dumplings are just the thing for a cozy fall or winter meal.

1. Cook the russet potato and sweet potato in a saucepan of boiling water until soft but not mushy, about 12 to 15 minutes. Drain well to remove as much moisture as possible and wipe the cooking pan dry. You can also bake the potatoes and do this step in advance.

2. Place the potatoes back into the dry pan and mash with a potato masher, or run the potatoes through a ricer into the pan. Add the ghee, salt, and nutmeg and mix to combine. Sift in the buckwheat flour and mix with a wooden spoon to form a soft dough.

3. With a small spoon, pinch one little dumpling-size bit of dough at a time and drop it into a lightly oiled steaming basket. Wet the spoon with water after shaping each dumpling to prevent sticking. In a pot big enough to accommodate the steaming basket, add water up to but not touching the bottom of the basket. Bring to a boil, then reduce the heat to a simmer. Place the basket with dumplings on top, cover, and steam them in batches for 7 minutes.

4. Distribute the dumplings among soup bowls and pour the hot vegetable broth over them. Season with salt and pepper, squeeze lemon juice over the bowls, garnish with thyme, and serve immediately. You can store the leftover dumplings in the refrigerator, covered, for a couple of days.

1 russet potato (about 7 oz [200 g]), peeled and diced

1 medium sweet potato (about 10 oz [285 g]), peeled and diced

2 tablespoons ghee (page 27) or olive oil

½ teaspoon sea salt, plus more to taste

⅛ teaspoon freshly grated nutmeg

¾ cups (105 g) buckwheat flour

About 4½ cups (about 1 liter) vegetable broth (page 28), warmed

Sea salt and freshly ground black pepper

1 lemon

Fresh thyme and/or other herbs for garnish

Creamy French Bean Soup

Serves 4

French or green beans are at their best when young and fresh. We have a small plot at a local community garden, and the amount of beautiful produce such a tiny piece of land yields constantly amazes me. Green beans are part of that Florida winter bounty, and I make this soup right after I pick my first harvest of the season. This simple and nutritious soup can be enjoyed hot or chilled.

1. Blanch the green beans in a saucepan of well-salted boiling water for 2 minutes. Transfer the beans to a bowl filled with ice water to stop the cooking. Let cool completely.

2. Drain the beans from the ice-water bath. Chop the beans roughly and place in a high-speed blender with the broth, almond milk, and basil and season with salt and pepper. Blend until smooth.

3. Squeeze a generous amount of lemon juice over the soup and stir to blend the flavors. Adjust the seasonings with salt and pepper.

4. If serving the soup warm, heat the soup gently over low heat without bringing it to a boil. Ladle the soup into bowls and garnish with the minced radishes and herbs. Alternatively, refrigerate the soup until chilled and serve cold.

Requires a high-speed blender

2½ pounds (1 kg 135 g) French beans, trimmed
1 cup (240 ml) vegetable broth (page 28)
1 cup (240 ml) almond milk (page 30) or other milk of choice
Handful of fresh basil leaves (optional)
Sea salt and freshly ground pepper
1 lemon
2 to 4 radishes, minced, for garnish
Fresh dill and/or chives for garnish

For the pumpkin seed cheese crackers

1 cup (160 g) pumpkin seeds, soaked in purified water for 4 hours

¼ cup (60 ml) purified water

2 tablespoons freshly squeezed lemon or lime juice

1 tablespoon nutritional yeast

¼ teaspoon sea salt

Requires a high-speed blender

For the apple anise soup

2 cups (500 ml) almond milk (page 30)

1 large fennel bulb, roughly chopped

1 large apple, cored and roughly chopped, one quarter reserved for garnish

Handful of fresh cilantro leaves

½ small chile, seeded

½ teaspoon ground coriander

Salt and freshly ground black pepper

Handful (about ¼ cup) pumpkin seeds, toasted (see page 12), or soaked and dehydrated (see page 36)

Drizzle of chili olive oil (olive oil mixed with chili powder to taste; optional)

Fresh mint and/or cilantro leaves for garnish

Apple Anise Soup
with pumpkin seed cheese crackers

Serves 4

I posted this recipe on my blog a few years ago and got so much positive response from those who tried it that I absolutely had to include it in this book. I remember having a hard time with the ratios and amount of spices at first, but I really wanted to make a soup with these ingredients. After several unsuccessful batches, I finally got it right, and we ate the whole pot for lunch. This soup is refreshing, aromatic, and simple. It is equally tasty served slightly warm, at room temperature, or chilled. It is especially delicious served with raw pumpkin seed cheese crackers on the side, though it can be omitted if you don't have a dehydrator.

TO MAKE THE PUMPKIN SEED CRACKERS

1. In a food processor, combine all the cheese cracker ingredients and process until smooth.

2. Spread in a thin layer onto Teflex-covered dehydrator trays. Dehydrate at 115°F (46°C) for 6 hours.

3. Flip over the sheet of cheese and peel away the Teflex. Break the cheese into cracker-size pieces and dehydrate for another 2 hours.

TO MAKE THE APPLE ANISE SOUP

1. In a high-speed blender, combine all the ingredients except the pumpkin seeds and chili olive oil and blend until smooth. Adjust the salt and spices to taste.

2. Cut the reserved apple into small cubes. Ladle the soup into serving bowls and garnish the bowls with the apple cubes, pumpkin seeds, and herbs. Drizzle with the chili olive oil and serve with pumpkin seed cheese crackers.

MAINS

Fingerling Potato and Rosemary Flatbread Pizza

Makes 1 pizza, about 11 inches (28 cm) in diameter

I was introduced to potato pizza during my first visit to Chicago. Masha and I were leaving a beautiful French antiques shop and realized how hungry we were. Thankfully, there was a good-looking Italian restaurant right across the street, and as it turned out it served the best pizza I had ever tasted. It had the most perfect thin crust and was covered with multicolored circles of very sweet fingerling potatoes. My version is inspired by the traditional dish, but also very far from it. It is easy to make and the crust (surprisingly) includes zucchini.

For the pizza crust

½ cup (60 g) rolled oats, ground into coarse flour in a food processor

½ cup (60 g) quinoa flakes

¼ cup (30 g) walnuts or pecans, ground into small pieces in a food processor

2½ tablespoons chia seeds

Pinch of sea salt

½ cup (125 ml) boiling water, plus more if needed

1 tablespoon olive oil

½ small or ¼ medium zucchini (about 2 oz [55 g]), to make about ⅓ cup finely shredded

For the topping

About 12½ ounces (350 g) multicolored fingerling potatoes or 3 medium Yukon gold potatoes, very thinly sliced with a sharp knife or on a mandoline

1½ tablespoons plus ¼ teaspoon sea salt

1 garlic head

½ tablespoon plus ¼ teaspoon olive oil, plus more for greasing the parchment paper

Freshly ground black pepper

3 fresh rosemary sprigs, chopped

4 to 6 small shiitake mushrooms, briefly rinsed, stems removed, sliced or left whole

⅛ medium yellow onion, thinly sliced

1 ounce (30 g) sheep's or goat's milk Greek feta cheese or other cheese of choice (optional)

TO PREPARE THE POTATOES AND ROAST THE GARLIC FOR THE TOPPING

1. Place the potato slices in a bowl, sprinkle with 1½ tablespoons salt, and cover with cold water. Let sit for about 1 hour.

2. Preheat the oven to 350°F (180°C).

3. Slice off the top of the garlic head to expose the insides. Sprinkle with ¼ teaspoon salt, the pepper, and ¼ teaspoon olive oil. Wrap in foil or parchment paper and roast for 25 to 30 minutes.

TO MAKE THE CRUST

1. In a large bowl, combine the oats, quinoa, walnuts, chia seeds, and salt. Pour the boiling water over the mixture, mix with a spoon, and let sit for 5 minutes.

2. Add the olive oil and zucchini and knead the dough until the ingredients are evenly mixed in, making a ball. Place the ball on a lightly oiled piece of parchment paper big enough to accommodate an 11-inch (28 cm) pizza. Flatten with the palm of your hand, cover with another square of parchment paper, then roll into a circle that is about 11 inches (28 cm). Peel away the top piece of parchment paper. If the dough separates at the edges, pinch it back together, and don't worry if the dough is not a perfect circle.

TO ASSEMBLE AND BAKE THE PIZZA

1. Preheat the oven to 500°F (260°C).

2. Drain and rinse the potato slices and pat them dry with paper towels. Squeeze the roasted garlic from its skin and smear half of it over the crust with a fork. Arrange the potato slices on the pizza crust, alternating the colors and overlapping the edges of the slices, making sure the whole crust is covered. Don't leave much of an edge so as to keep the crust from burning. Lightly brush with olive oil and sprinkle with salt and pepper.

3. Bake for 20 minutes. Remove the pizza from the oven and arrange the rest of the garlic on top, along with the rosemary, mushrooms, onions, and cheese, if using. Return the pizza to the oven and bake for another 10 minutes. Remove from the oven, let cool for about 5 minutes, cut into slices with a pizza cutter, and serve.

Beet and Buckwheat Gnocchi
with horseradish-cilantro pesto

Serves 2 to 4

These gnocchi are a rich magenta color, which makes them fun both to work with and to serve to guests. They are also nutritious and light and have a slightly sweet, earthy flavor. I always associate fresh horseradish with beets, as the two went hand in hand at our family table back home. The spicy, bright pesto complements the mild pasta, but any other pesto would be just as tasty.

TO MAKE THE HORSERADISH-CILANTRO PESTO

1. Toast the pine nuts on a dry skillet over medium heat until golden and fragrant, about 3 minutes, shaking the pan frequently. Alternatively, toast them in a preheated 350°F (180°C) oven for 5 to 7 minutes, stirring occasionally. Cool.

2. Combine the pine nuts in a food processor with the garlic and grind into a meal.

3. Add the horseradish, cilantro, and salt and continue grinding. With the machine running, add the olive oil in a steady stream through the hole in the lid and process until the ingredients are well combined. Serve the pesto immediately or refrigerate for up to 3 days. You can also freeze the pesto for about 1 month.

TO PREPARE THE VEGETABLES

1. Preheat the oven to 400°F (200°C).

2. Rinse and scrub clean the beet and sweet potato, then dry them with a dish towel. Trim the ends from the beet and wrap it in aluminum foil. Prick the skin of the sweet potato with a fork several times. Place the beet and sweet potato on a baking sheet and bake for 30 minutes. Check the potato; if it is tender throughout when pierced with a knife, remove it from the oven. If not, continue to bake for another 10 to 15 minutes, until tender. Check the beet after 45 minutes; if it is still hard in the middle, continue to bake for another 15 minutes or so, until soft throughout. Remove from the oven, unwrap, and let cool.

3. Peel the beet and finely grate it. Peel the sweet potato and mash it using a masher, fork, or potato ricer. In a medium bowl, combine the beet and mashed sweet potato into a smooth, homogenous puree. Measure 1 cup of the

For the horseradish-cilantro pesto
¼ cup (40 g) pine nuts

1 garlic clove, minced

1 teaspoon grated fresh horseradish

1 large bunch fresh cilantro, lower parts of stems removed and the rest torn (about 2 cups loosely packed)

½ teaspoon sea salt

¼ cup (60 ml) olive oil

For the gnocchi
1 small beet

1 medium sweet potato

1 tablespoon minced fresh sage, plus 3 to 5 leaves for infusing the ghee

¼ teaspoon sea salt

⅛ teaspoon freshly grated nutmeg

1 tablespoon melted ghee (page 27) or olive oil, plus 2 tablespoons for coating the gnocchi

¾ cup (105 g) to 1 cup (140 g) buckwheat flour, plus a little more if needed

Brown rice flour for rolling out the dough

3 to 4 fresh thyme sprigs

puree, reserving the amount left over (if any) for later. You can freeze it for next time you make gnocchi.

TO MAKE THE GNOCCHI

1. In a large bowl, combine the measured 1 cup of vegetable puree with the minced sage, salt, and nutmeg. Mix thoroughly. Add the melted ghee and blend it into the mixture. Gradually add the buckwheat flour, mixing the dough with a wooden spoon to incorporate. The dough should still be too sticky to knead with your hands but not too wet. Be careful not to add too much flour, as it will make the dough dry and heavy.

2. Generously sprinkle your working surface with brown rice flour and turn the dough onto it using a spoon. Sift some more flour on top to lightly cover the entire surface of the dough. Flour your hands and gently roll the dough in the flour, shaping it into a thick log. The dough will be very soft, but the surface should no longer be sticky.

3. Flour the blade of a knife and cut the log into 4 equal portions. Gently roll each portion into a ½-inch (about 1 cm) thick rope. Slice into 1-inch (about 2 cm) long pieces, periodically dusting the blade of your knife with flour. Turn these pieces on the cutting board to cover the freshly cut sides with flour. Gently press a floured fork into each bit of dough to create gnocchi's characteristic impression. Transfer the finished gnocchi to a floured plate or baking sheet.

4. In a pot with a steamer basket on top, add some water, low enough in the pot so it does not touch the bottom of the steamer basket. Bring to a boil, then reduce the heat to a simmer. Place the gnocchi into the steamer basket in a single layer. You may need to steam the gnocchi in two batches, depending on the size of the basket. Cover and steam the gnocchi for about 7 minutes.

5. Meanwhile, in a large skillet over medium-low heat, gently warm the remaining 2 tablespoons ghee with the sage leaves and thyme sprigs.

6. Using a spatula or spoon, remove the steamed gnocchi from the basket and add them to the pan with the herbs. Toss the gnocchi to coat, letting it absorb the herb flavors for a couple of minutes. Serve with the horseradish-cilantro pesto.

Note: You can eliminate step 5 by simply tossing the steamed gnocchi with the pesto and serving immediately. In this case, if you're steaming the gnocchi in batches, keep them warm in a warm oven (200°F [95°C]) until ready to serve.

Squash Blossom Quiche

Makes one 8 × 8-inch (20 cm) square or 9-inch (23 cm) round tart

In the vegetable gardens of my childhood I saw squash plants in bloom every summer, but I never knew their culinary potential. Eating them was not at all customary in our culture, and even now, when I mention this possibility to my mother, she shakes her head in disbelief. I, on the other hand, haven't been able to get enough of squash blossoms since my first sampling. They are whimsical and delicate, and they have a mild, flowery pumpkin flavor. I stuff the blossoms with a ricotta- or eggplant-based filling, sometimes even leaving them raw when they are extra fresh. They are also great lightly sautéed or baked into a tart, like I did for this recipe. Ricotta and zucchini pair so well together, especially when mixed with lots of fresh herbs and citrus.

For the crust

4 tablespoons coconut oil, melted, plus more for greasing the pan

4 tablespoons ghee (page 27), at room temperature

⅔ cup (80 g) quinoa flour

⅓ cup (60 g) brown rice flour

¼ cup (30 g) tapioca starch

1 teaspoon ground coriander

¼ teaspoon sea salt

Freshly ground black pepper

3 to 5 tablespoons ice water

For the filling

1¼ teaspoons sea salt, divided, plus more for sprinkling on top of the tart

2 small zucchinis (about 11 oz [315 g]), finely shredded on the smallest

holes of a box grater, to make about 2 cups

2 cups (18 oz [510 g]) ricotta cheese, either homemade (page 26) or store-bought, drained overnight (see page 26 for instructions on draining)

4 tablespoons chopped fresh parsley

2 tablespoons chopped fresh mint

1 teaspoon fresh thyme leaves

1 teaspoon freshly squeezed lemon juice

Zest of 1 lemon

1 tablespoon olive oil, divided

Freshly ground black pepper

About 8 squash blossoms, gently cleaned with a damp paper towel

TO PREPARE THE CRUST

1. In a small bowl, combine the coconut oil and ghee thoroughly. Spoon the mixture into a small, shallow dish and place into the freezer for about 10 minutes, until hardened. Lightly oil a tart pan.

2. In a food processor, combine the flours, tapioca starch, coriander, salt, and pepper to taste and pulse several times to combine. Take the hardened ghee mixture out of the freezer and cut it in the dish into ½-inch (1¼ cm) cubes. Add it to the flour mixture and pulse 10 to 15 times until the ghee cubes are ground into lentil-size pieces.

3. Add 3 tablespoons ice water and pulse several times to bring the dough together. Check the dough with your fingers; it should stick when pressed together. If not, add more ice water, 1 tablespoon at a time, and pulse again.

4. Put the dough on a work surface (it will be crumbly at this point) and quickly knead together, forming a ball. Flatten the ball with the palm of your hand and press into the tart mold, starting with the bottom center and pressing it out to the sides until you have an evenly thick crust. Prick the bottom crust with a fork several times and chill in the refrigerator for 30 minutes.

TO PREPARE THE FILLING AND BAKE THE QUICHE

1. Preheat the oven to 400°F (200°C).

2. Place the shredded zucchini in a colander over a bowl or the sink, sprinkle with 1 teaspoon of the salt, and let drain for 20 minutes. Gently squeeze the zucchini between your fingers over the sink, small handfuls at a time. Then wrap the zucchini in several layers of paper towels and twist slightly so the paper towels absorb as much moisture as possible.

3. In a large bowl, combine the drained ricotta, shredded zucchini, remaining ¼ teaspoon salt, the parsley, mint, thyme, lemon juice and zest, ½ tablespoon of the olive oil, and a grinding of black pepper. Gently mix with a wooden spoon to combine. Spoon the filling into the chilled crust, bringing it all the way to the top. Smooth the surface.

4. Arrange the squash blossoms on top, gently pressing them into the filling. Brush with the remaining ½ tablespoon olive oil, then sprinkle with salt and pepper. Bake for 30 to 35 minutes, until the crust is golden brown. Check periodically, especially toward the end, monitoring the blossoms; if they start to turn dark brown or burn, cover the tart with foil and finish baking. Remove from the oven and let cool. Slice and serve with a salad.

Note: If you don't have squash blossoms, top the tart with an additional small zucchini (about 3½ oz [100 g]). Slice it thinly (2 mm) on a mandoline and arrange the slices on top of the ricotta, gently pressing them into the filling. Brush with olive oil, sprinkle with salt and pepper, and bake the tart as described in the recipe.

Fava Bean Quinoa Cakes
with kale, ginger, and garam masala

Makes about 16 cakes

In these cakes, garam masala, fresh ginger, and herbs give quinoa and mild vegetables just enough of a kick to make the flavor multilayered and delicious. The cakes are simple in preparation, light, nutritious, and convenient enough to fit into Paloma's lunch box. You can substitute peas for the fava beans, and other greens for the kale if you like.

1. In a medium saucepan, combine the quinoa with 1 cup water, add a generous pinch of salt, and bring to a boil. Lower the heat, cover, and simmer for 20 minutes. Remove from the heat and let cool. You will have about 2 cups of cooked quinoa.

2. Bring a large pot of well-salted water to a boil. In the meantime, prepare a large bowl of ice water. Blanch the fava beans (or peas) for 1 minute. Remove them from the boiling water with a slotted spoon and transfer to the ice-water bath to stop the cooking process. Blanch the kale for 1 minute, drain it in a colander and transfer it into the ice bath as well. When cooled completely, drain all the vegetables in a colander. Remove the outer skin of the fava beans by gently pressing against the sides of each bean with your fingers until the bean pops out (there is no need to peel the peas).

3. Working with a small batch at a time, thoroughly squeeze out the excess water from the blanched kale with your hands. Chop it finely; you will have about 1 to 1½ tightly packed cups of kale. Put it into a food processor along with the fava beans (or peas), shallot, garlic, ginger, parsley, mint, garam masala, and salt and process to a chunky puree.

4. Preheat oven to 375°F (190°C).

5. In a food processor or coffee grinder, grind the pistachios into a meal. Combine the ground pistachios with the flax meal in a medium bowl. Measure ¼ cup of the mixture and set it aside. Add the sesame seeds to the rest of the pistachio-flax mixture and set aside as well; this will be your coating.

6. Transfer the vegetable mixture to a large bowl. Mix in the quinoa, ghee, and reserved ¼ cup pistachio-flax mixture and season with salt and pepper. Mix everything together very thoroughly with your hands, kneading the mixture between your fingers so the ingredients are melded.

7. Scoop out ¼ cup of the mixture at a time and form oval-shaped or round flattened patties. Press the mixture between the palms of your hands, making sure the cakes hold their shape nicely. Roll each cake in the sesame-pistachio

For the cakes
½ heaping cup (110 g) dried quinoa
1½ cups (225 g) fresh (from about 1½ lb [680 g] pods) or frozen shelled fava beans, or
1½ cups (220 g) fresh or frozen English peas
1 large bunch (about 12 oz [350 g]) curly kale, stems removed
1 small shallot, finely chopped
1 garlic clove, minced
1 tablespoon minced fresh ginger
2 tablespoons minced fresh parsley
2 tablespoons minced fresh mint
½ teaspoon garam masala
1 teaspoon sea salt, plus more to taste
½ tablespoon ghee (page 27) or olive oil
Freshly ground black pepper

For the sesame-pistachio coating
¼ cup (40 g) pistachio nuts or pumpkin seeds
⅓ cup (45 g) flaxseed meal
¼ cup (40 g) sesame seeds

coating to cover the surface. Place the cakes on a parchment paper–covered baking sheet without overcrowding them.

8. Bake for 10 minutes on each side. For a golden brown finish, broil the cakes for 1 minute on each side.

9. Serve with a green salad side and/or Greek-style yogurt mixed with chopped fresh herbs and a squeeze of lime juice.

Note: You can add about ½ cup sweet potato puree (from 1 small sweet potato) to the cake mixture for additional moisture and some sweetness.

Tarragon Millet and Pear Stuffed Squash

Serves 4 to 8

4 tablespoons grapeseed
oil, ghee (page 27),
or other oil of choice,
divided

2 medium red kuri (or
2 small butternut
or 2 medium acorn)
squashes, cut in half,
seeds removed

Sea salt and freshly ground
black pepper

1 teaspoon cumin seeds

1 teaspoon coriander seeds

1 teaspoon pink
peppercorns, plus more
for garnish

¼ teaspoon black
peppercorns

1 tablespoon fresh thyme
leaves, divided

1 leek, white and tender
green parts only, thinly
sliced

1 shallot, diced

1 large fennel bulb, shaved
with a vegetable peeler
or very thinly sliced on a
mandoline

3 medium parsnips, diced

¼ teaspoon paprika

1 bunch fresh tarragon,
stems removed,
leaves chopped (5 to 6
tablespoons), divided

1 cup (180 g) millet

2 cups (500 ml) hot purified
water

3 ripe but firm pears, such
as Bosc, cored (1 sliced
and 2 cubed)

1 tablespoon freshly
squeezed lemon juice

Zest of 1 lemon

My mother's stuffed summer vegetables make up the best dish in her reper-toire. She usually prepares a brilliant assortment of tomatoes, bell peppers, zucchini, and eggplant in one giant baking dish, so we don't have to choose just one and can taste them all. I could never conquer the stuffed summer veggie category as well as my mother, so I focus my stuffing recipes on winter squashes.

This aromatic dish takes on the flavors of fresh tarragon, fennel, and a variety of spices, all balanced by the sweetness of red kuri squash and pear.

1. Preheat the oven to 425°F (215°C).

2. Rub 2 tablespoons grapeseed oil over the squashes and sprinkle the flesh with salt and pepper. Place cut side down on an aluminum foil–covered baking sheet. Pierce the skin a few times with a fork and bake for 20 minutes. Using a spatula or oven mitt, flip the squash halves over and bake for another 10 minutes or more, depending on the size of the squash, until the flesh is soft and yields when pierced with a fork. Lower the oven temperature to 375°F (190°C).

3. While the squash is roasting, crush and coarsely grind the cumin seeds, coriander seeds, and pink and black peppercorns with a mortar and pestle. Alternatively, grind all the spices in a dedicated coffee grinder. In a large saucepan, warm the remaining 2 tablespoons oil over medium heat. Add the freshly ground spices with half of the thyme and sauté for about 2 minutes, until fragrant.

4. Add the leek and shallot to the pan and sauté for 2 minutes. Add the fennel, parsnips, paprika, and one-third of the tarragon, then sauté for 2 minutes. Add the millet, followed by the hot water and 2 teaspoons salt. Stir together to incorporate and bring to a gentle boil. Lower the heat, cover the pan, and simmer for 20 to 25 minutes, until the millet is cooked.

5. Remove the pan from the heat. Stir in the pear cubes and lemon juice and the rest of the thyme, most of the tarragon, and most of the lemon zest, reserving just enough for garnish. Fill the cavities of the squashes with the stuffing, building a small mound on top. Slip the pear slices into the stuffing on top of each squash half. Place the stuffed squashes on the baking sheet and return them to the oven for 5 to 7 minutes.

6. Remove the stuffed squash from the oven. Garnish with the remaining thyme, tarragon, pink peppercorns, and lemon zest, and let cool slightly before serving.

Coconut Black Rice with Grilled Peaches

1 cup (215 g) heirloom forbidden black rice

1¾ cups (440 ml) unsweetened full-fat canned coconut milk

4 or 5 Kaffir lime leaves

Pinch of sea salt

4 large ripe peaches

1 lime

Handful of mixed fresh mint and basil leaves, torn

Honey for drizzling

If you want to make this dish extra special and are ready for the challenge of opening a fresh coconut, make your own coconut milk from a young Thai coconut (see page 18). Otherwise, canned coconut milk will work just as well.

Serves 4

When peaches come into season, I center many meals around them. Everything from crumbles to pies and salads to salsas turns peachy. Outdoor grilling with friends is a gratifying, summer-specific activity, and this simple dish is perfect for such a setting.

The flavor of Kaffir lime leaves is somewhere between lemongrass and lime, which adds fresh dimension to this dish. You can find Kaffir lime leaves at Asian markets; they often come freshly frozen, so check in the frozen aisle.

1. Combine the rice, coconut milk, Kaffir lime leaves, and salt in a medium saucepan. Bring to a gentle boil. Lower the heat and simmer, covered, for 30 minutes. Remove from the heat and let stand, covered, for a few minutes.

2. Meanwhile, cut the peaches in half, remove the pits, and drizzle with honey. Preheat the outdoor grill on medium high for 6 to 8 minutes. Grill peaches lightly for 3 to 4 minutes on each side.

3. Remove the Kaffir lime leaves from the rice. Squeeze the juice from the lime into the rice and fluff with a fork. Add the mint and basil, reserving some for garnish.

4. Divide the rice among plates or bowls and place a grilled peach on top of each one. Drizzle with honey and garnish with more herbs.

Note: In the absence of a grill, roast the peaches in the oven at 425°F (218°C) for 15 to 20 minutes.

Colorful Tacos

with corn tortillas, sweet potatoes, eggplant, and poblano chiles

Makes about 10 tacos

I was introduced to tacos during my first year in the United States and crave them often. Ernie can still tell you about the time when I was pregnant with Paloma when I had him driving around town trying to find tacos that were to my liking. These tacos are filled with a rainbow of vegetables, while still full of trademark Mexican ingredients like poblanos, chipotle, lime, and cilantro.

It's easy to make taco shells with masa harina (lime-treated corn flour) at home, but store-bought tortillas work for this recipe as well. If you can't find purple masa harina, feel free to use all yellow masa harina.

1. Preheat the oven to 325°F (165°C).

2. Place the cherry tomatoes in a medium oiled baking dish, sprinkle with olive oil and some salt and pepper, and roast for 1 to 1½ hours, until the tomatoes are soft. While the tomatoes are roasting, prepare the eggplant and tortilla dough.

3. Cut each eggplant into ¾-inch (2 cm) thick cubes. Place in a colander over a bowl or the sink and generously sprinkle with salt. Let the eggplant sit for 30 minutes.

4. If using both the yellow and purple masa harina, combine 1 cup of each color with ⅛ teaspoon of the baking soda in two separate bowls. Then divide the amount of water in half (¾ cup) and dissolve ¼ teaspoon of salt in each portion. Add the salted water into bowls with the masa harina gradually, whisk to combine, and let sit for 5 minutes.

If using just the yellow masa harina, combine 2 cups of it with ¼ teaspoon baking soda. Dissolve ½ teaspoon of salt in 1½ cups of water. Add the water into the flour gradually, whisk to combine, and let sit for 5 minutes.

5. Knead the dough for several minutes, adding more water if too dry, or more masa harina if too moist. Cover and let rest while you prepare the filling.

6. When the tomatoes are done, remove them from the oven and set aside. Increase the oven temperature to 400°F (200°C).

7. Peel the sweet potatoes and cut them into ¾-inch (2 cm) cubes. Place the sweet potatoes and eggplant cubes into a large bowl, squeeze 1½ limes over them, add chipotle, olive oil, coriander, and sea salt and stir to coat. Spread the mixture onto a parchment paper–lined baking sheet. Roast for 25 minutes,

About 1½ pounds (680 g) cherry tomatoes

6 tablespoons olive oil, divided, plus more for sprinkling the tomatoes and greasing the baking dish

Sea salt and freshly ground black pepper

2 medium eggplants (about 2¼ lb [1 kg 40 g] total)

1 cup (120 g) yellow masa harina

1 cup (120 g) purple masa harina

¼ teaspoon baking soda

1½ cups (360 ml) hot water, plus more if needed

2 medium sweet potatoes

2 limes

1¼ teaspoon ground chipotle chile, or to taste

1½ teaspoons ground coriander

2 medium poblano chiles

Leaves from 1 bunch fresh cilantro (about ½ cup)

turning the cubes and rotating the sheet halfway through roasting, until cooked throughout and soft when pricked with a fork. Remove from the oven, cover, and set aside. Turn the oven to broil.

8. Place the poblanos on an aluminum foil–lined baking sheet and set them under the broiler. Check and turn every 1 to 2 minutes as their skin burns, until they are blackened all over. Remove the poblanos from the oven and place into a plastic bag or a bowl and cover it with plastic wrap. Let cool.

9. Meanwhile, prepare the tortillas. Pinch a piece of dough slightly bigger than a golf ball and shape it into a ball. Place it in the center of a piece of parchment paper big enough to accommodate a 6-inch (15 cm) tortilla and flatten the ball with the palm of your hand. Cover the dough with a second piece of parchment paper. Place a flat-bottom bowl on top and press it into the dough using the weight of your body. Then use a rolling pin to roll it out more, to make a 6-inch (15 cm) round tortilla. Repeat until all the dough is used. Stack the tortillas on top of each other, with pieces of parchment paper layered in between.

10. Heat a heavy-duty skillet over medium-high heat (a cast-iron pan is ideal). Cook one tortilla at a time for 1 to 2 minutes on each side. Stack them on top of each other in a bowl or on a plate and keep warm, covered with a lid, close to the stove.

11. Peel the burnt skin from the poblanos, then remove the seeds and membranes from the inside (you might want to wear plastic gloves to protect your hands). Cut the flesh into medium pieces.

12. Fill each tortilla with the eggplant–sweet potato mixture, followed by poblano pieces and cilantro leaves. Top with a couple of roasted cherry tomatoes. Garnish with more cilantro leaves and a squeeze of lime juice. It is best to assemble your tortillas right before eating. You can also serve all filling components separately, aside a warm stack of tortillas, so everyone can assemble their tacos as they'd like.

Note: Substitute or eliminate different filling components according to what you have on hand or to your liking. Beans, radishes, shredded cabbage, mushrooms, avocado slices, or guacamole would work great in these tacos. Top with cheese, sour cream, or Greek yogurt if you like.

Citrus Broccolini with Cardamom Tofu

1 package (14 oz [397 g])
   firm tofu
1 bunch (about 10 oz [285
   g]) broccolini

For the marinade
Juice and zest of 2 limes
Juice and zest of 1 lemon
Seeds of 7 cardamom pods,
   crushed in a mortar and
   pestle
⅛ teaspoon red pepper
   flakes
2 tablespoons coconut
   sugar
4 tablespoons olive oil, plus
   more for greasing the
   baking dish
¼ teaspoon sea salt
1 bunch cilantro, leaves
   and stems (about 1 cup)
1 tablespoon purified water
Handful almonds, toasted
   (see Note) and chopped

Serves 4

I love cooking with tofu, as its texture and ability to absorb any flavor allow so much creativity in the kitchen. The flavor of this marinade is sensational—the combination of cardamom and citrus is vibrant and sunny, perfect for a summer meal.

1. Drain the tofu and place it on a plate. Cover with another plate and put some weight on it, such as a glass jar filled with water. Let it drain for about 2 hours.

2. In a medium bowl, mix the citrus juices, cardamom, red pepper flakes, coconut sugar, olive oil, and salt. Pour into a food processor, add the cilantro and water, and pulse to incorporate. Reserve ½ cup of the dressing for later.

3. Pour away the water drained from the tofu. In a medium dish, crumble the tofu with your fingers. Pour the remaining dressing over the tofu and leave to marinate for 30 minutes to 1 hour. (You can do these steps in advance and marinate the tofu overnight.)

4. Preheat the oven to 425°F (215°C).

5. Blanch the broccolini in a large pot full of well-salted water for 4 to 5 minutes. Transfer to an ice-water bath to stop the cooking. Remove the broccolini from the water once cool, squeeze out the excess water, and pat dry with paper towels.

6. Place the broccolini in a lightly oiled baking dish, drizzle the reserved ½ cup of dressing over it, and top with marinated tofu. Bake for 10 minutes.

7. Sprinkle with the toasted and chopped almonds and serve immediately.

Note: You can toast nuts and seeds two ways. Roast them in your oven at 350°F (175°C) for 5 to 10 minutes, stirring once or twice, until golden brown. Or toast them on a dry skillet over medium heat, shaking the pan frequently to stir. Roasting gives you a more even color and a smaller chance of burning. Toasting on the stovetop demands constant shaking of the pan and a somewhat uneven browning of the nuts or seeds.

Cauliflower Pie
with a sweet potato crust

Makes one 9-inch (18 cm) pie

This recipe is inspired by Mollie Katzen's cauliflower pie, which I made often when I first became interested in vegetarian cooking. The crust is made from Yukon gold potatoes and sweet potatoes and resembles my homemade potato latkes, my ultimate guilty pleasure. I always buy colorful cauliflower—purple, yellow, green—when it's available, but just one type of cauliflower would be equally delicious.

For the crust
2 medium Yukon gold potatoes (about
    10½ oz [300 g])
1 small sweet potato (about 7 oz [210 g])
½ teaspoon sea salt
¼ medium yellow onion
1 large egg
Freshly ground black pepper
1 tablespoon olive oil, plus more for
    greasing the pie plate

For the filling
1½ pounds (680 g) cauliflower florets
    of various colors, equal to 1 medium
    cauliflower head, cut into small
    florets

½ teaspoon sea salt, plus more for
    blanching
2 ounces (60 g) Gruyère cheese,
    shredded (about ½ cup)
2 teaspoons cumin seeds, ground
    in a mortar with a pestle or in a
    dedicated coffee grinder
About 5 sprigs fresh thyme leaves or ½
    teaspoon dried thyme
2 tablespoons chopped fresh parsley
2 small garlic cloves, minced
¼ teaspoon paprika
Freshly ground black pepper
¼ cup (60 ml) unsweetened full-fat
    canned coconut milk
1 large egg

TO PREPARE AND BAKE THE CRUST

1. Fit your food processor with the shredder attachment. Peel the Yukon gold potatoes, then shred them; you should have about 1½ cups of shredded potatoes. Peel then shred the sweet potatoes; you should have about 1½ cups of shredded sweet potatoes. Alternatively, shred both using the large-holed side of a box grater. Transfer the shredded Yukon gold and sweet potatoes to a colander and mix with the salt. Place the colander over a bowl and let sit for 15 minutes.

2. Preheat the oven to 400°F (200°C).

3. Shred the onion using the same food processor attachment or the large holes of a box grater. Squeeze the excess liquid out of the shredded potatoes using your hands. Place the potatoes in a large bowl with the shredded onion.

4. Separate the egg, reserving the yolk for the filling. Add the egg white to the potatoes and onions, then add some pepper and mix thoroughly to combine.

5. Thoroughly oil a nonstick pie plate. Transfer the potato mixture into the pan and build the crust, distributing it evenly across the bottom and extending the mixture up the sides of the pan. Bake for 20 minutes. Remove from the oven, brush with olive oil, and bake for 10 more minutes. Remove the crust from the oven and lower the temperature to 375°F (190°C).

TO PREPARE THE FILLING AND BAKE THE PIE

1. While the crust is baking, blanch the cauliflower florets in a pot of well-salted water for 2 minutes, then transfer into an ice-water bath. Once cool, drain the cauliflower over a colander and place onto several layers of paper towels to dry.

2. Sprinkle half of the cheese over the crust. In a large bowl, combine the cauliflower pieces with the cumin, thyme, parsley, garlic, paprika, salt, and some pepper. Mix well to combine. Spoon the filling into the crust and sprinkle with the rest of the cheese.

3. Whisk together the egg, the remaining yolk from the crust, and the coconut milk. Pour the mixture evenly over the filling. Bake for 35 to 40 minutes, until the filling is set and the top is slightly golden. Let cool before slicing and serve with a large green salad.

Broccoli Rabe Focaccia

1 cup (120 g) rolled oats, pulsed into a coarse flour in a food processor

1 cup (120 g) quinoa flakes

½ cup (60 g) pecans or walnuts, ground into meal in a food processor

⅓ cup (55 g) chia seeds

1 teaspoon sea salt, plus more for the broccoli rabe

1 cup (240 ml) boiling water

2 tablespoons olive oil, plus more for greasing the parchment paper and drizzling on the broccoli rabe

About 2½ cups (9½ oz [270 g]) roughly chopped cauliflower florets

¼ bunch broccoli rabe (about 5 oz [140 g]), roughly chopped

1 garlic clove, minced

Pinch of red pepper flakes

Serves 4 to 6

This dish is quick to prepare and can be a satisfying snack, lunch, or even a light dinner. Don't expect this dough to be much like traditional focaccia—and the cauliflower gives it a nice softness and some thickness, so it is not quite flatbread. Broccoli rabe is a slightly spicy green, which complements the mild dough, but you can substitute kale for the broccoli rabe if it is not available.

1. Preheat the oven to 375°F (190°C).

2. In a large bowl, combine the oat flour, quinoa flakes, pecans, chia seeds, and salt. Pour the boiling water over the mixture and mix to combine. Let sit for about 5 minutes. Add the olive oil and mix with your hands until a soft dough is formed.

3. In a food processor, pulse the cauliflower into small pieces. Add the cauliflower to the dough, mix with your hands to incorporate, and form a ball. Flatten the dough on a piece of lightly oiled parchment paper, cover with another piece of oiled parchment paper, and roll into a ½-inch (1½ cm) thick rectangle. Peel away the top sheet of parchment paper. If the edges become separated, pinch them together with your fingers. Do not worry if the rectangle is not perfect; just make sure the dough's thickness is fairly even. Score the dough into squares and bake the crust for 40 minutes or until the edges are golden brown.

4. While the crust is baking, in a medium bowl, combine the broccoli rabe with the garlic and pepper flakes and lightly drizzle with oil. Rub the oil into the broccoli rabe with your hands, thoroughly mixing in the pepper flakes and garlic.

5. Remove the crust from the oven and top it with the broccoli rabe. Bake for another 10 minutes until the broccoli rabe is wilted. Break into squares and serve warm.

Pumpkin Seed Falafel with Grilled Peach Salsa

Makes about twenty 1¼-inch (3½ cm) diameter falafel balls

Falafel is second only to hummus on my husband's list of favorite foods. As for me, I had never heard of chickpeas, let alone falafel, before moving to the United States and meeting Ernie two years later. Since then, we've shared plenty of falafel, made easier since he seems to know where to find falafel in every town we visit.

   I bake falafel instead of frying it, and I use plenty of herbs, lemon, and spices. Freshly ground spices are essential for achieving the fullest flavor, but you can substitute preground spices for convenience. The juicy peach salsa nicely complements the spicy falafel, but if peaches are not in season, try serving the falafel with fresh vegetables. Cucumbers and radishes with a simple tzatziki sauce and fresh mint and lime juice make a nice choice, or serve with guacamole and tomato salsa.

Note: If you decide to cook with dried chickpeas, plan ahead and soak them in water overnight.

For the grilled peach salsa
3 ripe peaches, cut in half and pitted
1 to 1½ jalapeño chiles
¼ medium red onion
2 tablespoons freshly squeezed lime juice
1 tablespoon olive oil
1 tablespoon walnut or hazelnut oil
½ tablespoon honey
Pinch of sea salt
Freshly ground black pepper
Handful of fresh mint leaves, chopped

For the tahini sauce
⅓ cup (75 g) sesame tahini (page 32)
⅓ cup (80 ml) purified water
⅛ teaspoon red pepper flakes
1 teaspoon honey
Pinch of sea salt

For the falafel
½ cup (100 g) dried chickpeas or 1¼ cups (325 g) canned chickpeas

1 tablespoon plus 1½ teaspoons sea salt, divided
½ cup (80 g) raw pumpkin seeds
3½ tablespoons flax or chia meal, divided
2½ tablespoons sesame seeds
½ tablespoon cumin seeds
1 teaspoon coriander seeds
½ teaspoon mustard seeds
Seeds of 2 cardamom pods
¼ teaspoon red pepper flakes
3 tablespoons sesame tahini (page 32)
3 tablespoons olive oil
3 tablespoons freshly squeezed lemon juice
2 teaspoons coconut sugar
1 large garlic clove, minced
½ bunch fresh cilantro, harder, lower stems removed and discarded, then roughly chopped (about 1 cup)
2 to 3 fresh tarragon sprigs, leaves minced
5 to 7 fresh mint leaves, minced

TO MAKE THE SALSA

1. Grill the peaches for 3 to 4 minutes on each side on an outdoor or indoor grill. Remove and set aside. Grill the jalapeños and onion until the jalapeño skins are burnt and the onion is soft. Alternatively, use the oven: Broil the jalapeños until their skins are burnt, 1 to 2 minutes on each side, and roast the peaches and onion at 400°F (200°C) for 20 minutes on an aluminum foil–covered baking sheet. Remove from the oven and let cool.

2. Meanwhile, whisk together the lime juice, olive oil, walnut oil, honey, salt, and some pepper in a small bowl to make the dressing.

3. Once the peaches and jalapeño have cooled, slice the peaches, then remove the skins and seeds from the jalapeños (you may want to wear disposable gloves to protect your hands) and chop them roughly. Dice the onion. In a medium bowl, combine the peach slices, jalapeño, onion, and mint. Pour the dressing over and gently toss to coat.

TO MAKE THE TAHINI SAUCE

Combine all the ingredients in a blender and blend until smooth.

TO MAKE THE FALAFEL

1. Soak the dried chickpeas in plenty of purified water for 8 hours or overnight. Drain and rinse thoroughly. Place in a medium saucepan, cover with 5 cups of purified water, and bring to a boil. Lower the heat and simmer, uncovered, for 20 to 30 minutes (see Note on page 103), or until soft, adding about 1 tablespoon of the salt during the last 10 minutes. Drain and cool. If using canned chickpeas, simply drain and rinse them.

2. Preheat the oven to 375°F (190°C).

3. In a food processor, grind the pumpkin seeds into a coarse meal and transfer to a medium bowl. Reserve 2 tablespoons of the pumpkin seeds in a small bowl and add 1½ tablespoons of the flax meal and the sesame seeds. Mix to combine and set aside for coating the falafel.

4. Using a designated coffee grinder, grind the cumin, coriander, mustard, and cardamom seeds and red pepper flakes. In a medium bowl, combine the spice mixture with the tahini, olive oil, lemon juice, coconut sugar, and remaining 1½ teaspoons sea salt.

5. Place the cooked chickpeas, spicy tahini mixture, remaining pumpkin seeds, 2 tablespoons flax meal, the garlic, cilantro, tarragon, and mint in a food processor and pulse several times to combine. Scrape the sides of the machine with a spoon or spatula if needed. The mixture should be well mixed but still chunky. Taste for salt and add more if needed. Transfer to a medium bowl.

6. Line a baking sheet with parchment paper and start forming the falafel. Scoop about 1 generous tablespoon of the chickpea batter for each falafel and form a ball about 1¼ inches (3¼ cm) in diameter. Roll each falafel in the pumpkin seed-sesame-flax coating and place on the baking sheet. Repeat until all of the batter is used up. Put the sheet into the oven and bake for 15 minutes, turning the falafel every 5 minutes for even color. Remove from the oven and let cool. Serve stuffed into warm pita bread pockets, lettuce leaves, or other wraps of choice, 2 to 3 falafels per wrap. Top with the tahini sauce and peach salsa.

Note: You can make this falafel with sprouted chickpeas; the process is similar to the Roasted Kala Chana Hummus recipe (page 101): Bake the sprouted chickpeas in half of the spicy tahini mixture made in step 4 at 400°F (200°C) for 30 minutes covered, stirring halfway through. Lower the oven temperature to 375°F (190°C) and proceed to step 5, pulsing the baked sprouted chickpeas with the remaining spicy tahini mixture, 2 tablespoons olive oil, and the rest of the ingredients listed. Continue with the recipe as directed.

Black Bean Pasta with Black Sesame Sauce

with wilted dandelion greens and Bing cherries

Serves 4 to 6

For the black sesame paste

¼ cup (30 g) walnuts

¾ cup (120 g) black sesame seeds

2 tablespoons coconut sugar

2 tablespoons apple cider vinegar

2 tablespoons freshly squeezed lime juice

2 teaspoons walnut or hazelnut oil

½ teaspoon toasted sesame oil

⅛ teaspoon cayenne pepper

Generous pinch of sea salt

For the pasta

1 large bunch (about 9 oz [250 g]) dandelion greens

3 cups (15 oz [420 g]) pitted Bing cherries

1 package (7.05 oz [200 g]) black bean spaghetti or other spaghetti of choice

When I discovered black bean spaghetti in the gluten-free aisle of the grocery store, I was intrigued by the ingredients list—nothing more than black beans and water. The noodles have a pleasantly soft but slightly chewy texture and mild taste. You can always use buckwheat soba noodles or another pasta of choice, but this is a lovely, nutritious way to test your palate.

This dish is inspired by sour cherry ravioli, or *vareniki,* a summer treat from my childhood. Back then, I couldn't get enough of these pillows of pasta dough, filled with dark cherries and served with a spoonful of sugar and sour cream on top. Because making ravioli can be involved, a shortcut treat was any kind of noodles mixed with pitted sour cherries, butter, and sugar. I still dream about these flavors. Use sour cherries if you can, but sweet Bing cherries work well too. The lightly blanched dandelion greens add plenty of nutrients to the meal.

1. In a small skillet, toast the walnuts over medium heat, shaking the pan often, until lightly browned and fragrant. Remove from the skillet and set aside to cool. In the same skillet, toast the black sesame seeds, stirring or shaking the pan constantly for 1 to 2 minutes. Take care not to burn them; it is hard to tell when black sesame seeds are ready because of their color, so you must go by smell. Once you smell the warm aroma of lightly toasted sesame, immediately remove the skillet from the heat.

2. Place the toasted walnuts onto a clean kitchen towel and rub to remove the skins. Chop roughly. Reserve 2 tablespoons each chopped walnuts and toasted sesame seeds for garnish. In a coffee grinder, grind the rest of the walnuts and sesame seeds into a fine meal. Put in a bowl and mix with the rest of the ingredients to form a paste.

3. Bring a large pot of well-salted water to a boil and blanch the dandelion greens for 30 seconds. Using a slotted spoon, immediately transfer them into an ice-water bath to stop the cooking. Once cold, drain and squeeze out the water excess with your fingers. Roughly chop and set aside.

4. Cook the pasta in a pot with 2 quarts of salted boiling water for 6 to 8 minutes, or according to the package instructions. Drain, reserving about 1 cup of the cooking water. Briefly rinse the pasta with cold water and transfer to a pot or a large bowl. Add the dandelion greens.

5. Dilute the black sesame paste with ¾ cup of the pasta cooking liquid and mix thoroughly. Add it to the pasta together with the cherries, and mix to coat. Distribute between plates, garnish with the reserved chopped walnuts and sesame seeds, and serve.

Chickpea Crepes with Mango Salsa

For the mango salsa

1 large ripe mango, peeled, pitted, and cubed

1 small cucumber, peeled, seeded, and cubed (about 1 cup)

¼ cup finely chopped red onion

Leaves from ½ bunch cilantro, roughly chopped (about ¼ cup)

1 tablespoon chopped seeded jalapeño chile

1 tablespoon freshly squeezed lime juice

Sea salt

For the chickpea crepes

2 cups (240 g) chickpea flour

3 teaspoons black sesame seeds (optional)

1½ teaspoons ground turmeric

2 teaspoons sea salt

½ small red chile, seeded and chopped

2½ cups (600 ml) purified water

Grapeseed oil for frying

Makes 10 crepes

Crepes, or *blini*, as we call them, may be the ultimate comfort food for any Russian. The variety of recipes is endless, as is the list of fillings and ways to serve them. My mother makes the most delicate buttermilk-based crepes and serves them with a colorful display of sweet and savory small plates of caviar, smoked fish, soft cheeses, sour cream, jams, and honey.

Crepes made with chickpea flour do not taste anything like our *blini*, but they have their own unique, exciting flavor that I immediately fell in love with. The spicy notes of turmeric and chile balance perfectly with the juicy mango salsa.

TO MAKE THE MANGO SALSA

Combine the mango, cucumber, onion, cilantro, and jalapeño in a bowl. Add the lime juice, season with salt, and mix gently. The salsa will keep, refrigerated, for up to 3 days.

TO MAKE THE CREPES

1. In a large bowl, mix together all the crepe ingredients except the water. Gradually pour in the water, whisking the mixture as you go, until it forms a smooth batter. Let the batter sit for 30 minutes, covered.

2. Heat an 8-inch nonstick sauté pan over medium heat. Add about 2 teaspoons grapeseed oil to the hot pan.

3. Whisk the batter again. Add about ⅓ cup of the batter to the hot pan while swirling it. Cook the crepe for about 1 minute, until the surface is bubbly and the edges begin to turn a golden brown in color. Using a spatula, separate the edges from the pan, then carefully and quickly flip the crepe over (I usually use my hands) and cook until slightly golden on the other side. (The first crepe is a test to help you determine the amount of batter needed for each crepe and the right temperature. Don't worry if it's not perfect or sticks a little.) Add more oil before cooking each crepe.

4. As the crepes are cooked, stack them on a plate and cover them with a lid or another plate to keep them warm. Serve immediately with the salsa on the side or rolled into the crepes.

Asparagus and Kohlrabi Tart

Makes one 4½ × 13½-inch (11 × 35 cm) rectangular tart

Kohlrabi is a curious-looking brassica with a pleasant, cabbage-like flavor that goes very well with asparagus. Look for the smallest kohlrabi, as they are the most tender and juicy. If you can't find kohlrabi, add 2 medium potatoes to the filling ingredients. I like to use white asparagus on the bottom of the tart and very young green asparagus on top for a playful visual effect, but any fresh asparagus in season will work well.

TO PREPARE AND BAKE THE CRUST

1. Preheat the oven to 375°F (190°C).

2. In a food processor, grind the pecans into a coarse flour and transfer to a large bowl. Partially grind ½ cup (60 g) of the oats in the food processor to the consistency of a very coarse, chunky flour. Add to the bowl with the ground pecans, followed by the rest of the oats, the chia seeds, and salt. Pour the boiling water over the mixture, mix well, and let sit for about 5 minutes.

3. Add the olive oil and knead with your hands to form a soft and sticky dough. Using wet hands and a wet spoon, press into a lightly greased tart pan. Start with the bottom and extend to the sides, distributing the dough evenly. Make sure the crust is of an even thickness throughout.

4. Bake uncovered for 30 minutes, then remove from the oven and let cool.

TO PREPARE THE VEGETABLES

1. Drain and rinse the beans. In a medium saucepan, cover the beans with plenty of salted water and bring to a boil. Lower the heat and simmer for about 30 minutes, until completely cooked and soft. Drain and let cool. Or if using canned beans, simply drain them.

2. Peel and slice the kohlrabi into 4 to 5 slices each (about ⅓-inch [8 mm] thick). Arrange on a parchment paper–covered baking sheet. Brush both sides with 1 tablespoon of olive oil and sprinkle with salt and pepper.

3. When the crust is ready, increase the oven temperature to 450°F (230°C). Bake the kohlrabi for 20 minutes, or until tender when pricked with a fork, flipping the slices halfway through. Lower the oven temperature to 375°F (190°C).

4. While the kohlrabi is roasting, grind the coriander, cumin, mustard, and cardamom seeds and red pepper flakes in a mortar with a pestle or in a

For the crust

Generous ⅓ cup (40 g) pecans or walnuts

1 cup (120 g) rolled oats

2 tablespoons chia seeds

¼ teaspoon sea salt

⅔ cup (160 ml) boiling water

2 teaspoons olive oil, plus more for greasing the tart pan

For the filling

½ cup (100 g) dried cannellini beans, soaked in purified water overnight, or 1⅓ cups canned cannellini or other white beans

Sea salt

3 small (1 lb [450 g]) kohlrabi (about the size of a small apple)

2 tablespoons olive oil, divided

Freshly ground black pepper

1 teaspoon coriander seeds

½ teaspoon cumin seeds

¼ teaspoon mustard seeds

Seeds of 1 cardamom pod

⅛ teaspoon red pepper flakes

1 garlic clove, minced

Handful (about ¼ cup) of fresh parsley leaves, chopped

1 ounce (30 g) feta cheese, preferably goat's milk and/or sheep's milk feta

1 bunch each white and green asparagus, or 2 bunches of one kind (about 1 lb [450 g] total)

dedicated coffee grinder and set aside. Set a large pot of well-salted water to a boil for blanching the asparagus.

5. Roughly chop the kohlrabi slices and add to the food processor along with beans, three-quarters of the spice mixture, the garlic, parsley, and cheese and season with salt and pepper. Pulse several times until you have a chunky puree.

6. Slice the tough ends off each asparagus spear. Blanch them in the boiling water for 2 minutes, then transfer to an ice-water bath to stop the cooking. Remove from the water and pat dry with paper towels before assembling the tart.

TO ASSEMBLE AND BAKE THE TART

1. Arrange a single layer of white or green asparagus on the bottom of the crust. Lightly brush with half of the remaining olive oil and sprinkle with salt, pepper, and half of the remaining spice mixture.

2. Spoon the kohlrabi mixture on top of the asparagus, pressing carefully to fill the crust to the top. Even it out with a spoon. Depending on the thickness of the asparagus spears, you may or may not have some extra. Arrange the green or white asparagus snugly on top, gently pressing each spear into the puree. You may or may not need all of it, depending on the thickness of the asparagus spears. Aim for very young, thin asparagus for better presentation and taste.

3. Brush with the remaining oil and sprinkle with salt and pepper and the remaining spice mixture. Bake for 20 minutes, then turn the oven to broil, and broil for 1 to 2 minutes. Let cool, then unmold, slice, and serve.

Butternut Squash and Sage Fritters

1½ tablespoons olive oil, divided

½ medium yellow onion, finely chopped

1 large garlic clove, minced

2 cups (about 14½ oz [410 g]) packed finely shredded butternut squash

1 large egg

Large pinch of sea salt

Freshly ground black pepper

1½ tablespoons minced fresh sage (from about 5 sage leaves)

1 tablespoon minced fresh flat-leaf parsley

¼ teaspoon smoked paprika

Dash of freshly grated nutmeg

1½ ounces (45 g) feta cheese, preferably goat's milk and/or sheep's milk feta, crumbled

½ cup (50 g) hazelnut flour or almond flour

Makes about 12 fritters

I have a deep fondness for vegetable pancakes or fritters; they were one of the tastiest and simplest meals of my childhood. My mother made them with zucchini in summer and pumpkin in fall and winter, or we would enjoy potato pancakes, or *draniki*, the dish so dear to most Eastern European cultures.

These baked butternut squash fritters satisfy my craving for vegetable pancakes and deliver a strong fall flavor. You can also make them with zucchini in the summer instead of butternut squash—just squeeze out the excess water. For the summery variation, eliminate the sage and nutmeg and add 1 tablespoon each minced mint and dill and use almond flour rather than hazelnut flour.

1. Warm ½ tablespoon of the olive oil in a small sauté pan over medium-low heat. Add the onion and garlic and sauté for 4 to 5 minutes, until translucent. Set aside to cool.

2. Preheat the oven to 400°F (200°C).

3. Wrap the shredded butternut squash in several layers of paper towels and squeeze gently so the paper towels can absorb the excess liquid. Remove the paper towels and place the squash in a medium bowl with the egg, salt, pepper, sage, parsley, paprika, nutmeg, cheese, and hazelnut flour. Add the onion and garlic and mix to combine.

4. Line a baking sheet with lightly oiled parchment paper. With your hands, shape the squash mixture into patties and arrange them on the baking sheet about 1½ inches (4 cm) apart. If the batter doesn't stick together or is too wet, add a little more flour. Brush the patties with half of the remaining olive oil and bake for 10 minutes.

5. Remove the sheet from the oven and flip the patties using a thin spatula. Brush the other side of the patties with the remaining olive oil and bake for another 10 minutes. Serve with sour cream or yogurt and/or a simple green salad on the side.

For a vegan variation: Roast ½ cup hazelnuts in a 350°F (180°C) oven for 7 to 10 minutes. Let the nuts cool, then remove the skins by rubbing them with a kitchen towel. Grind the hazelnuts into small pieces in a food processor. Add the hazelnut meal to the shredded squash along with salt, spices, herbs, and sautéed vegetables. Add 1 tablespoon ground chia seeds and ¼ cup buckwheat flour. Mix well, then form the patties and bake as directed above.

Heirloom Tomato, Olive, and Basil Tofu Soufflé

2 (12.3 oz [349 g]) packages firm or extra-firm silken tofu

2 tablespoons nut butter of choice or sesame tahini, or 1 tablespoon of each

1 tablespoon olive oil, plus more for brushing on top and greasing the baking dish

Zest of 1 lemon

2 tablespoons freshly squeezed lemon juice

1 small garlic clove, roughly chopped

¼ teaspoon sea salt, plus more for sprinkling on top

Freshly ground black pepper

1 cup packed fresh basil leaves, torn

6 assorted olives, such as black and green Cerignola and/or Castelvetrano, pitted and roughly chopped

About 2 cups (300 g) ripe heirloom cherry tomatoes

½ each yellow and red small ripe heirloom tomatoes, or one of any color, sliced

Several sprigs of fresh thyme (optional)

Serves 4

Makes one 8 × 8 inch (20 cm) square or 9-inch (23 cm) round baking dish

This recipe was my solution to a very desirable problem: I had lots of very ripe, delicious tomatoes on hand and needed to use them up. The key to success here is the sweet heirloom tomatoes at the peak of the season. I highly recommend waiting until summer to make this dish.

1. Preheat the oven to 375°F (190°C).

2. Wrap each block of tofu in several layers of paper towels and let sit for about 10 minutes, letting the paper towels absorb excess liquid.

3. Unwrap the tofu, then roughly chop it. Place it in a food processor along with the nut butter, olive oil, lemon zest and juice, garlic, salt, and some pepper and process until smooth.

4. Transfer the tofu mixture into a bowl. Add the basil, half of the olives, and about half of the cherry tomatoes. Spoon the mixture into a lightly oiled baking dish and smooth out the top. Arrange the heirloom tomato slices and the remaining cherry tomatoes and olives on top, pressing them lightly into the tofu mixture.

5. Brush with olive oil, sprinkle with salt and pepper, and garnish with thyme sprigs, if using. Bake for 25 to 30 minutes, until the edges are golden brown. Turn on the broiler and broil for 1 to 2 minutes, until the top is golden and the tomatoes look cooked. Let cool slightly before serving.

Mushroom and Rutabaga Tartlets

with fresh herbs and purple potatoes

Makes six 4-inch (10 cm) tarts

Forest mushrooms are one of the foods from Russia I miss the most. Nothing can re-create the experience of foraging for wild mushrooms and then savoring their earthy flavors. To make mushroom hunting safe, one must be an expert in distinguishing edible mushrooms from poisonous ones, as my father was. He knew where to pick delicious mushrooms almost all year long. From the first morels of spring to the oyster mushrooms of mild winter months, my father supplied our family with the freshest mushroom crop throughout the year.

Chanterelles and shiitakes come the closest to replicating these legendary harvests.

Rutabaga is a nutritious root vegetable with a flavor somewhere between cabbage and turnips. You can use potatoes only for the filling if you want to keep things simpler. If you don't have all of the herbs for the mushroom marinade, don't let that stop you—improvisation is welcome.

For the filling

1 small (about 10 oz [280 g]) rutabaga

3 or 4 small (about 12 oz [340 g]) purple potatoes or Yukon gold potatoes

About 6 ounces (170 g) mixed chanterelle or shiitake mushrooms

3 tablespoons minced fresh parsley leaves, divided

1 tablespoon minced fresh dill

Leaves from 1 sprig fresh rosemary, minced

3 or 4 fresh sage leaves, minced

Leaves from 3 fresh thyme sprigs

Handful of fresh basil leaves, minced

3 tablespoons olive oil, divided

3 tablespoons freshly squeezed lemon juice

Sea salt and freshly ground black pepper

2 large garlic cloves, minced

2 ounces (60 g) feta cheese, preferably goat's milk and/or sheep's milk feta, crumbled (optional)

For the crust

4 tablespoons coconut oil, melted, plus more for greasing the tart pans

4 tablespoons ghee (page 27), at room temperature

1 tablespoon ground chia seeds

5 to 6 tablespoons ice water

⅔ cup (95 g) quinoa flour

½ cup (90 g) brown rice flour

⅓ cup (40 g) tapioca starch

¼ teaspoon sea salt

Freshly ground black pepper

½ tablespoon chopped fresh rosemary

TO PREPARE THE VEGETABLES

1. Preheat the oven to 375°F (190°C).

2. Wrap the rutabaga in aluminum foil and prick the potatoes with a fork several times. Place the potatoes and rutabaga on a baking sheet and put it in the oven. Bake the potatoes for 30 to 40 minutes, piercing with a fork to test for tenderness. Remove from the oven when they are soft throughout and set aside. Keep the rutabaga in the oven, baking for about 1 hour and 45 minutes total time, until tender throughout when a knife is inserted into it. Set aside.

3. While the rutabaga and potatoes are baking, briefly wash the mushrooms and squeeze out any excess water. Remove the stems from the shiitakes, slice the larger mushrooms, and place all of them into a medium bowl. Reserve 2 tablespoons of the parsley for later and add the remaining herbs, 2 tablespoons of the olive oil, the lemon juice, and 2 generous pinches of salt and pepper to the mushrooms. Mix to coat and set aside while you prepare the crust.

Note: You can prepare the vegetables the day before and store them refrigerated in a covered container.

TO PREPARE AND BAKE THE CRUST

1. In a small bowl, thoroughly mix together the coconut oil and ghee. Spoon the mixture into a small, shallow dish and place in the freezer for about 10 minutes, until hardened. Lightly oil the tart pans.

2. In another small bowl, combine the ground chia seeds with 1 tablespoon of the ice water. Mix the ingredients into a paste and refrigerate.

3. In a food processor, combine the flours, tapioca starch, salt, pepper, and rosemary and pulse several times to mix. Remove the hardened ghee mixture from the freezer and cut it in the dish into ½-inch (1¼ cm) cubes. Add the cubes to the flour mixture and pulse 10 to 15 times, until the ghee is ground into lentil-size pieces.

4. Remove the chia paste from the refrigerator and add it to the food processor, along with 4 tablespoons ice water. Pulse several times to bring the dough together. Check the dough with your fingers; it should stick when pressed together. If not, add 1 more tablespoon ice water and pulse again.

5. Put the dough onto a work surface (it will be crumbly at this point) and quickly knead together. Shape the dough into a thick log and cut it into 6 equal parts. Flatten each portion with the palm of your hand and press into the oiled tart pans. Starting with the bottom, extend it to the sides until you have an evenly thick crust. Prick with a fork several times and chill in the refrigerator for 30 minutes.

6. Preheat the oven to 375°F (190°C).

7. Cover the chilled crusts with parchment paper and place baking beans inside. Blind-bake the crusts for 20 minutes, then remove from the oven and set aside. Increase the oven temperature to 400°F (200°C).

TO ASSEMBLE AND BAKE THE TARTLETS

1. While the crust is baking, peel the baked rutabaga and potatoes and thinly slice them. When the crusts are cool enough to handle, arrange the vegetable slices on the bottom of each tartlet. Alternate the potato and rutabaga slices, overlapping the edges slightly. Lightly brush each layer with the remaining 1 tablespoon olive oil and sprinkle with salt and pepper, the reserved parsley, the garlic, and cheese, if using. When the tartlets are almost filled, pile the mushrooms on top.

2. Bake for 15 minutes until the crust is golden and mushrooms look cooked. Remove from the oven and let the tartlets cool before unmolding.

Zucchini Spaghetti with Nectarines and Pumpkin Seed Pesto

For the pumpkin seed pesto

1 cup (160 g) raw unsalted pumpkin seeds

¼ teaspoon sea salt

3 tablespoons olive oil, divided

1 cup packed opal or regular fresh basil leaves

2 tablespoons purified water

1 tablespoon freshly squeezed lemon juice

½ garlic clove, minced

For the zucchini spaghetti

2 small to medium zucchinis (about 1½ lb [680 g])

2 nectarines, pitted and sliced

Opal or regular fresh basil leaves for garnish

Serves 4

I stumbled upon the idea of raw food accidentally, while searching for ways to further improve my health after Paloma was born. The novel techniques and nourishing ingredients fed my curiosity for a long time. Zucchini noodles with marinara sauce was one of the first raw dishes I ever tried, and I was impressed and persuaded to experiment more. The best way to make the noodles is with a special tool called a spiral slicer or spiralizer. It is affordable and very easy to operate. Alternatively, you can use a mandoline or a julienne slicer.

Note: There is a lot of room for creativity when it comes to dishes like this one. Here I combined the zucchini spaghetti with a pesto made from toasted pumpkin seeds and opal basil, accompanied by juicy nectarine slices. You can experiment with different herbs, such as parsley, dill, or cilantro instead of the basil and any number of nuts instead of the pumpkin seeds. The pesto is also delicious on crackers or Quick Spelt Bread (see page 315).

TO MAKE THE PESTO

1. Preheat the oven to 375°F (190°C).

2. In a medium bowl, combine the pumpkin seeds with the salt and 1 tablespoon of the olive oil. Mix well to coat. Spread on a parchment paper–covered baking sheet and toast for 10 minutes, or until the seeds are puffed up and golden. Remove from the oven and let cool.

3. In a food processor, grind the toasted pumpkin seeds to the size of small breadcrumbs. Add the remaining 2 tablespoons olive oil, the basil, water, lemon juice, and garlic and blend to a smooth paste. Use immediately or refrigerate for up to 3 days.

TO ASSEMBLE

Slice the zucchini with a spiral slicer (you should get about 5 cups of spaghetti). Place into a bowl and mix in about 5 tablespoons of the pesto. Divide among serving bowls, arrange the nectarine slices on top, and garnish with basil and small dollops of pesto.

Caramelized Fennel and Fig Pizza

Makes 2 medium pizzas

I could never pick a favorite fruit; any fruit in season becomes *the one*. If I absolutely had to choose, I would choose figs.

Figs bring me back to our summer stays in a vacation town on the Black Sea where my aunt lived. They grew wild there, ripened to a honey-like sweetness by the warm summer sun and salty sea breeze. We never thought to cook with them, enjoying them as nature made them: fresh from the tree. Years later, I learned about using figs in sweet and savory dishes through traveling and seeing how they were used in various cuisines. Now, when fig season arrives in late summer and early fall, my family goes through many boxes a week. The figs find their way into jams, cakes, salads, breakfast cereal, and on top of pizza. If figs are unavailable, you can substitute thinly sliced apples and a sprinkle of cinnamon.

I use a very simple pizza crust here—no yeast, gluten, eggs, or dairy. You can use this simple crust with any of your favorite pizza toppings; just be sure to cover the crust completely with toppings to prevent the edges from hardening or burning.

TO ROAST THE FENNEL AND MAKE THE PIZZA DOUGH

1. Preheat the oven to 415°F (210°C).

2. Brush both sides of the fennel slices with olive oil and lay them on a parchment paper–covered baking sheet. Sprinkle some salt and pepper on top. Roast for 20 to 30 minutes, rotating every 10 to 15 minutes, until softened.

3. To make the crust, mix together the water, salt, and 1½ tablespoons of the coconut sugar in a jar with a tight-fitting lid. Shake until the salt and sugar are dissolved. Add the vinegar and shake lightly to mix. Measure 1 cup of the liquid and set aside.

4. Sift 1½ cups of the flour into a large bowl, then add the baking soda, 4 tablespoons of the olive oil, and the remaining 1 tablespoon coconut sugar. Gradually pour in 1 cup of the liquid, mixing to combine. The dough will be liquidy at this point.

5. Start adding more flour by sifting it into the bowl, ½ cup at a time, mixing it in with a wooden spoon as you go. When the dough is no longer too sticky to be kneaded by hand, knead it quickly for no more than 2 minutes. Make sure to dust your hands and the surface of the dough with flour. The dough should be very soft and may be slightly sticky at this stage. It is important to

For the topping

2 large fennel bulbs, sliced into ¼-inch (6 mm) thick slices, green fronds reserved

1 tablespoon olive oil

Sea salt and freshly ground black pepper

14 to 16 ripe figs

1 to 2 ounces (30 to 60 g) feta cheese, preferably goat's milk and/or sheep's milk feta shredded or crumbled (optional)

For the crust

1½ cups (360 ml) purified water

¾ tablespoon sea salt

2½ tablespoons coconut sugar or other sweetener, divided

1 tablespoon apple cider vinegar

3 cups (420 g) buckwheat flour, plus more for dusting, divided

½ teaspoon baking soda

5 tablespoons olive oil, divided

add the flour just a little at a time; if not, it may become too stiff, which will be hard to fix, even by adding more liquid.

6. When you are finished kneading, divide the dough into 2 equal portions and shape each portion into a ball. Place each ball onto the center of a piece of plastic wrap and flatten into a disk with the palm of your hand. Cover with more plastic wrap and refrigerate for at least 30 minutes. You can prepare the dough in advance and refrigerate it overnight.

TO ASSEMBLE AND BAKE THE PIZZAS

1. Preheat the oven to 395°F (200°C).

2. Dust a rolling pin with a little bit of flour. Roll each piece of dough on a separate piece of parchment paper into a ¼-inch (6 mm) thick pizza crust. Brush with the remaining 1 tablespoon olive oil.

3. Bake for 10 minutes, one crust at a time. Remove from the oven and top with the fennel, then the figs and cheese, if using. Don't leave too much of the border uncovered to prevent the dough from drying and hardening. Bake for another 12 minutes, one pizza at a time. Top with the fennel fronds and other greens, such as arugula, and some black pepper and let cool slightly before slicing.

Celeriac Chickpea Stew
with slow-roasted tomatoes

For the slow-roasted tomatoes

¼ cup (60 g) olive oil

1 tablespoon balsamic vinegar

½ tablespoon coconut sugar

½ teaspoon sea salt, plus more for sprinkling on top

4 garlic cloves, minced

Leaves of several fresh thyme sprigs

1 pound (454 g) cherry or grape tomatoes, preferably on the vine

Freshly ground black pepper

For the chickpeas and celery root

2 cups (400 g) chickpeas, soaked overnight or sprouted (see page 36)

1½ medium yellow onions, chopped, divided

About 14 fresh thyme sprigs, divided

3 bay leaves

1 large (about 1½ lb [680 g]) celeriac, peeled, cut into 1-inch (2½ cm) cubes

Sea salt to taste

½ chile, seeded and roughly chopped

2 garlic cloves, chopped

3 tablespoons olive oil

1 cup packed fresh basil leaves (optional)

Serves 6 to 8

This simple but flavorful dish can be a great side dish or its own meal. Sweet slow-roasted tomatoes offset the spicy notes of chile in the chickpeas. Celeriac, or celery root, is a versatile vegetable that adds flavor and nourishment.

TO ROAST THE TOMATOES

1. Preheat the oven to 325°F (160°C).

2. In a small bowl, combine the olive oil, vinegar, coconut sugar, salt, garlic, and thyme. Place the tomatoes into a shallow oiled baking dish and pour the mixture over them. Add the thyme sprigs and sprinkle with a little more salt and some pepper.

3. Place in the oven and bake for 1½ hours, or until the tomatoes are soft. Remove from the oven and set aside.

TO PREPARE THE CHICKPEAS AND ASSEMBLE THE DISH

1. Place the chickpeas, ½ onion, 8 sprigs thyme, and the bay leaves in a large saucepan. Cover with a large amount of water and bring to a boil, then lower the heat and simmer, uncovered, for 20 to 30 minutes, or until almost soft (see Note on page 103).

2. Add the celeriac and salt and simmer for another 8 to 10 minutes, until the celeriac and chickpeas are tender throughout. Reserve 1¼ cups of the cooking liquid, then drain.

3. In a food processor, combine the remaining onions and thyme, the chile, and garlic, and pulse into a pulp.

4. In a large skillet, heat the olive oil over medium heat, add the spicy pulp, and cook for 5 to 7 minutes, stirring occasionally. Add the chickpeas, celeriac, and the reserved cooking liquid and cook, partially covered, for 5 to 7 minutes, until most of the liquid evaporates and the chickpeas are very soft.

5. Remove from the heat and add the basil and juices from the roasted tomatoes. Adjust the salt and pepper, top with the roasted tomatoes, and serve.

Mediterranean Dolmas

Makes about 21 dolmas

This dolma is bursting with fresh and vibrant flavors and is great as an appetizer at parties or even a light main dish for a more casual meal. If fresh grape leaves are readily available, marinate them yourself in olive oil and balsamic vinegar and/or lemon juice. Marinated grape leaves are usually available at health food and some regular grocery stores and sold in glass jars next to olives and other preserved vegetables.

For the herb and sesame sauce

⅔ cup (105 g) sesame seeds

½ cup packed fresh parsley, hard stems removed

½ cup packed fresh dill, hard stems removed

1 cup packed fresh cilantro

Handful of fresh mint leaves

⅓ cup (85 ml) olive oil

1 teaspoon sea salt, plus more to taste

1 cup (240 ml) purified water, plus more if needed

For the dolmas

1 cup (about 150 g) cherry tomatoes, or ½ cup (80 g) sun-dried tomatoes, soaked in purified water for 1 hour, drained, and chopped

5 to 8 fresh thyme sprigs (optional)

3 tablespoons olive oil, plus more for coating the dolmas

2 tablespoons balsamic vinegar (optional)

Sea salt and freshly ground black pepper

1½ cups sprouted quinoa (see page 37; from about ¾ cup dried quinoa) or 1 ½ cups cooked quinoa (from about ⅓ cup dried quinoa)

5 or 6 olives, such as Cerignola and/or Castelvetrano, pitted and chopped

1 small cucumber, peeled, seeded, and cut into small cubes (about 1 cup)

1 small shallot, minced

1 small garlic clove, minced

½ small jalapeño or other chile, seeded and minced

Zest of 1 lemon

2 tablespoons freshly squeezed lemon juice

2 tablespoons chopped fresh dill

2 tablespoons chopped fresh mint

2 tablespoons chopped fresh parsley

20 to 25 marinated grape leaves, depending on their size

TO MAKE THE HERB AND SESAME SAUCE

In a medium skillet, heat the sesame seeds over medium heat and toast until golden, stirring or shaking the pan frequently. Remove from the heat and cool, then place them in a high-speed blender with the remaining sauce ingredients and blend until smooth. The sauce will keep refrigerated for up to 3 days.

TO PREPARE THE FILLING AND ROLL THE DOLMAS

1. If using cherry tomatoes, preheat the oven to 275°F (135°C).

2. Cut the cherry tomatoes in half vertically and place on a parchment paper–lined baking sheet. Top with the thyme, sprinkle with 1 tablespoon of the olive oil, the vinegar, and some salt and pepper. Bake for 1 to 2 hours, until partially dried. Remove the thyme and let cool, then quarter each tomato half. Alternatively, use the soaked sun-dried tomatoes.

3. In a large bowl, combine the tomatoes, quinoa, olives, cucumber, shallot, garlic, jalapeño, lemon zest and juice, dill, mint, parsley, the 2 remaining tablespoons olive oil, and some salt and pepper. Mix gently to incorporate all the juices and set aside.

4. Briefly rinse the grape leaves and pat dry with paper towels.

5. Put 1 to 2 tablespoons of the filling (depending on the leaf size) in the center of each leaf and fold. Begin with the stem end, followed by the sides, then roll into a tight cylinder.

6. Lightly brush with olive oil to coat and set aside for 30 minutes to 1 hour. Serve with the herb and sesame sauce. The dolmas will keep refrigerated for up to 3 days.

Note: This recipe is extremely versatile and easy to modify. You can tweak the filling ingredients without compromising the flavor. Add more tomatoes or eliminate them entirely, for instance, and you'll still end up with a great-tasting dish. I encourage you to experiment and adjust according to what is available or on hand.

3

Teatime & Sweets

IN OUR HOME, WE OFTEN BEGIN AND END OUR DAY WITH TEA, drink it at every meal, and even take a cup or two in between. If I need to wake up, I usually drink green tea in the warm weather, black in the winter. There is chamomile or lavender tea for winding down, herbal teas for aiding digestion, and rooibos and mate as great caffeine-free boosts. I also like to make ginger or basil tea by simply brewing fresh ginger root or basil leaves in hot water. The possibilities are endless.

The samovar is a traditional appliance for heating water, and it has been a crucial element of Russian teatime until recently. These urn-like objects are truly artisanal, and they have become the main symbol of Russian hospitality. Originally the samovar was heated with charcoal, and a dedicated old leather boot was worn whenever the hot air needed pumping within to keep the coals going. The care and pride associated with samovars show how seriously our culture treats the custom of tea drinking. Nowadays we have an electric samovar. While not as authentic, it does the trick when gathering friends and sharing many laughs.

My parents' country house, or *dacha,* had the ideal courtyard for summer teatime. My parents decided to purchase the property after my mother retired and finally had time to plant her dream garden. It was also the perfect pastime for the grandchildren, and Masha still refers to the country house as her favorite place in the world, having practically grown up there. Our dacha was located outside of town, near a large forest, on Cherry Street. It consisted of a two-story brick house with a moss green roof, a small backyard off to the side, a wooden tool shack, an outdoor shower, and a garden in the back. My mother, always having had a green thumb, did an admirable job taking care of the garden almost exclusively on her own. She grew beautiful vegetables, berries and other fruits, and flowers. Among my favorites was a miniature sour cherry tree, which blossomed pink in the spring and yielded a delicious crop in the summer, as well as the bushes of black, red, and white currants that lined the whole perimeter of the garden. For teatime, we liked to fold out a table in the courtyard, bring out the electric samovar, and enjoy the sweet summer crop, whether on its own or in baked goods, over a few cups of perfectly brewed tea.

Tea warms the soul, comforts the mind, and brings people together. Making tea gives us the chance to pause and unwind. I confess, I cannot enjoy even the most decadent of desserts without a hot cup of tea. A sip between bites makes the treat melt on your tongue, which enhances its flavor and makes the sensory experience that much more pleasurable.

In this chapter, you will find desserts that can be enjoyed with tea or without, and most are nutritious enough to be eaten for breakfast. Sweets generally have the reputation of an unhealthy indulgence. By using the best of what nature has to offer and working with the seasons, I strive to steer my desserts away from sinful and toward nourishing. I use the least amount of sweetener possible, and the best quality of it as is appropriate. The sweetener frames the intended flavor rather than overpowers it. I also enjoy incorporating spices and herbs into desserts, as much as I do with savory dishes, to find new, interesting flavor combinations. To me dessert is the culmination of a meal, and I love to play with colors, textures, and shapes to make every dessert a celebration.

Mango Lime Tartlets

Makes seven 5-inch (13 cm) tartlets

There are more than one hundred known varieties of mango. To me, the best mango is any ripe one in season. In spring, you can find me at the Asian market twice a week buying a whole box of small champagne mangoes at a time. Later in the summer, I keep my eyes open for local Florida mangoes. If I'm lucky, I'll get some from a neighbor's tree.

So inspired by my love of mango, I created two versions of these tartlets: one raw, one baked.

I have made this recipe with other fruits in season, though I'm partial to the mango-lime combo. Try strawberries, peaches, apples, or apricots. Adjust the size of the tartlet to the size of the fruit. You can substitute lemon for the lime, and soak the chia seeds in fresh apple or pear juice.

TO PREPARE THE TOPPING

1. Zest and juice the lime. Place the zest in a small bowl, cover with plastic, and set aside for garnish. In another small dish, whisk the lime juice with the honey and set aside.

2. Peel the mangoes. Cut the flesh along the flat sides of the pit to get two even halves. (The center pit slab will still be fleshy.) Slice each mango half very thinly (about 3 mm thick) lengthwise. Then cut each slice in half. Set aside.

3. Cut the rest of the flesh off the pit and reserve for the crust.

TO PREPARE THE CRUST

1. Zest and juice the limes. Place the zest in a small bowl, cover with plastic, and set aside. Chop the reserved mango flesh; you should have about 1 cup. In a blender, combine the chopped mango with the lime juice and blend until smooth. In a medium bowl, thoroughly combine the mixture with the chia seeds and let sit for 15 minutes, or until a gel forms.

2. Meanwhile, mix together the coconut oil, almond butter, honey, 1/3 cup of the coconut sugar, and vanilla in a medium bowl. Add the chia gel to the mixture, stirring to combine well.

3. In a blender or food processor, pulse the quinoa flakes into flour (you should end up with approximately 1½ cups). In a large bowl, combine the quinoa, coconut flour, salt, and baking soda, mixing to incorporate. Add the wet ingredients to the dry mixture, mixing it until it resembles a sticky cookie dough. The dough may seem too wet at first, but it will thicken and become drier after about 5 minutes. If it remains too wet, add small amounts of the

For the mango-lime topping

1 lime
1 tablespoon honey
2 large or 4 small mangoes (about 2 lb [900 g] total)

For the crust

2 limes
3 tablespoons chia seeds
5 tablespoons coconut oil, melted
¼ cup almond butter or other nut butter
¼ cup honey
1/3 cup (45 g) plus 3 tablespoons coconut sugar, divided
½ tablespoon vanilla extract
2 cups (240 g) quinoa flakes
½ cup (60 g) coconut flour
¼ teaspoon sea salt
½ teaspoon baking soda
Brown rice flour for rolling the crust
1/3 cup unsalted pistachio nuts, plus more for garnish

coconut or quinoa flake flour, but avoid adding too much. Shape the dough into 5 even-size balls and set aside.

TO ASSEMBLE AND BAKE THE TARTLETS

1. Preheat the oven to 350°F (175°C).

2. Cover a baking sheet with parchment paper. Lightly dust your working surface and rolling pin with brown rice flour. Flatten and roll the dough on the working surface, one ball at a time, until the balls are approximately ¼ inch (6 mm) thick. Cut out 5-inch (13 cm) circles with a cookie cutter or a small bowl, tracing it with a knife (a small tart pan also works great). Reshape and re-roll the dough until you cut 7 rounds total. Place each crust on the prepared baking sheet as you go.

3. Pulse the pistachios in a food processor into fairly small pieces and reserve 1 tablespoon for garnish. In a medium bowl, combine the remaining 3 tablespoons coconut sugar with the remaining pistachios and reserved zest from 2 limes. Divide the mixture among the tartlets and sprinkle to cover the surface, leaving a small border free of topping around the edges.

4. Arrange the mango slices on top in a spiral, overlapping the edges. Place the flat, cut edge of each slice facing out and the pointed end facing the center of the tartlet. Brush the mango with the reserved lime-honey mixture.

5. Bake for 25 minutes, or until the edges are golden. Garnish with the reserved zest of 1 lime and the pistachios. Let rest briefly on the sheet, then carefully transfer to a cooling rack with a wide pie server (tartlets can be fragile when still hot). Let cool completely before serving.

TO MAKE THE RAW VERSION

Grind the coconut sugar in a coffee grinder. Replace the quinoa flakes with 1½ cups oat flour (preferably sprouted) and the coconut oil with the same amount of melted cocoa butter. Eliminate the baking soda. Otherwise, follow the same prep and assembly instructions as above.

Place the tartlets on Teflex-lined dehydrator trays and dehydrate at 115°F (45°C) for 8 to 12 hours or overnight. Transfer the tartlets onto mesh screen–covered dehydrator trays and dehydrate for a couple more hours, or until firm enough to handle but not too dry. The raw version keeps well refrigerated for up to 2 weeks.

Roasted Plum Ice Cream

2 pounds (910 g) ripe black plums, halved and pitted

10 cardamom pods (or fewer for a milder flavor), crushed with a mortar and pestle

2 cups (500 ml) unsweetened full-fat canned coconut milk

2 tablespoons grated fresh ginger

2 tablespoons plum brandy (optional)

Pinch of sea salt

¾ to 1 cup (210 to 280 ml) honey (depending on how sour your plums are and how sweet you like your ice cream)

Serves 6

After tasting this ice cream, my friend Elena's nine-year-old son announced he no longer wanted to eat store-bought ice cream. The flavor is rich and multilayered in the best way. All you need to ensure success—and a delicious, unique ice cream—are ripe plums in season.

For best results, roast the plums and prepare the ice cream base the night before to give it a chance to chill well.

1. Preheat the oven to 375°F (190°C) and cover a baking sheet with aluminum foil.

2. Place the plums, cut side up, on the baking sheet and roast for 15 to 20 minutes, until soft and jammy. Loosely wrap the foil liner around them and set aside to cool.

3. Remove the green cardamom pods from the seeds and discard the pods. Place the cardamom seeds and coconut milk in a medium saucepan. Bring to a boil, remove from the heat, cover, and let the cardamom infuse for 30 minutes.

4. Combine the plums, ginger, and brandy, if using, in a blender and blend until smooth, then add the coconut-cardamom milk and a pinch of sea salt and blend to combine. Strain the mixture, stir in the honey, and chill well in the refrigerator for several hours or overnight.

5. Pour the mixture into the bowl of an ice cream maker and churn for 25 minutes, or according to the manufacturer's instructions. Freeze for at least 2 to 3 hours before serving.

Note: Ever since purchasing an ice cream maker, I often wonder how we lived without it for so long. This modest investment was a small price to pay for so much joy and so many satisfied cravings. All the wild flavor combinations you envision for your frozen treats become possible to make at home with this simple device.

If you don't have an ice cream maker, cool the mixture completely and freeze in a container. After about 45 minutes, when the ice cream has begun to solidify around the edges, stir it to break down any frozen segments, then return it to the freezer. Stir the ice cream again every 30 minutes or so, until it is evenly frozen throughout. This will take 2 to 3 hours.

Rum and Raisin Bundt Cakes

Makes 3 small (4-inch [10 cm]) cakes

Glazed rum and raisin cakes, or *baba,* were a popular bakery item when I was a child. Even our school cafeteria served them regularly. This recipe is my offering of a much healthier version of that comforting childhood treat. These cakes are studded with rum-soaked raisins and topped with a coconut glaze. They are best eaten fresh, and within two days . . . which is never a problem in our family. The cakes rarely last through the evening.

The longer the raisins are soaked in rum, the more flavor they will absorb. Overnight is optimal.

1. Soak the raisins in the rum for several hours or overnight.

2. Preheat the oven to 400°F (200°C).

3. Cut the sweet potato in half lengthwise, then place the halves on a baking sheet cut side down. Bake for 30 minutes, or until tender. Let cool, remove the skin, place in a bowl, and mash with a fork. Set aside. Lower the oven temperature to 350°F (180°C).

4. Oil the cake pans, then lightly dust them with brown rice flour. In a medium bowl using a hand blender, beat the egg with the coconut sugar until foamy, creamy, and increased in volume. Add the sweet potato puree, ¼ cup of the coconut milk, the olive oil, and 1 teaspoon of the vanilla and blend to combine thoroughly. Put the remaining ½ cup coconut milk in the freezer.

5. In a large bowl, combine the brown rice flour, oat flour, almond flour, tapioca starch, salt, baking powder, baking soda, and cinnamon. Add the wet ingredients to the dry mixture, then add the raisins and rum. Mix into a wet and sticky dough. Using a small spoon and well-floured hands, spoon the dough into each of the cake forms, filling them two-thirds full.

6. Bake for 20 to 25 minutes, until a toothpick poked into the center comes out clean. Let the cakes cool a little on a cooling rack, then unmold. Place the cakes on a cooling rack to cool completely.

7. To prepare the glaze, remove the coconut milk from the freezer and whisk it with the honey and the remaining 1 teaspoon vanilla. If the coconut milk is icy or lumpy, give the mixture a quick whirl in a blender. Keep the mixture refrigerated until the cakes have cooled completely, then liberally pour the glaze over them. Garnish with fresh berries, if you'd like.

1 cup (120 g) raisins
⅓ cup (80 ml) rum
1 medium sweet potato
2 tablespoons olive oil, plus more for greasing the cake pans
¾ cup (135 g) brown rice flour, plus more for dusting the cake pans and your hands
1 large egg
¼ cup (35 g) coconut sugar
¾ cup (190 ml) unsweetened full-fat canned coconut milk, divided
2 teaspoons vanilla extract, divided
¼ cup plus 2 tablespoons (40 g) oat flour
¼ cup (25 g) almond flour
¼ cup (40 g) tapioca starch
½ teaspoon sea salt
1 teaspoon baking powder
½ teaspoon baking soda
¼ teaspoon ground cinnamon
½ tablespoon honey
Fresh berries for garnish (optional)

Rhubarb and Rosemary Tart
infused with Grand Marnier and orange

Makes one 9-inch (23 cm) tart

Somehow rhubarb eluded me most of my life. My first taste of rhubarb was only recently, in a dessert that featured it marinated in Grand Marnier, honey, and rosemary. I knew instantly that I'd been missing out—and that I needed to re-create a version of this delight for myself. Rhubarb's main flavor is an aromatic sourness, and I love how the liqueur and rosemary work with the rhubarb's nature to give this tart its unique flavor.

Note: Macerating the rhubarb makes it flexible enough to arrange in a circular pattern. Plan ahead and let it macerate the night before for convenience.

TO PREPARE THE RHUBARB

1. Slice the rhubarb stalks into thin strips, 4 to 6 strips per stalk. Bruise 3 rosemary sprigs with the back of a chef's knife. Place the rhubarb into a shallow dish, add the rosemary sprigs, and cover with ¾ cup of the coconut sugar, mixing to coat. Cover and let macerate for 4 to 5 hours or overnight in the refrigerator.

2. Drain the rhubarb, reserving the soaking liquid. In a medium saucepan, mix the soaking liquid and soaked rosemary with the remaining ¼ cup coconut sugar, the orange zest and juice, and Grand Marnier. Bring to a boil over medium-high heat and boil for 10 to 15 minutes, until syrupy and reduced to about ¼ cup. Add the remaining 3 sprigs rosemary, cover, and let infuse while you bake the tart. You will use this orange-rosemary glaze during assembly.

TO PREPARE THE CRUST

1. Pour the coconut oil into a small shallow dish and place in the freezer for 10 to 15 minutes, until hardened. Lightly grease the tart pan.

2. In a food processor, combine the flours, tapioca starch, coconut sugar, rosemary, and salt and pulse several times to mix. Remove the hardened coconut oil from the freezer and cut it into small cubes. Add it to the flour mixture and pulse until the coconut oil is ground into tiny granules and incorporated into the flour. The mixture will resemble sand.

3. Add 4 tablespoons ice water to the food processor and pulse several times to bring the dough together. Check the dough with your fingers; it should

For the rhubarb filling
1½ pounds (680 g) rhubarb
6 fresh rosemary sprigs, divided
1 cup (140 g) coconut sugar, divided
Zest of 1 orange
1 cup (240 ml) freshly squeezed orange juice
2 teaspoons Grand Marnier

For the crust
½ cup (120 ml) coconut oil, melted, plus more for oiling the pan
½ cup (70 g) buckwheat flour
½ cup (90 g) brown rice flour
¼ cup (30 g) tapioca starch
2 tablespoons coconut sugar
1 teaspoon minced fresh rosemary
¼ teaspoon sea salt
4 to 5 tablespoons ice water

For assembling
5 tablespoons coconut sugar
1 tablespoon chopped fresh rosemary
2 tablespoons almond flour

stick when pressed together. If not, add 1 more tablespoon ice water and pulse again.

4. Turn the dough onto a work surface (it will be crumbly) and quickly knead it into a ball. Flatten it with the palm of your hand and press it into the tart pan. Starting at the center, push the dough out to the sides, covering the bottom until the crust is even. Prick with a fork several times and chill in the refrigerator for 30 minutes.

TO ASSEMBLE AND BAKE THE TART

1. Preheat the oven to 375°F (190°C).

2. In a small bowl, mix the coconut sugar and chopped rosemary.

3. Take the crust out of the refrigerator and sprinkle with the almond flour. Snugly arrange the drained rhubarb in a circular pattern to fill the tart. Sprinkle the rosemary-sugar mixture on top. Bake for 40 minutes, or until the crust is golden brown and the rhubarb is soft and caramelized. Let cool, then brush the rhubarb with the orange-rosemary glaze. Unmold, slice, and serve with a cup of freshly brewed tea.

Fig Cupcakes

Makes 10 cupcakes

One night I dreamed of a cupcake with a whole fig baked into it. This sort of thing happens to me quite a lot, and I often wake up determined to cook whatever it is I saw in my dream.

A whole fruit encased in baked dough makes for an exciting pastry. The fruit transforms, with its sweet juices caramelizing and getting absorbed into the pastry, but still holds its shape. The wait for fig season to make these cupcakes is worth it—figs are just the right size, texture, and sweetness for this baking trick.

For the vanilla frosting

Requires a high-speed blender

1 cup (150 g) raw cashews, soaked in
   purified water for 4 hours
¾ cup (190 ml) plus 2 tablespoons
   unsweetened full-fat canned
   coconut milk, plus more if needed
¼ cup (75 g) light agave syrup or liquid
   honey
3 tablespoons freshly squeezed lemon
   juice
Seeds of 1 vanilla bean
Small pinch of sea salt
½ cup (125 ml) coconut oil, melted

For the cupcakes

1 cup (100 g) almond flour
½ cup (90 g) brown rice flour
¼ cup (30 g) millet flour
¼ cup (30 g) coconut flour
1 tablespoon arrowroot powder
½ teaspoon baking powder
¼ teaspoon baking soda
¼ teaspoon sea salt
Zest of 1 lemon
1 tablespoon coconut oil
1 cup (240 ml) unsweetened full-fat
   canned coconut milk
¼ cup (70 ml) honey
2 tablespoons freshly squeezed lemon
   juice
10 small ripe figs, stems cut off

TO MAKE THE VANILLA FROSTING

1. Drain and rinse the cashews. In a high-speed blender, combine the cashews with the coconut milk, agave, lemon juice, vanilla seeds, and salt and blend until creamy and smooth. Stop the blender, add the coconut oil, and blend to incorporate.

2. Place the frosting in the freezer to thicken for about 30 minutes while you are baking the cupcakes, until it is thickened and firm to the touch but not frozen.

TO MAKE THE CUPCAKES

1. Preheat the oven to 350°F (180°C). Lightly grease 10 holes of a 12-hole muffin pan or line them with silicone or paper liners (silicone liners will work best; if you are using paper, oil with nonstick cooking spray).

2. In a large bowl, combine the flours, arrowroot powder, baking powder, baking soda, salt, and lemon zest. Add the coconut oil and work it in to combine. Set aside.

3. In a medium bowl, combine the coconut milk, honey, and lemon juice. Add the wet ingredients to the dry mixture and mix, making a soft, sticky dough.

4. Using a wet spoon, fill the muffin holes with the dough about one-third of the way, helping arrange the dough inside the liners with wet fingers if necessary. Insert 1 fig per cupcake into the dough, pressing gently, making sure that the fig is almost at the bottom of the cupcake but not all the way through it. Add more dough on top to enclose the fig completely.

5. Bake for 20 to 25 minutes, until the tops are golden. Remove from the oven and cool completely on a cooling rack. If you used silicone liners, remove them; it's not necessary to remove paper liners.

TO FROST THE CUPCAKES

Place the vanilla frosting in a pastry bag and press it down toward the tip of the bag. Pipe some cream on top of each cupcake to form good-looking peaks. Keep refrigerated.

Lemongrass Raspberry Trifle

with cardamom custard cream

Makes 6 individual glasses (3¼ inches tall, 2½ inches in diameter)

During my first years in the United States, I fell in love with Nigella Lawson's cookbooks, in particular her recipe for a raspberry lemongrass dessert. Recently, while developing the menu for an Ayurveda-inspired birthday party, the idea of making a trifle infused with lemongrass and spices came to me, evoking Nigella's genius combination. The trifle tastes rich, but is very light and nutritious.

Each step in this recipe is not long on its own, but combined it could turn into a half-day affair. To simplify the presentation, the individual serving glasses can be eliminated and the layers can be arranged in one large glass bowl. Any way you decide to present it, you will not regret the effort.

I offer two ways to make this treat—cooked and raw. Both of them are favorites, and equally delicious.

For the crumbles

¾ cup (90 g) rolled oats

½ cup (60 g) quinoa flakes

¼ cup (35 g) amaranth flour or other gluten-free flour, such as millet, quinoa, or buckwheat flour

3 tablespoons coconut oil

2 tablespoons honey

¼ teaspoon sea salt

1 teaspoon vanilla extract or the seeds of ½ vanilla bean

For the raspberry layer

4 stalks lemongrass, or more to taste

1 cup (240 ml) purified water

⅓ cup honey or other sweetener of choice

3½ cups (15 oz [420 g]) raspberries

For the cardamom custard creme

2 cups (500 ml) almond milk (page 30)

1 tablespoon vegan gelatin (see page 21) or 1 ounce (30 g) dried Irish moss (see Notes)

½ cup (120 ml) purified water

2 to 3 large very moist and soft dates, pitted and chopped (¼ cup) (see Notes)

⅓ cup (100 ml) agave syrup

2 teaspoons vanilla extract

Seeds of 2 or 3 whole cardamom pods, ground with a mortar and pestle (see Notes) or ¼ teaspoon ground cardamom

½ cup (120 ml) coconut oil, melted

Notes: Dry dates can be soaked in purified water overnight to plump them up.

If you are using a high-speed blender, there is no need to pre-grind the cardamom; you can throw the whole seeds in with the rest of the ingredients.

Irish moss requires a high-speed blender.

TO PREPARE AND BAKE THE CRUMBLES

1. Preheat the oven to 350°F (180°C). Line a baking sheet with parchment paper.

2. Combine all the ingredients in a food processor and pulse until crumbly. Make sure that the oats and quinoa flakes are broken down into very small, breadcrumb-like pieces.

3. Transfer the mixture to the lined baking sheet in one even layer. Bake for 12 to 15 minutes, until golden, stirring two or three times to ensure even baking. Remove from the oven and cool completely.

TO PREPARE THE RASPBERRY LAYER

1. Cut each lemongrass stalk into 2-inch (5 cm) pieces, then cut each piece in half lengthwise. Bruise them with the handle of a chef's knife. Combine the water and honey in a medium saucepan, add the lemongrass, bring to a boil, then reduce the heat and simmer for 2 to 3 minutes. Remove from the heat, cover, and infuse for 30 minutes. Strain the lemongrass syrup into a medium bowl, discarding the lemongrass.

2. In the same saucepan, combine 2½ cups of the raspberries and ¾ cup of lemongrass syrup and bring to a rolling boil. Mash the berries with a fork until the mixture thickens and reaches a chunky jam-like consistency. It should take only a couple of minutes. Remove from the heat and stir in the remaining 1 cup raspberries, mashing them slightly. Remove from the heat to cool.

TO MAKE THE CARDAMOM CUSTARD CREME

1. This step varies by which thickener you are using:

Vegan gelatin and any kind of blender: Bring all 2 cups of the almond milk to a boil in a medium saucepan. Add the gelatin and whisk to dissolve completely. Pour it into a blender, add the water, dates, agave, vanilla, and cardamom, and blend until smooth, then add the coconut oil and blend to incorporate.

Irish moss and a high-speed blender: Rinse the Irish moss under cool water to remove as much salt and debris as you can, then place it in a large bowl. Soak in plenty of hot water for at least 10 minutes. Irish moss will expand in size significantly, so make sure that it is completely covered with water. Add more water as needed. Drain and rinse the Irish moss again, making sure it is completely clean. In a high-speed blender, combine the Irish moss with the almond milk, water, dates, agave, vanilla, and cardamom and blend until smooth, then add the coconut oil and blend to incorporate.

2. For both thickeners: Pour the mixture into a medium bowl, cover, and let cool and thicken a little while you begin to assemble the trifle. Make sure not to leave the creme in the refrigerator too long at this stage, as you don't want it to thicken too soon.

TO ASSEMBLE

1. Reserve some crumbles for garnish. Pour ¼ cup of the crumbles for each glass (one portion at a time) into a small strainer and dunk them into the raspberry mixture. Spoon the raspberry-dunked crumbles into the bottom of each glass and drizzle lightly with the remaining lemongrass syrup.

2. Spoon the raspberry mixture on top of the crumbles, dividing it evenly among the glasses. Top with cardamom custard creme. Refrigerate until the creme is set, about 2 to 4 hours or overnight. Garnish with the reserved crumbles and reserved raspberries.

TO MAKE THE RAW VERSION

1. For raw crumbles, soak ¾ cup raw buckwheat groats for about 1 hour. Rinse very well. In a food processor, combine the buckwheat with ½ cup powdered coconut sugar and 1 teaspoon vanilla extract. Pulse into a slightly chunky puree. Spread on a Teflex-lined dehydrator tray and dehydrate for 8 hours or overnight. Flip carefully, peel away the Teflex, and dehydrate for 2 to 3 more hours, until crisp. Break into small pieces and divide among glasses.

2. For the raspberry layer, blend 3 cups of raspberries with 2 stalks of lemongrass. Strain out the solids and add honey to taste. Chop the remaining ½ cup raspberries and add them to the raspberry puree. Spoon on top of the buckwheat crumbles. Slightly lift and drop each glass several times to coax the raspberry puree down into the crumble layer.

3. For the cardamom creme layer, use the Irish moss variation. Pour over the raspberry layer and refrigerate until set, 2 to 4 hours or overnight. Garnish with crushed pistachios and fresh raspberries.

Note: If you're not a strict vegetarian and decide to use regular gelatin, increase the amount to 5 teaspoons and simply add with the rest of the creme's ingredients and blend until smooth.

Berry and Chocolate Crisp
with a minty lime creme

Makes six 7-ounce (200 g) ramekins or one 9-inch (23 cm) pie

Crisps are some of the simplest and most comforting desserts. Plus, providing the fruit you use is fresh and in season, they are almost foolproof.

This crisp becomes decadent when the oozing baked berries blend with the dark chocolate, orange, and molasses-like flavor of coconut sugar. The minty creme adds an interesting cool and tart note, but any crumble is delicious on its own or with vanilla ice cream on the side.

For the minty lime creme
Requires a high-speed blender

1 cup (150 g) raw cashews or cashew
  pieces, soaked in purified water for
  2 hours, drained, and rinsed
Zest and juice of 2 limes
¼ cup (60 ml) purified water
¼ cup (70 g) light agave syrup or honey
Large handful of fresh mint leaves
¼ avocado (optional)

For the filling
2 cups fresh blueberries
2 cups fresh blackberries
½ cup coconut sugar

½ tablespoon vanilla extract or seeds
  of 1 vanilla bean
Zest of 1 orange
1½ tablespoons freshly squeezed
  orange juice

For the crisp
Generous ½ cup (60 g) walnuts or
  pecans
½ cup (50 g) hazelnut or almond flour
2 tablespoons (30 ml) maple syrup or
  honey
Small pinch of sea salt
¼ cup (45 g) good-quality chopped
  dark chocolate or chocolate chips,
  chilled for 30 minutes
Coconut oil for greasing the ramekins
  or pie dish

TO MAKE THE MINTY LIME CREME

Combine all the ingredients in a high-speed blender and blend until completely smooth, adding more water if needed. It will keep refrigerated for up to 3 days.

TO PREPARE THE FILLING

In a large bowl, gently toss the berries with the rest of the ingredients and set aside to macerate while you prepare the crumbles.

TO PREPARE AND BAKE THE CRUMBLES

1. Preheat the oven to 300°F (150°C).

2. In a food processor, grind the walnuts until their oil releases and they are the size of coarse breadcrumbs. In a medium bowl, mix the walnuts with the hazelnut flour, maple syrup, and salt until the mixture becomes crumbly.

3. Spread the mixture evenly on a parchment paper–covered baking sheet and bake for 10 to 15 minutes, until golden brown. Monitor the baking and stir the crumbles frequently to prevent them from burning. Break and separate large pieces into smaller crumbles as you stir. Remove from the oven and cool completely. You can put the crumbles in the freezer while you grind the chocolate.

4. Increase the oven temperature to 350°F (175°C).

TO ASSEMBLE AND BAKE THE CRISP

1. Grind the chilled chocolate into tiny granules in a food processor. Mix the chocolate into the crisp and combine thoroughly.

2. Lightly oil the ramekins or pie pan with coconut oil. Gently stir the berries, then divide them among the ramekins or pour into the pie pan. Top with the chocolate crumbles and bake for 25 to 30 minutes, until the fruit is bubbling through the crumbles. Let cool slightly. Serve with the minty lime creme, yogurt, or vanilla ice cream.

TO MAKE A RAW VERSION

Place the nut crumbles onto Teflex-covered dehydrator trays and dehydrate at 115°F (46°C) for 24 hours, or until crisp. Follow the same instructions for mixing the berries as for the baked version, then place the berries in a shallow dish and dehydrate for 4 hours, stirring occasionally. Let the crumbles cool completely. Use raw chocolate (page 32), and make sure it is chilled thoroughly before grinding it into very small pieces in a food processor. Combine with the crumbles. Divide the berries among ramekins, top with the crumbles, place in the dehydrator, and dehydrate at 115°F (46°C) until the chocolate is melted and the berries are warm, about 30 minutes.

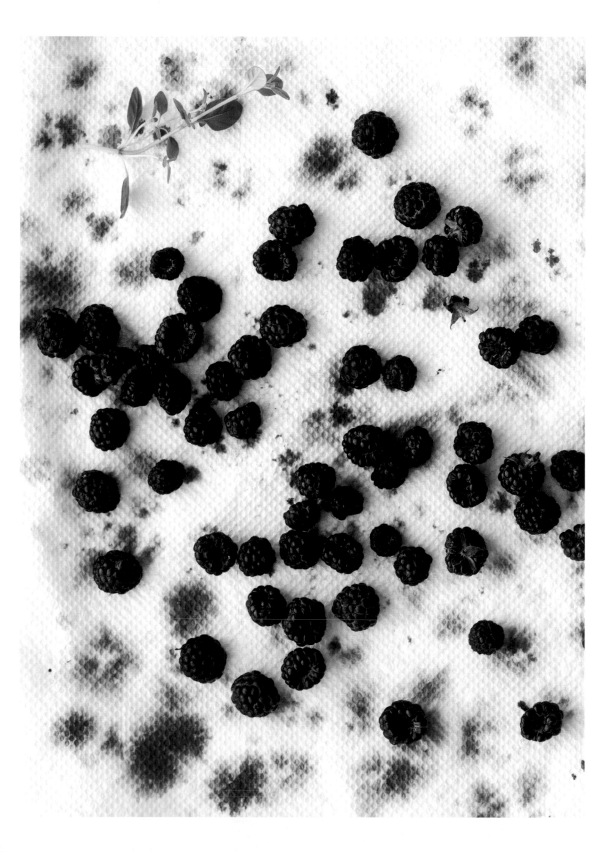

Lemon Bars

Makes 18 bars

While we were writing this book, we filled a binder with recipes and printed photographs to have an idea of what the finished cookbook will look like. Paloma loves to look through this binder and make comments, as she's tasted almost everything pictured (some recipes more than once). One of the games she likes to play is pointing out what she wants to eat that day, like she is ordering from her personal menu. She flips through the pages with the air of an important food critic and very often stops at these lemon bars, declaring, *"Here, I want you to make these."* Neither Paloma nor any of our friends seems to be able to get enough of these. The combination of zesty, smooth lemon mousse and the crumbly shortbread is completely irresistible, especially when the mousse is made with Meyer lemons.

Requires a high-speed blender

For the pistachio and millet shortbread

½ cup (80 g) raw pistachio nuts
6 tablespoons almond butter (page 30)
2 tablespoons ghee (page 27), at room temperature, or coconut oil, melted
¼ cup (70 ml) honey
1 teaspoon vanilla extract
½ cup (90 g) brown rice flour
¼ cup (45 g) millet flour
3 tablespoons tapioca starch
Pinch of sea salt

For the lemon mousse

¾ cup (135 g) white chocolate chips or chopped white chocolate
2 teaspoons vegan gelatin (see page 21), or 1 ounce (30 g) dried Irish moss
½ cup (75 g) raw cashews, soaked in purified water for 4 hours
¾ cup (180 ml) unsweetened almond milk
Zest of 2 lemons (about 2 tablespoons)
½ cup (120 ml) freshly squeezed lemon juice
1½ tablespoons honey
1 teaspoon coconut oil
⅛ teaspoon ground turmeric (optional)

TO PREPARE AND BAKE THE SHORTBREAD

1. Place the pistachios in the freezer for 10 to 15 minutes. In a medium bowl using a hand mixer, cream the almond butter and ghee with the honey and vanilla. In a food processor, grind the pistachios into a meal, taking care to not turn them into butter (chilling them in the freezer helps prevent that). Combine the ground pistachios, flours, tapioca starch, and salt in a large bowl, then add the cream. Mix with a spoon until just blended, then knead the mixture into a sticky dough with your hands.

2. Line an 8 × 8-inch (21 × 21 cm) baking pan with a piece of parchment paper, extending it up all the sides. Press the dough into the bottom of the pan

in an even layer and prick the dough several times with a fork. Refrigerate for 30 minutes.

3. Preheat the oven to 350°F (180°C).

4. Remove the pan from the refrigerator and bake for 10 to 12 minutes, until the edges are slightly golden. Remove from the oven and cool in the pan on a wire rack.

TO MAKE THE LEMON MOUSSE

1. Slowly melt the white chocolate in a double boiler over low heat. White chocolate often doesn't melt as evenly as dark chocolate, so stir it while it's melting to make sure it stays smooth. Drain and rinse the cashews.

Note: If you are not a strict vegetarian and decide to use regular gelatin, simply add the same amount (2 teaspoons) of it to a blender with the rest of the lemon mousse ingredients.

2. This step varies according to the thickener you are using:

Vegan gelatin: Bring the almond milk to a boil in a small saucepan. Add the vegan gelatin and whisk until dissolved. Pour into a high-speed blender, add the melted white chocolate, cashews, almond milk, lemon zest and juice, honey, coconut oil, and turmeric, if using, and blend until very smooth.

Irish moss: Rinse the Irish moss under cool water to remove as much salt and debris as you can, then place in a large bowl. Soak in plenty of hot water for at least 10 minutes. Irish moss will expand in size significantly, so make sure that it is completely covered with water. Add more water as needed. Drain and rinse the Irish moss again, making sure it is completely clean. Place in a high-speed blender with the melted white chocolate, cashews, almond milk, lemon zest and juice, honey, coconut oil, and turmeric, if using, and blend until very smooth.

3. For both thickeners: Pour the mixture into a medium bowl. Let sit in the refrigerator, stirring occasionally, until the mousse begins to thicken but is still pourable.

TO ASSEMBLE

1. Pour or spoon the mousse over the cooled shortbread, still in the pan. Refrigerate overnight.

2. Remove the pan from the refrigerator. Holding the ends of the parchment paper, lift the lemon bars out of the pan and carefully transfer the whole bars onto a large cutting board. Using a very sharp knife, make two cuts crosswise and one cut lengthwise for 6 large pieces. Cut each large piece lengthwise into 3 pieces for 18 bars total. Wipe the knife clean after each cut. The bars will keep refrigerated in an airtight glass container for up to 1 week. Layer parchment paper between the bars if you are storing them on top of each other to keep them from sticking.

Persimmon and Chocolate Loaf

Makes one 8½ × 4½-inch (21½ × 11½ cm) loaf or 12 muffins

Back home, persimmons were so inexpensive and abundant, sold on every street corner in winter, that I took them for granted. Ripe persimmons in Florida are elusive; they are somewhat rare and not cheap. Nevertheless, when the season comes, I stock up on Fuyu persimmons at our local Asian market.

Chocolate and persimmons are a match made in heaven. Baked persimmon tastes like a cross between pumpkin and quince, and it pairs beautifully with rich chocolate. When persimmons are not in season, substitute one medium shredded apple for the persimmon and don't place any fruit on top. You can also make this into muffins.

1. Place the chocolate in the freezer while gathering the rest of the ingredients. In a large bowl, mix the flours, quinoa flakes, cocoa powder, baking powder, baking soda, and salt. In a food processor, grind the chocolate into the smallest pieces possible without overheating it. Toss the chocolate with the flour mixture and set aside.

2. Grate the pear and 1 persimmon or apple—do not worry about peeling the fruit—and set aside. In a small bowl, beat the egg with the coconut sugar using a hand mixer until light, foamy, and doubled in volume. In another small bowl, mash the banana with a fork, then add to the egg mixture. Add the vanilla and coconut oil and mix with a hand mixer to combine.

3. Preheat the oven to 350°F (180°C).

4. Add the wet mixture to the dry ingredients, followed by the shredded fruits. Mix with a fork to combine.

If you are making a loaf, spoon the batter into a lightly oiled loaf pan. Arrange 2 persimmons on top of the loaf, pressing them just over halfway into the batter and leaving the tops peeking out on top. Bake for 1 hour, or until the top is dry and firm to the touch. This cake is so moist and the melted chocolate so gooey that a toothpick inserted won't ever be completely dry, even when the loaf is cooled. Let the loaf cool almost completely inside the pan and then invert it onto a cooling rack to cool completely before slicing.

If you are making muffins, distribute the batter across a lightly oiled or lined muffin tin. Bake for 30 minutes until a toothpick inserted in the center comes out clean. Let the muffins cool inside the pan briefly, then place on a cooling rack to cool completely. They will keep refrigerated in an airtight container for up to 3 days.

¼ cup (50 g) good-quality chopped dark chocolate or chocolate chips

½ cup (70 g) buckwheat flour

¾ cup (115 g) hazelnut flour

½ cup (70 g) quinoa flakes

3 tablespoons unsweetened cocoa powder

1 teaspoon baking powder

½ teaspoon baking soda

¼ teaspoon sea salt

1 large ripe pear

3 ripe Fuyu persimmons if making a loaf, or 1 ripe Fuyu persimmon if making muffins, or 1 medium apple

1 large egg

¼ cup (35 g) coconut sugar

1 ripe banana

½ tablespoon vanilla extract

¼ cup (60 ml) coconut oil, melted, plus more for greasing the pan

There are two types of persimmons commonly sold in the United States—Fuyu and Hachiya. Fuyu are squat and stay somewhat hard even when ripe. Hachiya are elongated, almost like plum tomatoes, and must be eaten only when extremely soft to completely lose the astringency characteristic to unripe persimmons. Hachiya is sweeter and my personal favorite, but also much harder to find fully ripe.

Apple and Blackberry Cobbler

For the crust

1 cup (100 g) almond flour

½ cup (90 g) brown rice flour

⅛ teaspoon sea salt

¼ teaspoon baking soda

¼ cup (60 ml) melted coconut oil or ghee (page 27), at room temperature, plus more for oiling the pie pan

2 tablespoons honey

1 teaspoon vanilla extract

For the filling

5 to 7 apples, such as Pink Lady, Honeycrisp, or Granny Smith, peeled, cored, and thinly sliced

1½ cups (about 6 oz [170 g]) blackberries

¼ cup (70 ml) honey

Zest of 1 orange

1 tablespoon freshly squeezed orange juice

Seeds of 1 vanilla bean or ½ tablespoon vanilla extract

1 teaspoon ground cinnamon

½ teaspoon freshly grated nutmeg

½ tablespoon arrowroot powder (optional)

Serves 6

Makes one 10-inch pie pan

Anytime I bake with apples, I think of my maternal grandmother, Nina, and her otherworldly apple pie. Nina's apple pie consisted of a layer of tender shortbread, saturated with the juice from shredded apples, topped with feather-light peaks of meringue. To my amazement, my grandmother never used any kind of machine to beat her egg whites, just a fork, and made it seem effortless. Her pies always turned out incredibly light, not overly sweet, and melt-in-your-mouth delicious. She added wild blackberries in season if there were any left over from our foraging escapades.

1. Preheat the oven to 350°F (180°C).

2. In a medium bowl, combine all the crust ingredients and mix them into a soft dough. Divide in half and shape each into a ball. Flatten each ball with the palm of your hand and wrap each disk in plastic wrap. Refrigerate the crust while you prepare the filling.

3. In a large bowl, combine all the filling ingredients and gently toss to coat the apples. Spoon the filling into a lightly oiled 10-inch (26 cm) pie or baking dish. Working with one half of the dough at a time, crumble it on top of the filling. You can also arrange the dough in a basket weave pattern, as shown. Slice off a 1-inch (2½ cm) piece of the dough disk, then quickly roll it between your palms into a rope and lay it on top of the filling, close to the edge. Continue shaping the rest of the dough, covering the surface first in parallel strips, then overlaying perpendicular strips. The dough is very tender and tears easily, so don't worry about making it perfectly even; the cobbler should look rustic.

4. Bake the cobbler for 25 minutes. Remove the cobbler from the oven, cover it with aluminum foil, then bake for another 10 minutes until golden brown. Remove from the oven and cool before serving. The cobbler is delicious on its own or served with a scoop of vanilla ice cream on the side.

Thumbprint Cookies
with apricot puree and roasted strawberry jam

Makes about 38 cookies

This is a variation of a *kurabie*, or thumbprint cookie, which was one of my teatime favorites growing up. I added sesame tahini and fresh vanilla bean to this version, which bring more (grownup) complexity to the childhood memories. Here I used dried apricot puree and roasted strawberry jam; however, feel free to top them with any of your favorite jams or even leave them plain. Dip these cookies in tea or almond milk as you savor them and they will melt in your mouth.

For the apricot puree
Makes 1 cup

¾ cup (165 g) dried unsulphured apricots
1 cup (240 ml) hot purified water
½ tablespoon freshly squeezed lemon juice
1 teaspoon vanilla extract

For the roasted strawberry jam
Makes 1¼ cups

2 pounds (1 kg 135 g) strawberries, halved
½ cup (35 g) coconut sugar
1 vanilla bean (optional)
1 tablespoon freshly squeezed lemon juice

For the thumbprint cookies

7 tablespoons almond butter
5 tablespoons sesame tahini
4 tablespoons ghee (page 27), at room temperature, or melted coconut oil
½ cup (140 ml) honey
1 vanilla bean (optional)
1 cup (100 g) almond flour
1 cup (180 g) brown rice flour
½ cup (60 g) oat flour
¼ cup (30 g) tapioca starch
½ teaspoon sea salt
½ cup apricot puree (see above)
½ cup strawberry jam (see above)

TO MAKE THE APRICOT PUREE

1. Soak the apricots in a bowl with the hot water for 2 hours. Drain, reserving 3 tablespoons of the soaking liquid.

2. In a food processor, combine the apricots with the reserved soaking liquid, the lemon juice, and vanilla and process until smooth.

TO MAKE THE ROASTED STRAWBERRY JAM

1. In a large bowl, combine the strawberries and coconut sugar. Scrape the seeds from the vanilla bean, if using, add to the strawberries, and stir everything to coat. Add the vanilla bean and let the strawberries macerate for about 10 minutes while you preheat the oven to 250°F (120°C). Mix the lemon juice into the strawberries.

2. Transfer the strawberries to a parchment paper–covered baking sheet, spreading them evenly. Roast for about 2 hours until carmelized. Scrape all the cooked fruit and the caramelized juices into a bowl. Remove the vanilla bean. Mash with a potato masher for a chunky jam or puree in a food processor for a smoother jam.

TO MAKE THE THUMBPRINT COOKIES

1. In the bowl of a stand mixer fitted with the paddle attachment, combine the almond butter, tahini, and ghee. Add the honey and seeds from the vanilla bean. Beat until well combined, light, and fluffy, about 2 minutes, scraping the sides of the bowl if needed. Add the flours, tapioca starch, and salt and mix well to form a soft, sticky dough.

Alternatively, use a hand mixer to cream the butters with the honey and vanilla seeds in a medium bowl. In a large bowl, combine the flours, tapioca starch, and salt, then add the buttery cream. Mix with a spoon, then knead with your hands into a soft, sticky dough.

2. Divide the dough into 4 equal portions and shape each into a ball. Place each ball on a piece of plastic wrap and flatten it slightly with the palm of your hand. Cover with another piece of plastic wrap. With a rolling pin, flatten each ball into a $^3/_8$-inch (1 cm) thick circle. Place each circle of dough on a flat even surface such as a baking sheet. Refrigerate for 1 hour.

3. Preheat the oven to 350°F (180°C). Line a baking sheet with parchment paper.

4. Working with one portion of the dough at a time, remove the top layer of plastic. Using any shape cookie cutter you like, cut as many cookies as possible and transfer them to the baking sheet, leaving about an inch between each cookie. Reshape and reroll the rest of the dough, reusing the plastic wrap. Repeat with each remaining portion of dough. You may need 2 sheets, depending on the sheet size.

5. Using your thumb, make a slight indentation in the middle of each cookie. Pile ½ teaspoon of jam or puree on top of the indentation. Bake for 10 minutes until lightly golden on the bottom; do not overbake or they become hard.

6. Remove the cookies from the oven and let them cool on the sheets for 10 minutes. They will be very soft when still hot. They will keep, stored in an airtight container, for up to 3 days.

Pink Salt and Chocolate Mousse Tart

Makes one 9-inch (23 cm) tart

Sea salt–sprinkled chocolate brightens even the darkest of days. This tart usually doesn't last more than an evening in our home full of chocolate lovers. As with several other desserts in this book, I usually make it with Irish moss, although you can use gelatin instead. You can substitute any other salt you like—fleur de sel, gray, smoked, or a combination—for the pink Himalayan salt. If you are not a fan of the sweet and salty combination, you can eliminate the salt from the recipe.

Requires a high-speed blender

For the hazelnut crust

½ cup (150 ml) coconut oil, melted, plus more for oiling the tart pan

1 tablespoon ground chia seeds

2 to 3 tablespoons ice water

½ cup (70 g) amaranth flour

⅓ cup (60 g) brown rice flour

¼ cup (25 g) hazelnut flour

¼ cup (40 g) tapioca starch

2 tablespoons coconut sugar

¼ teaspoon salt

For the chocolate mousse

1 cup (170 g) good-quality chopped dark chocolate or chocolate chips, or ¾ cup (170 g) raw chocolate (page 32)

½ cup (70 g) raw cashews, soaked in purified water for 4 hours

1 tablespoon vegan gelatin (see page 21) or 0.8 ounce (22 g) Irish moss

1⅔ cups (420 ml) unsweetened almond milk

1½ tablespoons coconut sugar

1½ tablespoons coconut oil, melted

For assembly

Himalayan pink salt

Small chocolate candies (optional)

TO PREPARE AND BAKE THE CRUST

1. Pour the coconut oil into a small shallow dish and place in the freezer for 10 to 15 minutes, until hardened. Lightly oil the tart pan.

2. In a small bowl, mix the ground chia seeds with 1 tablespoon of the ice water, forming a paste. Place in the refrigerator.

3. In a food processor, combine the flours, tapioca starch, coconut sugar, and salt and pulse several times to combine. Take the hardened coconut oil out of the freezer and cut it in the dish into ¼-inch (½ cm) cubes. Add it to the flour mixture and pulse until the cubes are finely ground and incorporated into the flour and the mixture resembles sand.

4. Take the chia paste out of the refrigerator and add to the food processor, along with 1 tablespoon ice water. Pulse several times to bring the dough together. Check the dough with your fingers; it should stick when pressed together. If not, add more ice water, 1 tablespoon at a time, and pulse more.

5. Turn the dough onto a work surface (it will be crumbly) and quickly knead it into a ball. Flatten it with the palm of your hand and press it into the oiled tart pan. Starting at the center, press the dough out to the sides, covering the bottom until the crust is even. Prick with a fork several times and chill in the refrigerator for 30 minutes.

6. Preheat the oven to 350°F (180°C).

7. Cover the chilled crust with parchment paper and place baking beans inside. Blind-bake for 20 minutes. Remove the parchment paper and baking beans and bake, uncovered, for 10 to 15 minutes, until the crust is golden brown. Let the crust cool completely on a cooling rack and leave it in the mold.

TO MAKE THE CHOCOLATE MOUSSE

1. Melt the dark chocolate in a double boiler over low heat or make the raw chocolate. Drain and rinse the cashews.

Note: If you aren't vegetarian and decide to use regular gelatin, simply combine the same amount (1 tablespoon) of it with the rest of the mousse ingredients in a high-speed blender until smooth.

2. This step varies according to the thickener you are using:

Vegan gelatin: Bring the almond milk to a boil in a small saucepan. Add the gelatin and whisk until dissolved. Pour into a high-speed blender, add the melted chocolate, cashews, coconut sugar, and coconut oil, and blend until smooth.

Irish moss: Rinse the Irish moss under cool water to remove as much salt and debris as you can, then place in a large bowl. Soak in plenty of hot water for at least 10 minutes. Irish moss will expand in size significantly, so make sure that it is completely covered with water. Add more water as needed. Drain and rinse the Irish moss again, making sure it is completely clean. Place in a high-speed blender, add the melted chocolate, cashews, almond milk, coconut sugar, and coconut oil, and blend until smooth.

3. For both thickeners: Pour the mixture into a medium bowl and refrigerate until it begins to thicken but is still pourable. Stir and check periodically, making sure that it doesn't set completely.

TO ASSEMBLE

1. Pour or scoop the mousse into the crust, smoothing it with a spoon. Sprinkle with salt and garnish with chocolate candies, if using.

2. Refrigerate the tart until the mousse is completely set, several hours or overnight. It should be thick and firm. Serve cold.

Earl Grey Poached Pears with Hazelnut Panna Cotta

Serves 8

This is an autumnal dessert full of comforting flavors. It can be an elegant alternative to cake or pie when served at a dinner party. I love using tea leaves in my cooking as a way of introducing new, deep flavors into a dish, and the hint of bergamot in Earl Grey combines so well with the poached pear. This panna cotta can be exceptionally nutritious if you use Irish moss as a thickener.

Works best with a high-speed blender

For the panna cotta
2 cups (300 g) untoasted hazelnuts
4 cups (960 ml) purified water
6 teaspoons vegan gelatin (see page 21), or 42 g (1½ oz) dried Irish moss
½ teaspoon ground cinnamon
¼ teaspoon freshly grated nutmeg
Seeds of 2 or 3 cardamom pods, ground in a mortar and pestle (see Note), or ¼ teaspoon ground cardamom
6 tablespoons honey
6 tablespoons coconut oil

For the pears
Zest of 2 oranges
2 cups (510 ml) freshly squeezed orange juice
2 cups (480 ml) purified water
¼ cup loose Earl Grey tea leaves
1 cup (140 g) coconut sugar
1 cinnamon stick
3 cloves
1-inch (2½ cm) piece fresh ginger
4 ripe but firm pears, peeled, halved, and cored

For assembly
½ cup (150 g) toasted hazelnuts (see page 12), chopped

Note: If you are using a high-speed blender, there is no need to pre-grind the cardamom; you can throw the whole seeds in with the rest of the ingredients.

TO MAKE THE HAZELNUT MILK

1. Combine the hazelnuts and water in a high-speed blender (for best results) and blend until smooth. Let rest for 10 minutes for the flavor to infuse. Strain the milk through a nut milk bag or several layers of cheesecloth and discard the pulp. You should have 3½ cups strained hazelnut milk (alternatively, you can use 3½ cups store-bought nut milk).

2. This step varies according to which thickener you are using:

Vegan gelatin and any kind of blender: Bring the hazelnut milk to a boil in a small saucepan. Add the gelatin and whisk to dissolve completely. Pour it into the blender, add the remaining ingredients, and blend until smooth.

Irish moss and a high-speed blender: Rinse the Irish moss under cool water to remove as much salt and debris as you can, then place in a large bowl. Soak in plenty of hot water for at least 10 minutes. Irish moss will expand in size significantly, so make sure it is completely covered with water. Add more water as needed. Drain and rinse the Irish moss again, making sure it is completely clean. Combine the Irish moss with the remaining ingredients in a high-speed blender and blend until completely smooth.

3. For both thickeners: Divide the mixture among 8 serving bowls that are big enough to accommodate ½ pear. Cover the bowls with plastic wrap and refrigerate until firm.

Keep the panna cotta refrigerated until you are ready to serve.

TO POACH THE PEARS

In a large saucepan, combine all the ingredients except the pears. Bring the liquid to a boil, stirring to dissolve the sugar. Add the pears, lower the heat, and simmer for 15 minutes, or until the pears are tender. Remove them from the saucepan and let them cool to room temperature.

TO MAKE THE SPICY SYRUP

Strain the poaching liquid and pour it back into the same saucepan; return the cinnamon stick and ginger to the pan. Bring to a boil over medium-high heat and cook until the liquid is syrupy and reduces to about 1 cup, about 15 minutes. Stir and check for thickness often. The syrup will thicken further when it cools. The syrup will keep refrigerated for up to 3 days.

TO ASSEMBLE

Arrange a pear half on top of each panna cotta. Drizzle with the spicy syrup and sprinkle with the toasted hazelnuts.

Note: If you are not vegetarian and decide to use regular gelatin as a thickener, add 10 teaspoons of it with the rest of the panna cotta ingredients and blend until smooth.

Swirled Açaí and White Chocolate Cheesecake

Makes one 8- to 9-inch (20 to 23 cm) cheesecake

If you've never made or tasted a no-bake, dairy-free cheesecake, you're in for a surprise. The filling turns out creamy, yet very light and fluffy, and no one will suspect that it is not made of traditional cheesecake ingredients. All you need for success is a good high-speed blender; otherwise the recipe is uncomplicated and very versatile.

Açaí puree can be found in the freezer section of your natural grocery store. It is a convenient add-in for smoothies and desserts. The flavor of açaí is magical; it resembles blueberries and chocolate mixed together, especially when sweetened. Açaí berries are harvested from the rain forest of Brazil and are remarkably rich in antioxidants, essential amino acids, and valuable trace minerals. You can substitute açaí powder for açaí puree; just add 1 tablespoon at a time when making the filling until you like the taste and color. I also include blueberry powder for a richer color, but it is completely optional.

TO MAKE THE CRUST

Combine all the crust ingredients in a food processor and process until the mixture becomes crumbly and sticks together when lightly pressed between your fingers. Assemble a springform pan with the bottom flipped upside down, with the lip facing down (for easier serving). Lightly oil the inside of the form with coconut oil. Press the crust mixture into the bottom of the form, pressing firmly to make a compact and even layer. Set aside.

TO MAKE THE FILLING

1. Drain and rinse the cashews. In a high-speed blender, combine the cashews with the almond milk, agave, vanilla, lemon juice, and salt and blend until smooth. Add the cocoa butter and blend to incorporate. Reserve 2 cups of the filling in a medium bowl and ¼ cup of the filling in a small bowl. Pour the rest of the filling into the springform over the crust. Do not rinse the blender. Slightly lift and drop the springform onto your work surface to release trapped air bubbles.

2. Run the frozen açaí packs under hot water, then break the puree into small pieces while it is still in the packs. Cut open one side of each bag and drop all the açaí pieces into the blender with the reserved 2 cups filling and the blueberry powder, if using. Blend until smooth, and taste. If it doesn't taste distinct or sweet enough, add more sweetener, a tiny pinch of salt, and/or another squeeze of lemon juice.

Requires a high-speed blender

For the crust

1¼ cups (175 g) raw almonds

1 tablespoon cacao nibs

2 tablespoons unsweetened cocoa powder

About 5 large soft dates, pitted and chopped (½ cup packed)

1 teaspoon vanilla extract

Pinch of sea salt

Coconut oil for oiling the pan

For the filling

3 cups (450 g) raw cashews or cashew pieces, soaked in purified water for 4 hours

2 cups (500 ml) almond milk (page 30)

¾ cup (225 ml) agave syrup, honey, or other sweetener of choice

¼ cup (60 ml) vanilla extract

3 tablespoons freshly squeezed lemon juice

Pinch of sea salt

1 cup (80 g) shaved food-grade cocoa butter, gently melted in a double boiler

2 small packs of frozen unsweetened açaí puree (3½ ounces [100 g] each)

1 to 2 teaspoons blueberry powder (optional, for richer color)

3. Before pouring the açaí layer, reserve 2 to 4 tablespoons of the açaí filling in a small bowl (you should have a small amount of both colors reserved). Start pouring the açaí mixture into the springform with confidence, creating enough pouring force so the purple filling penetrates the white filling. Pour the açaí filling evenly over the whole cake surface so it fills in evenly in the pan. When you have just ½ cup of the açaí filling left, pour the rest very lightly, leaving just a touch of the violet açaí color on the surface. Quickly draw a chopstick through the swirl pattern. Take care not to overdo it, as it is easy to blend the colors too much. Use the reserved filling of both colors to add to and fix the swirled design if needed.

4. Freeze the cheesecake for 2 to 3 hours, until firm throughout. Remove the springform, but keep the cheesecake on the inverted base. The cheesecake keeps well, covered and refrigerated, for at least 4 days.

Note: In place of açaí, feel free to use less exotic berries such as fresh blueberries, strawberries, raspberries, blackberries, or even cherries. Just blend them into a puree first, making sure to strain out any seeds. The swirling of the layers is optional as well; the two layers can just sit on top of each other, or you can make the cheesecake all one flavor/color.

The cocoa butter can be replaced with coconut oil, though you will lose the white chocolate flavor.

Autumn Sorbet Trio

Requires a high-speed blender

For the Concord grape sorbet

4 cups (about 700 g) Concord grapes

1 cup (240 ml) purified water

⅔ cup (200 ml) agave syrup, plus more to taste

For the muscadine grape sorbet

4 cups (about 800 g) green or purples muscadine grapes

1 cup (240 ml) purified water

¾ cup (225 ml) agave syrup, plus more to taste

For the pear sorbet

4 medium ripe, sweet pears, peeled, cored, and roughly chopped

1 tablespoon freshly squeezed lemon juice

¼ cup (75 ml) agave syrup

¼ cup (60 ml) purified water

Serves 8 to 10

We had a natural Concord grape vine canopy over the courtyard at our summer dacha in Russia. From late summer and deep into autumn, bunches of grapes were readily available for picking and eating on the spot. The rest went into jams and homemade wine.

If you've never tasted Concord grapes, you must do so at least once. They have a distinct, rich flavor and beautiful deep purple color, all qualities perfect for sorbet. Both Concord and muscadine grapes are highly nutritious, with an impressive antioxidant count, mostly concentrated in their skins. When making these sorbets, I blend the grapes whole—skin, seeds, and all—to get the full health benefits. The sweet grape sorbets contrast well with the subtle taste of pear for the ultimate early fall indulgence.

Chilling the sorbet mixtures overnight will ensure the best freezing results.

TO MAKE THE CONCORD GRAPE SORBET

1. Combine all the ingredients in a high-speed blender and blend well. Strain to remove the solids and discard them. Refrigerate until well chilled, preferably overnight.

2. Churn in an ice cream maker for 25 minutes, or according to the manufacturer's instructions. Freeze for at least 2 hours before serving.

TO MAKE THE MUSCADINE GRAPE SORBET

1. Combine all the ingredients in a high-speed blender and blend well. Strain to remove the solids and discard them. Refrigerate until well chilled, preferably overnight.

2. Churn in an ice cream maker for 25 minutes, or according to the manufacturer's instructions. Freeze for at least 2 hours before serving.

TO MAKE THE PEAR SORBET

1. Combine all the ingredients in a high-speed blender and blend until smooth. Refrigerate until well chilled, preferably overnight.

2. Churn in an ice cream maker for 25 minutes, or according to the manufacturer's instructions. Freeze for at least 2 hours before serving.

Note: If you don't have an ice cream machine, you can still enjoy these frozen treats in the form of ice pops. Simply pour the fruit mixtures into ice pop molds (see Avocado and Strawberry Ice Pops, page 274, for instructions) and freeze. Ice pops will not be as creamy as sorbet, but they will be just as delicious.

Blood Orange Chocolate Cakes

Makes four 3¾-inch (9 cm) cakes

To me, the pairing of chocolate and orange is one of the best in the world of flavors. These cakes are about the size of a large orange and very striking in appearance. Blood oranges are fascinating because of the deep, fiery red color of their flesh. They are great for decorative use in desserts, and they are very sweet and citrusy. The cakes are layered, which makes for a nice surprise when cutting into them. Use regular oranges if blood oranges are unavailable. Just like the Black and White Chocolate Cups (page 267), they are even better the next day, after some time in the refrigerator.

Requires a high-speed blender

For the chocolate cake
¾ cup (75 g) almond flour
⅓ cup (60 g) plus 1 tablespoon brown rice flour
⅓ cup (40 g) plus 1 tablespoon coconut flour
1 tablespoon arrowroot powder
1 teaspoon baking powder
½ teaspoon baking soda
⅛ teaspoon sea salt
1 tablespoon coconut oil, melted, plus more for oiling the springform
¾ cup (140 g) good-quality chopped dark chocolate or chocolate chips, placed in the freezer for 30 minutes

2½ tablespoons unsweetened cocoa powder
1½ tablespoons coconut sugar
1 cup (240 ml) unsweetened full-fat canned coconut milk
⅓ cup (90 ml) plus 1 tablespoon honey

For the orange frosting and to assemble
3 to 4 blood oranges
1 cup (150 g) raw cashews, soaked in purified water for 4 hours
Scant ¼ cup (75 ml) agave syrup
½ tablespoon vanilla extract
Small pinch of sea salt
½ cup (125 ml) coconut oil, melted

TO PREPARE AND BAKE THE CAKE

1. Preheat the oven to 350°F (180°C).

2. While the chocolate is chilling in the freezer, mix the flours, arrowroot powder, baking powder, baking soda, and salt in a large bowl. Add the coconut oil and work it in with a wooden spoon. Take the chocolate out of the freezer and transfer to the bowl of a food processor. Grind the chocolate into the smallest pieces your food processor can make without overheating it. Add the ground chocolate, cocoa powder, and coconut sugar to the bowl with the flours and mix to combine.

3. In a separate medium bowl, whisk together the coconut milk and honey until well mixed. Pour the wet ingredients into the dry ingredients and mix with a fork to combine. The batter will be soft and wet.

4. Assemble a 10-inch (25 cm) springform pan with the bottom flipped upside down and the lip facing down, for easier handling. Lightly oil the inside of the form with coconut oil. Spoon the batter inside the pan, spreading it evenly. Bake for 25 to 30 minutes, until the surface is dry to the touch. It is not necessary to check for doneness with a toothpick. Remove from the oven and let cool completely on a cooling rack while you prepare the frosting. Once cooled, remove the springform and place the cake in the refrigerator for at least 30 minutes. You can also bake the cake in advance and refrigerate covered until ready to be cut and frosted.

TO PREPARE THE FROSTING

1. Zest all the oranges and place the zest in the blender. Juice 1 of the oranges, measure ½ cup juice, and pour it into the blender. Drain and rinse the cashews and add them into the blender along with the agave, vanilla, and salt. Blend until smooth, then add the coconut oil and blend to incorporate.

2. Pour the frosting into a medium bowl, cover with plastic, and place in the freezer for 30 minutes to 1 hour, until firm. Make sure the frosting does not freeze; move it to the refrigerator when it is firm.

TO ASSEMBLE THE CAKES

1. Remove the chocolate cake from the refrigerator and carefully transfer it (use a cake lifter if you have one) onto a large cutting board. Cut 8 circles out of the cake, using a 2¾-inch (7 cm) cookie cutter or a ring mold, or by tracing a circle with a sharp knife. Don't worry if the edges are not perfect. Place 4 of the cut circles onto an individual square of parchment paper, big enough to accommodate 1 cake. Those will be the bottom layers of your cakes. Set the remaining 4 circles aside.

2. Collect the pieces and crumbles left after cutting out the circles into an airtight glass container and keep refrigerated. You can snack on them when a chocolate craving hits or use them to make the Black and White Chocolate Cups (page 267).

3. Slice the remaining 2 or 3 blood oranges into ¼-inch (6 mm) slices. Cut the rim off each slice and pat dry with paper towels to remove any extra juice.

4. Take the frosting out of the freezer and begin to frost your cakes, one at a time. Make a middle layer first, applying 1½ to 2 tablespoons of the frosting on each of the 4 circles. Top them with the remaining 4 circles and frost the cakes to cover completely. The frosting doesn't have to be applied perfectly smooth, as it will be covered with the orange slices for the most part.

5. Garnish each cake with 5 orange slices, arranging them on the sides of the cake so that they extend to the top and round the edges. Refrigerate each cake after assembly and remove from the refrigerator right before serving.

Apricot and Lavender Tart

Makes one 9-inch (23 cm) tart

At their ripest, apricots are one of the most beautiful and flavorful summer fruits. When I was a child, we ate them right off wildly growing apricot trees or in the form of my mother's fancy apricot preserves. My mother would leave the apricot whole, carefully removing the pit. She cracked the pit open and removed the almond-like kernel from inside of the pit, then slipped the kernel back inside the apricot before preserving them in a thick, sweet syrup. This flourish improved the apricot flavor while adding a delightful element of surprise.

This tart is very simple and fresh, with an unexpected highlight of lavender flowers. Make sure to use only the ripest apricots. You can also substitute other fruit combinations for the apricots: try pear-ginger or mango-lime, or make a simple apple tart using the recipe's crust.

For the crust
½ cup (150 ml) coconut oil, melted,
 plus more for greasing the tart pan
½ cup (70 g) quinoa flour
½ cup (90 g) brown rice flour
¼ cup (30 g) tapioca starch
2 tablespoons coconut sugar
1 teaspoon dried lavender flowers
¼ teaspoon sea salt
4 to 5 tablespoons ice water

For the filling
¼ cup (35 g) coconut sugar
1 teaspoon dried lavender flowers
11 ripe apricots, cut in half, pits
 removed
1 tablespoons almond flour

TO PREPARE THE CRUST

1. Pour the coconut oil into a small shallow dish and place in the freezer for 10 to 15 minutes, until hardened. Lightly grease the tart pan.

2. In a food processor, combine the flours, tapioca starch, coconut sugar, lavender, and salt and pulse several times to mix. Take the hardened coconut oil out of the freezer and cut it in the dish into ¼-inch (½ cm) cubes. Add it to the flour mixture and pulse until the coconut oil cubes are ground into tiny granules and incorporated into the flour and the mixture resembles sand.

3. Add 4 tablespoons ice water to the food processor and pulse several times to bring the dough together. Check the dough with your fingers; it should stick when pressed together. If not, add 1 more tablespoon ice water and pulse again.

4. Put the dough on a work surface (it will be crumbly at this point) and quickly knead together, forming a ball. Flatten it with the palm of your hand

and press into the oiled tart pan. Starting with the bottom, extend it to the sides until you have an evenly thick crust. Prick with a fork several times and chill in the refrigerator for 30 minutes.

TO ASSEMBLE AND BAKE THE TART

1. Preheat the oven to 375°F (190°C).

2. In a designated coffee grinder, grind the coconut sugar with the lavender.

3. Thinly slice each apricot half lengthwise to make half-moons. Sprinkle the crust with the almond flour. Arrange the apricot slices inside the crust in a circle, overlapping, with the skin side facing up. When all of the crust is covered, dust it with half of the lavender sugar. Continue with the rest of apricots, arranging them in a second layer in the same fashion. Finish by dusting the remaining lavender sugar on top.

4. Bake for 30 to 35 minutes, until the crust is golden brown and the apricots are caramelized. Cool on a cooling rack before unmolding and slicing. Serve on its own or with a scoop of ice cream on the side.

Cacao Nib Cookies

with dried currants

1¼ cups (225 g) brown rice flour

½ cup (70 g) quinoa flour

¼ cup (25 g) almond flour

¼ cup (30 g) coconut flour

¼ teaspoon sea salt

1 teaspoon baking powder

½ teaspoon baking soda

3 tablespoons coconut oil, melted

½ cup (125 ml) unsweetened almond milk

½ cup (125 ml) unsweetened full-fat canned coconut milk

½ cup (70 g) plus 1 tablespoon powdered coconut sugar

½ tablespoon vanilla extract

½ cup (70 g) cacao nibs

⅓ cup (40 g) dried currants

1 tablespoon cocoa powder

Makes about 20 small cookies

The cookies that I grew up with are very different from traditional American cookies; they were mostly shortbread, plain, or filled with various fruit jams. Over the years, I've learned to like the softer texture of an American cookie, while still wishing they contained half the sugar. These cacao nib cookies are crusty on the outside, while soft and crumbly on the inside: a perfect balance.

Dried currants can be found in the bulk section of most health food stores; you can use raisins if you cannot find currants.

1. Preheat the oven to 350°F (180°C).

2. In a large bowl, combine the flours, salt, baking powder, and baking soda. Add the coconut oil and work it into the dry mixture. In a medium bowl, combine the almond milk and coconut milk, ½ cup of the coconut sugar, and the vanilla. Mix well to combine. Pour the wet ingredients into the dry mixture, add the cacao nibs and currants, and combine thoroughly, taking care not to overmix the batter.

3. Line a baking sheet with parchment paper and fill a bowl with water. Dip a small ice cream scoop (1¾ inches [4½ cm] in diameter works best) into the water, fill it with cookie dough, one scoop at a time, and place on the sheet, leaving some space between the cookies. Dip the ice cream scoop in water between each scoop. Place the sheet in the oven and bake for 20 minutes, or until a toothpick inserted in the middle of a cookie comes out clean. Be careful to not overbake, as the cookies can easily become dry.

4. While the cookies are in the oven, mix the remaining 1 tablespoon powdered coconut sugar with cocoa powder in a small bowl. Remove the cookies from the oven, cool slightly on the sheet, then using a fine-mesh strainer or sifter, sprinkle the sugar-cocoa mixture on top.

Note: These cookies are on the less sweet side; if you like a sweeter cookie, reduce the amount of cacao nibs and add more coconut sugar.

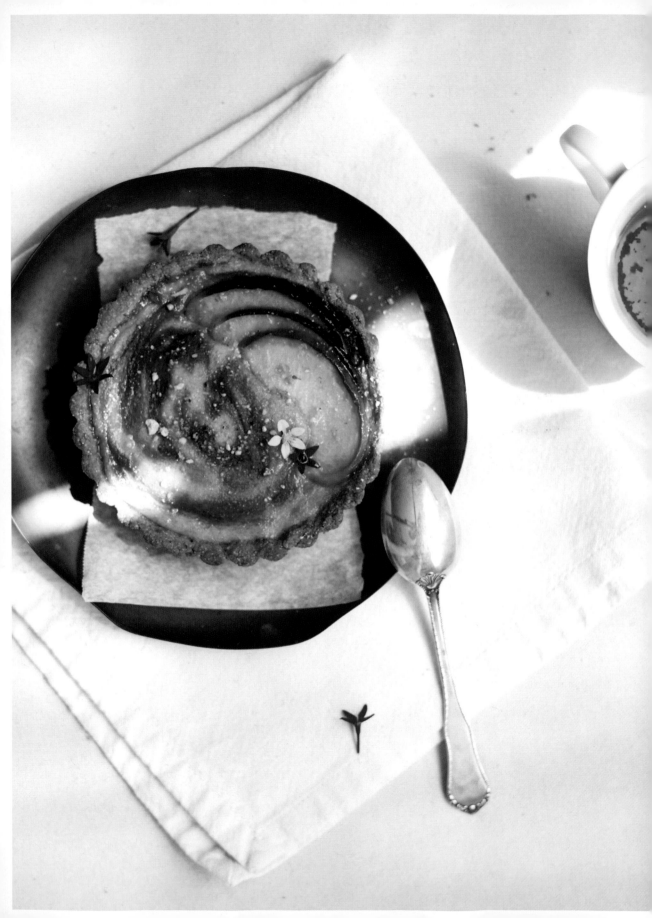

Peach and Raspberry Tartlets

Makes six 4-inch (10 cm) tartlets

In summer I revisit the combination of raspberries and peaches time and time again. The two fruits complement each other perfectly, both tastewise and visually. These tartlets are light and healthy, with the minimum amount of sweetener and with chia seeds for a thickener.

I like to create swirled patterns in the raspberry mousse and peach puree—there is a lot of potential for making these very pretty.

TO PREPARE AND BAKE THE CRUST

1. Pour the coconut oil into a small shallow dish and place in the freezer for 10 to 15 minutes, until hardened. Lightly grease the tart pans.

2. In a food processor, combine the flours, tapioca starch, coconut sugar, and salt and pulse several times to mix. Take the hardened coconut oil out of the freezer and cut it in the dish into ¼-inch (½ cm) cubes. Add it to the flour mixture and pulse until the coconut oil cubes are ground into tiny granules and incorporated into the flour and the mixture resembles sand.

3. Add 4 tablespoons ice water to the food processor and pulse several times to bring the dough together. Check the dough with your fingers; it should stick when pressed together. If not, add 1 more tablespoon ice water and pulse more.

4. Put the dough onto a work surface (it will be crumbly at this point) and quickly knead together. Form a thick log and cut into 6 even pieces. Flatten each portion with the palm of your hand and press into the oiled tart pans. Starting with the bottom, extend it to the sides until you have an evenly thick crust. Prick with a fork several times and chill in the refrigerator for 30 minutes.

5. Preheat the oven to 375°F (190°C).

6. Cover the chilled crusts with parchment paper and place baking beans inside. Blind-bake for 15 minutes, then lower the oven temperature to 350°F (180°C). Remove the baking beans and parchment paper and bake for another 5 minutes. Remove from the oven and cool on a cooling rack.

For the crust
½ cup (150 ml) coconut oil, melted, plus more for greasing the tart pans
⅔ cup (65 g) oat flour
½ cup (90 g) brown rice flour
⅓ cup (40 g) tapioca starch
2 tablespoons coconut sugar
¼ teaspoon sea salt
4 to 5 tablespoons ice water

For the raspberry mousse
4 cups (about 480 g) fresh raspberries
4½ tablespoons ground chia seeds
4½ tablespoons honey

For assembly
3 to 4 ripe peaches
1 tablespoon honey
1 tablespoon almond flour
¼ cup whole raspberries (optional)

TO MAKE THE RASPBERRY MOUSSE

1. In a blender, blend the raspberries until smooth. Strain through a fine-mesh strainer to remove the seeds and discard them. You should end up with about 1½ cups strained raspberry puree.

2. Rinse the blender, add the raspberry puree, chia meal, and honey, and blend until smooth. Pour into a medium bowl and let sit for about 15 minutes to thicken.

TO ASSEMBLE AND BAKE THE TARTLETS

1. Preheat the oven to 400°F (200°C).

2. Peel, pit, and chop 1 peach. Place it in a blender or food processor, add the honey, and blend to a smooth puree. Pour into a small bowl and set aside.

3. Dust each crust with almond flour. Pit and thinly slice the remaining 2 to 3 peaches. Arrange the slices on the bottom of each tart in a single layer.

4. Spoon the raspberry mousse on top to fill the tarts completely. Drizzle the peach puree on top and create a pattern using a toothpick or a fork. Arrange the remaining peach slices and whole raspberries, if using, on top.

5. Bake for 15 to 20 minutes, until the surface of the filling feels dry and firm to the touch and the crust is golden. Cool on a cooling rack before unmolding and serving.

Black and White Chocolate Cups

Makes ten 6- or 8-ounce ramekins or small glasses

If you are looking for a new indulgence, look no further than these black and white mousse cakes, where rich, moist chocolate sponge cake is topped with vanilla and dark chocolate mousse cream. Red currants are a beautiful, tangy garnish.

Requires a high-speed blender

For the sponge cake
⅓ cup (85 ml) unsweetened full-fat canned coconut milk
¼ cup (60 ml) almond milk (see page 30 or unsweetened store-bought)
¼ cup (70 ml) honey
½ cup (50 g) almond flour
¼ cup (45 g) brown rice flour
¼ cup (30 g) coconut flour
½ tablespoon arrowroot powder
½ teaspoon baking powder
¼ teaspoon baking soda
⅛ teaspoon sea salt
½ tablespoon coconut oil, melted, plus more for oiling the ramekins
½ cup (95 g) good-quality chopped dark chocolate or chocolate chips, ground into tiny pieces in a food processor
2 tablespoons unsweetened cocoa powder
1 tablespoon coconut sugar

For the white chocolate and vanilla mousse
1 cup (180 g) good-quality white chocolate chips or chopped white chocolate
1 cup (240 ml) almond milk (page 30, or unsweetened store-bought)
1 teaspoon vegan gelatin (see page 21) or 17 grams (0.6 oz) dried Irish moss
½ cup (75 g) raw cashews, soaked in purified water for 4 hours
1 teaspoon coconut oil
Seeds of 1 vanilla bean

For the dark chocolate mousse
¾ cup (140 g) good-quality chopped dark chocolate or chocolate chips
1 teaspoon vegan gelatin or 11 grams (0.4 oz) dried Irish moss
½ cup (70 g) raw cashews, soaked in purified water for 4 hours
1 cup (240 ml) almond milk (page 30, or unsweetened store-bought)
1 teaspoon coconut oil

For garnish
Red currants or other berries (optional)

TO MAKE THE SPONGE CAKE

1. Preheat the oven to 350°F (180°C).

2. In a medium bowl, combine the coconut milk, almond milk, and honey. Set aside.

3. In a large bowl, combine the flours, arrowroot powder, baking powder, baking soda, and salt. Add the coconut oil and work it in. Then add the ground chocolate, cocoa powder, and coconut sugar, mixing thoroughly.

4. Add the wet ingredients to the dry mixture, mixing to form a soft, wet batter. Make sure you don't overwork it.

5. Lightly oil a 9-inch (23 cm) springform or cake pan with coconut oil and press the dough into the bottom of the pan. Do not press the dough too hard so it can stay fluffy. Bake for 20 minutes or until the surface is dry to the touch, remove from the oven, and cool completely on a cooling rack while you make the mousse.

TO MAKE THE WHITE CHOCOLATE MOUSSE

1. Melt the white chocolate in the top part of a double boiler over low heat, stirring until smooth. Drain and rinse the cashews.

2. This step varies according to which thickener you are using:

Vegan gelatin: Bring the almond milk to a boil in a small saucepan. Add the gelatin and whisk until dissolved. Pour into a high-speed blender, add the melted white chocolate, cashews, coconut oil, and vanilla seeds, and blend until smooth.

Irish moss: Rinse the Irish moss under cool water to remove as much salt and debris as you can, then place in a large bowl. Soak in plenty of hot water for at least 10 minutes. Irish moss will expand in size significantly, so make sure it is completely covered with water. Add more water if needed. Drain and rinse the Irish moss again, making sure it is completely clean. Place in a high-speed blender, add the melted white chocolate, cashews, almond milk, coconut oil, and vanilla seeds, and blend until smooth.

3. For both thickeners: Pour the mixture into a medium bowl. Do not rinse the blender. Let the mixture sit in the refrigerator, stirring periodically, until the mousse begins to thicken but is still pourable.

TO MAKE DARK CHOCOLATE MOUSSE

Follow the instructions for the white chocolate mousse, using the dark chocolate instead of the white chocolate and omitting the vanilla seeds.

TO ASSEMBLE THE MOUSSE CAKES

1. With a spoon, break apart and crumble the sponge cake, dividing it among 10 ramekins. Don't be shy about using your fingers. Fill the ramekins one-quarter to one-third full.

2. Spoon the dark chocolate mousse on top of the cake in each ramekin. Then follow by spooning in the white chocolate mousse, arranging it so the dark chocolate mousse is still visible in places. Garnish with red currants.

3. Refrigerate the cups for 2 to 3 hours or overnight, until the mousse is completely set. This dessert gets better the longer it's in the refrigerator, and will keep for up to a week. Keep refrigerated until ready to serve.

Note: If you're not vegetarian and decide to use regular gelatin, simply combine the same amount (1 teaspoon) with the rest of the mousse's ingredients in a high-speed blender until smooth.

4

Playtime

I HAVE TWO DAUGHTERS WHO ARE EIGHTEEN YEARS APART. They could not be more different. Masha, the oldest, is the perfect example of an introvert—soft-spoken, incredibly modest, and wise. She has always been artistic and loves to read and write. Raising a child who seemed to be more composed than myself from a very young age left me completely unprepared for the hurricane named Paloma. Coincidentally, the year my second daughter was born, there was an actual hurricane by that same name in the Atlantic Ocean. Paloma is four now, and I am still amazed by the amount of energy and demanding force that radiates from this child.

Raising my older daughter in Russia, I stuck to traditional Russian meals, similar to the ones I grew up on. Masha always had an aversion to meat and became a vegetarian the moment she moved to the United States and saw vegetarianism as a realistic possibility. My interest in cooking healthier meals started there and then. After learning a great deal about vegetarian cooking, I became curious about cooking without any animal products, and then the raw and gluten-free lifestyles. By the time Paloma was ready to eat solid foods, I had gained enough knowledge and experience to provide her with a balanced, mostly plant-based diet.

As parents, Ernie and I were quick to realize that Paloma needed to be occupied at all times if we wanted to survive. She started daycare very early and loved every minute of it. She embraces and thrives on every activity we offer her—Russian school, ice skating, ballet, gymnastics, swimming, and traveling.

As I spend a good amount of my time cooking, Paloma practically grew up around the kitchen table. Pots and pans were the best toys for a while, but soon enough I had to get more creative and present her with some real kitchen projects—stirring, cutting out cookies, sorting fruits and vegetables and whatnot. As active and at times impatient as Paloma is, she becomes attentive when cooking and sometimes even likes to wash the dishes. (We hope her interest in dishwashing will last into her teenage years.)

I try to use every opportunity to teach Paloma the names of ingredients, their colors, textures, and shapes. Every day when I pick Paloma up from school, she is curious about what I cooked that day and what to expect for dinner. I cannot say that raising a child eating healthy foods is always easy—it takes commitment and determination, but the results are very much worth the effort.

Health is the very thing that allows us to go through life happily and with the most energy, and every child deserves that opportunity. At school Paloma doesn't hesitate to brag about her Chickpea Chocolate Pops (page 296), proudly telling the teachers that they are not made from candy but beans. For birthday parties and sugar-laden holidays such as Halloween, I make sure to pack along nutritious treats. Quite honestly, she has little interest in regular cake or candy if a special treat is offered. This, of course, is not only due to luck but is no doubt the result of the consistency, dedication, and discipline that we as parents practiced throughout her first years of life.

Although we've been told never to play with our food, there are some situations when playing can result in a natural learning process.

Below are some helpful things that I've discovered in the four years of trying to raise Paloma to be a mindful and adventurous eater.

- Making healthy choices from the very beginning, right when introducing solid foods, is important. Children are more likely to grow up loving the foods that they are used to eating from early on.

- Be consistent with your approach. I cannot emphasize this enough: consistency is key in building good habits.

- Make trying foods a rule. Your child doesn't have to eat it if he doesn't like it, but he has to try it to decide whether he truly likes it or not. Soon enough, the rule of acquired taste may kick in.

- Do not make a big issue out of your child not eating something. Continue enjoying your meal and pleasant conversation at the table. Don't drop everything and start offering your child different foods in an attempt to get her to eat no matter what it takes. When a child is hungry, she will eat (providing that she is not sick, of course). You will do your child and yourself a big favor by staying calm and nonchalant about her protests. Next time she will know that this kind of behavior doesn't get results and may decide to eat dinner together with everybody else.

- Try not to use food as reward or punishment. This way your child will have an easier time building a healthy relationship with food and eating.

- If possible, sit at the table for a meal with the whole family at least once a day. Let your kids set the table, and make it festive. Help your child build positive memories around food.

- Bring healthy snacks or meals with you on the road and pack your child's school lunch to avoid the temptation of buying fast food or processed foods.

- Cultivate curiosity. Discuss food with your child, help him learn about it, and explain why it is good for him.

- Let your child participate in cooking. In my experience, this trick works wonders. She will be so much more likely to try something she participated in making and generally will develop a higher appreciation for the meal.

Avocado and Strawberry Ice Pops

2 large, ripe but firm Hass
  avocados
1 cup (240 ml) purified
  water
½ cup (150 ml) agave syrup
  or other sweetener of
  choice
2 tablespoons freshly
  squeezed lemon juice
About 5 strawberries,
  preferably organic,
  hulled

Makes 9 to 10 ice pops

Paloma is at an age when she demands to be involved in everything, and helping out in the kitchen has become one of her favorite activities.

These ice pops are an ideal treat to make with your child's extensive participation. They are quick and easy, and the result is colorful and rewarding. They will all but guarantee your child will know and like avocado. It is no secret that avocado is considered one of the best sources of healthy fats, and it is rich in vitamins C, K, and B$_6$, folate, fiber, and potassium. It also happens to be ideal in desserts, especially ice cream, because of its creamy texture and neutral taste.

1. If you are using wooden ice pop sticks, soak them in water for 2 to 3 hours before using.

2. Cut the avocados in half, remove the pits, and scoop out the flesh with a spoon. In a blender, combine the avocado with the water, agave, and lemon juice and blend until smooth.

3. Thinly slice the strawberries. Arrange the slices inside the ice pop molds, sticking them to the walls so they will be visible on the surface of the pops. Fill the molds with the avocado mixture, spooning just a little at a time, taking care not to create large air pockets. Once full, lift and gently drop the molds on the counter several times to eliminate any air bubbles. Cover with the lid and insert the sticks.

4. Freeze for at least 3 to 4 hours or overnight. Run hot water over the molds and the lid to remove the pops.

Everything Halva

Makes 24 small bars

Halva is one of my favorite desserts. Whenever I see those irregularly shaped blocks of nuts and sugar at Middle Eastern markets, I lose all willpower. I can't ever pick just one kind—sesame, sunflower, pistachio—they are all delicious in their own way. It's no surprise that I wanted to create a healthier alternative so I wouldn't feel a sugar overload after every burst of indulgence. This halva can be treated as a healthy snack bar and is great to make with kids. Let them measure and toss all the ingredients into the bowl, and teach them about each one along the way (see My Ingredients on page 7 and Resources on page 319).

5 large soft dates (about 120 g)

1 cup (120 g) raw walnuts

1 cup (150 g) raw hazelnuts

½ cup (75 g) raw sunflower seeds

½ cup (60 g) rolled oats

½ cup (80 g) raw Brazil nuts

Pinch of sea salt

2 tablespoons maca powder (optional)

3 tablespoons coconut butter or
    coconut oil

2 tablespoons sesame tahini (page 32)

¼ cup (40 g) pumpkin seeds

¼ cup (40 g) unhulled or hulled raw
    sesame seeds

¼ cup (40 g) hemp seeds

¼ cup (45 g) chia seeds

2 tablespoons quinoa puffs

⅓ cup (30 g) goji berries

1 heaping tablespoon cacao nibs

½ tablespoon bee pollen

3 tablespoons honey

1. Place the dates in a medium bowl and cover with purified water. Let them soak while you follow the next few steps. Make sure your dates are very fresh, soft, and moist; if they're not, soak them for several hours.

2. Preheat the oven to 350°F (180°C).

3. Spread the walnuts and hazelnuts on a baking sheet, place it in the oven, and toast the nuts for 10 minutes. Remove from the oven and let cool. Meanwhile, spread the sunflower seeds on a separate baking sheet and toast them for 5 minutes. Remove from the oven and let cool. Rub the toasted walnuts and hazelnuts with a kitchen towel to remove their skins.

4. Pulse the rolled oats in a food processor to partially grind them, about 10 pulses. Transfer into a large bowl. Add the walnuts, hazelnuts, sunflower seeds, Brazil nuts, and salt to the food processor and grind to the consistency of breadcrumbs. Drain the dates, remove the pits, and add to the nut mixture in the food processor, along with the maca powder, if using, the coconut butter, and tahini. Grind until well combined and as smooth as possible.

5. Add the remaining ingredients to the large bowl with the rolled oats, followed by the nut-date mixture. Using your hands, combine everything very well. The mixture should be sticky and hold together when pressed between your fingers.

6. Line an 8 × 8-inch (21 × 21 cm) baking pan with parchment paper extending up the sides. Press the mixture into the pan in an even layer and freeze for 1 hour. Remove the pan from the freezer, lift the halva out with the parchment paper, and place the halva on a cutting board. Carefully slice it into bars with a large, sharp knife. It will keep refrigerated in an airtight container for up to 3 weeks. You can also store the bars in the freezer; they don't harden completely, so you can eat them straight from the freezer.

Note: This recipe allows a ton of room for experimentation. You can modify the flavor by eliminating or adding different ingredients. Just make sure you keep the dry to wet ingredient ratio the same. Coconut flakes, hemp protein, flaxseeds, buckwheat crispies (page 34), pistachios, and dried fruits are some delicious alternative add-ins. Try raw walnuts, hazelnuts, and sunflower seeds or make the halva nut-free by using only sunflower and pumpkin seeds as a base.

Vegetable Miso Soup

Serves 8 to 10

I introduced Paloma to the tastes of spices and herbs very early on, right as she started eating solid foods. Our Russian nanny was in a constant state of shock from the variety of spices that went into the child's meals. Paloma was at ease with curry, ginger, jalapeño, coriander, cardamom, and cumin, to name just a few, and all kinds of herbs.

This miso soup is full of bright, healing flavors. I try to get as many different kinds and colors of vegetables as I can in this soup when making it with Paloma. She cuts the carrots into flower shapes with a cookie cutter, sorts the vegetables, and asks all kinds of questions—*Why is this cauliflower purple? Why are the noodles transparent? Why does lotus root have holes in it?*—making new discoveries in the world of food in the process.

3 lemongrass stalks

3-inch (7½ cm) piece fresh ginger

3 garlic cloves

1 small chile

10 tablespoons (generous ⅓ cup) miso paste, or to taste

5 Kaffir lime leaves (optional)

1 medium carrot

½ small zucchini

½ cup fresh or frozen green peas

Handful of sugar snap peas

Handful of snow peas

About ¼ broccoli head

¼ head each purple and yellow cauliflower, or ½ head white cauliflower

About 2 cups spinach leaves

About 1½ cups shiitake mushrooms (optional)

5 ounces (142 g, or ½ standard 10-oz package) clear mung bean vermicelli noodles or other noodles of choice

2 teaspoons salt

1 piece kombu (optional)

2 teaspoons dried wakame (optional)

1 lime

About 1½ cups fresh cilantro leaves

1 tablespoon toasted sesame seeds (optional)

1. Cut each lemongrass stalk into 2-inch (5 cm) pieces. Slice each piece lengthwise and bruise it with the back of a chef's knife. Peel and mince the ginger and garlic and seed and mince the chile. Pour 10 cups of water into a large pot and bring to a boil. Add the lemongrass, ginger, garlic, chile, and lime leaves. Cover and set aside to infuse for about 30 minutes. Remove the lemongrass with a slotted spoon.

2. Dissolve the miso paste in a small amount of spicy broth in a small bowl. Add mixture back to the broth, mix to combine.

3. Prepare all the vegetables: Thinly slice the carrots and then cut into shapes with a mini cookie cutter or shave with a vegetable peeler. Thinly slice

the zucchini, remove the strings from the sugar snap peas and snow peas, and chop the broccoli and cauliflower into small florets. Roughly chop the spinach, remove the stems from the shiitakes, and thickly slice the shiitakes. In a separate pot, bring another 10 cups of water to a boil. Add the salt and noodles and cook, stirring occasionally, for about 8 minutes, until soft. Drain and set aside.

4. Cut the kombu into ½-inch (1¼ cm) pieces (I use kitchen scissors). Add the noodles, all the vegetables, the kombu, and wakame to the miso broth and reheat until very hot but not boiling. Remove from the heat. Squeeze the juice from the lime over the soup and add ½ cup of the cilantro. Serve right away, garnished with the remaining cilantro and the sesame seeds, if using. You can also refrigerate the soup overnight and reheat it gently before serving.

Notes: This soup is very versatile and the recipe can be altered a few ways:

You can blanch all the vegetables before adding them to the broth if you like them on the softer side.

You can leave out the miso paste, which will result in a lighter, clearer broth. In this case, you'll need to add salt. The saltiness of different varieties of miso varies greatly. I use chickpea miso in this recipe; the amount used here is usually enough to season the broth without adding more salt.

Another option is to add a package of silken or regular tofu along with or instead of the clear noodles. If you don't have mung bean noodles, soba is a great alternative.

Last, you can add or leave out any vegetables according to your taste.

Thunderstorm Cookies
with mesquite powder and sesame tahini

Makes about 15 cookies

In Florida, summer is the rainy season. Thunderstorms are an almost daily occurrence, and they are the very noisy and colorful tropical kind. The summer Paloma turned four seemed particularly storm-heavy, perhaps because she started to be very afraid of thunder. Otherwise a very brave girl, she would spend hours weeping under a blanket, with her little hands over her ears. The situation soon became disruptive to our daily routine and something had to be done.

We decided to explore the rain, thunder, and lightning through a culinary art project. We made rain cloud stencils for cookies, which we then cut out, baked, and dipped into raw chocolate to signify the darkness of storm clouds. We built a stormy sky on card stock, with the cookies as clouds and sprinkles as raindrops. We then talked about the nature of thunder, lightning, and rain, and why rain is a good thing. Paloma ate the cookies during the next storm and miraculously, once something scary had become sweet, her fear melted away.

Use any cookie cutter to make these cookies or create your own shape. Note that the number of cookies will depend on the size and shape that you choose.

¾ cup (135 g) brown rice flour

¼ cup (25 g) almond flour

⅓ cup (40 g) tapioca starch

¼ cup (40 g) mesquite powder (page 21)

¼ cup (35 g) cacao nibs, ground into a coarse flour in a coffee grinder (optional)

¼ cup (70 ml) plus 2 tablespoons honey

4 tablespoons almond butter (page 30)

3 tablespoons sesame tahini (page 32)

1 teaspoon vanilla extract

¼ teaspoon sea salt

1 tablespoon ice water, plus more if needed

2 ounces (60 g) raw chocolate (page 32) or other good-quality chopped dark chocolate or chocolate chips

1. In a food processor, combine the flours, tapioca starch, mesquite powder, cacao nibs, if using, honey, almond butter, tahini, vanilla, and salt and process until thoroughly mixed. The mixture should stick together a little if pressed between your fingers. Add the water and mix again. Test the mixture: if it sticks easily when pressed with your fingers, transfer it to a large bowl. If not, add more ice water, 1 tablespoon at a time, until you have the right consistency.

2. Knead into a smooth, oily dough, divide it into 2 equal portions, and form each into a ball. Place each ball on its own piece of plastic wrap and flatten them with the palm of your hand. Cover each with another layer of plastic wrap and roll the dough into a ³/₈-inch (1 cm) thick circle. Carefully transfer the dough into the freezer, placing them on a flat surface such as a baking sheet. Chill the dough for 30 minutes.

3. Preheat the oven to 350°F (180°C).

4. Working with one piece at a time, unwrap the dough and cut as many cookies as you can with a cookie cutter or a small sharp knife. Place them on a parchment paper–covered baking sheet. Reshape, reroll, and recut the dough until all is used up. (Try cutting the dough into small triangles when there is not enough left for a whole cookie.)

5. Bake for 10 minutes, or until the bottoms are lightly browned. Take care not to overbake, or the cookies will turn very hard. Cool completely before dipping into the chocolate.

6. If you're making the raw chocolate at the same time as the cookies and it's not yet set, begin dipping your cookies into it. If not, slowly melt your chocolate in the top of a double boiler over low heat. Then dip the cookies in it, one at a time. You may want to use a small spoon to help the chocolate flow better.

7. Place the cookies on a parchment paper–covered cutting board that fits in your freezer. Chill in the freezer for about 10 minutes for the chocolate to set. The cookies are best eaten the day they are made, or you can store them in an airtight container at room temperature for up to 3 days.

Spinach and Quinoa Blinchiki

Makes about six 8-inch (20 cm) or eighteen 5-inch (12 cm) crepes

Blinchiki is an affectionate Russian term for crepes, one that Paloma uses often, as they are one of her favorite foods. If in doubt about what to feed her, *blinchiki* is always the answer. I keep several nutritious flours handy for emergency crepes. This recipe is a variation on the Chestnut and Buckwheat Crepes (page 59)—it's just as simple and full of nutrition. You can substitute any other mild green leafy vegetables for the spinach. These crepes are tasty enough to be eaten plain with a smear of ghee, or serve them with leeks and shiitakes (see page 59), fresh ricotta cheese (page 26), your favorite nut butter, and/or fresh fruit of your choice.

¾ cup (105 g) quinoa flour
½ teaspoon baking soda
½ teaspoon sea salt
1½ (375 ml) cups unsweetened almond milk, divided
About 1 cup (1 oz [30 g]) fresh spinach leaves
½ tablespoon ground chia seeds
1 tablespoon grapeseed oil, plus more for cooking the crepes

1. In a medium bowl, combine the quinoa flour, baking soda, and salt. In a small saucepan, warm 1 cup of the almond milk to about 105°F (40°C). In a blender, combine the almond milk with the spinach and chia meal and blend until smooth.

2. Pour the warm milk and spinach mixture over the dry ingredients and whisk until a smooth batter forms. Let stand for 30 minutes.

3. In a small saucepan, bring the remaining ½ cup almond milk to a boil. Add it to the batter and whisk to combine. Last, add the grapeseed oil and whisk together.

To make sturdier, less tender crepes, whisk one egg with the warm milk and spinach mixture and flour at step #2. This is also helpful if you are not very familiar with the crepe-making process.

4. Heat a nonstick skillet over medium heat. Add about 1 teaspoon oil for a 5-inch pan or about 2 teaspoons for an 8-inch pan. Start adding about ⅛ cup batter to a 5-inch pan or about ⅓ cup to an 8-inch pan at a time. Turn the pan as you pour, letting the batter flow over the entire surface of the pan. Don't worry if the first crepe is not perfect or sticks to the pan a little, as the first crepe is usually the test one.

5. Cook the crepe for about 1 minute, until the surface is bubbly and the edges begin to turn golden brown. Using a thin spatula, separate the edges from the pan and then the entire crepe, making sure that the batter is cooked enough to hold its shape. If not, leave it to cook a little longer. Flip the crepe and cook on the other side for about 1 minute. Continue cooking crepes in the same fashion until all the batter is used. I rarely add oil to the pan between crepes, but if you feel it is necessary to make things go smoother, add 1 to 2 teaspoons at a time. As the crepes come off the pan, stack them on a plate and keep them covered and warm, close to the stove. The less batter you use, the thinner your crepes will be. If the batter seems too thick, add more hot milk to the batter, 2 tablespoons at a time, and mix well.

Chickpea Chocolate Pops

½ cup (100 g) dried chickpeas, soaked in purified water overnight, or 1 cup canned chickpeas

2 tablespoons honey

2 tablespoons sesame tahini

1 tablespoon coconut oil, melted

1 tablespoon ground chia seeds

1 tablespoon cacao nibs or finely chopped chocolate

1 teaspoon vanilla extract

Small pinch of sea salt

About ¾ cup (5 oz [140 g]) raw chocolate (page 32) or good-quality chopped dark chocolate or chocolate chips (see Note)

Makes about 45 pops

Paloma has a funny idea of healthy eating, just from observing us and listening to our family talk about food. When offered sweets, she declines by saying that she only eats *good bad food*. She often makes sure that her doughnuts have *vitamins* in them.

These pops are a great example of how versatile chickpeas can be, even in desserts. They can be fun to make for a children's party or as edible gifts for the holidays.

1. If you are using dried chickpeas, drain and rinse them. Transfer to a medium saucepan, cover with a generous amount of water, and bring to a boil. Lower the heat and simmer, uncovered, until soft but not mushy. Drain over a colander and let sit over the sink or a bowl for 10 to 15 minutes. You want the chickpeas to be as dry as possible. Measure 1 cup of chickpeas. (Extra beans can be reserved for salads or other snacks.)

If you are using canned chickpeas, drain and rinse them. Measure 1 cup, then spread them on a few layers of paper towels so the liquid is absorbed.

2. Transfer the chickpeas into a food processor and add the remaining ingredients, except the raw chocolate. Process until smooth, scraping the sides of the bowl if needed. Spoon the mixture into a medium bowl, cover with plastic wrap, and refrigerate for 1 to 2 hours, until firm to the touch.

3. Remove the mixture from the refrigerator. Scoop out 1 teaspoon at a time, rolling it into a ball in your hands. Place each ball on a parchment paper–covered cutting board or a baking sheet that can fit in your freezer. Insert a toothpick or small wooden skewer into each ball and place them in the freezer for 30 minutes to 1 hour, until the surface is firm and the toothpicks are stable.

4. Prepare one portion of the raw chocolate or melt the chocolate of your choice in a double boiler. Remove the chickpea balls from the freezer and dip into the melted chocolate one at a time. Set them on a new piece of parchment paper on the board. When all of the balls have been covered in chocolate, return the board to the freezer for 5 to 10 minutes, until all the chocolate is set. Remove from the freezer and store in the refrigerator for up to 1 week.

Note: If using raw chocolate for dipping, pour the remaining chocolate into molds and freeze until set to make extra chocolate treats.

Carob Animal Cookies

with beets and red beans

Makes about 30 cookies

These cookies are kid-friendly and very nutritious, as they are full of fresh beet, bean protein, sesame tahini, and carob powder. If you use less carob and make the cookies round, they will look and taste somewhat like red velvet cookies.

   The secret to success is rolling the dough exactly to the thickness I recommend and not overbaking them. If you follow the instructions carefully, you'll get perfectly moist cookies with a nice chewy crust. And in case you do not yet have a menagerie of animal cookie cutters, use any other shapes instead.

7 tablespoons (slightly less than ½ cup) almond butter
¼ cup (55 g) sesame tahini
⅓ cup (75 g) ghee (page 27)
¾ cup (105 g) coconut sugar
2 tablespoons honey
½ cup shredded fresh beet
½ cup cooked or canned red kidney beans or other red beans of choice

1 teaspoon vanilla extract
1 cup (180 g) brown rice flour
1 cup (100 g) almond flour
½ cup (60 g) oat flour
¼ cup (30 g) tapioca starch
¼ cup (25 g) carob powder (see Note)
½ teaspoon sea salt

Whenever I bake these cookies, I most often use animal-shaped cookie cutters: owl, goat, horse, dragonfly, pig, squirrel, and rooster. Paloma gets to choose which animals go into her lunch box for the next day. For some reason, a squirrel or goat always wins.

1. In a medium bowl, combine the almond butter, tahini, and ghee. Add the coconut sugar and honey and beat with a hand mixer until light and fluffy, starting at a low speed to prevent the sugar from splashing, then gradually increasing the speed to maximum. Stop the mixer halfway through and scrape the sides of the bowl with a spatula.

2. Place the shredded beet and red beans into the bowl of a food processor. Add the buttery mixture, vanilla, and brown rice flour. Blend until smooth, scraping the sides of the bowl if needed.

3. In a large bowl, combine the almond flour, oat flour, tapioca starch, carob powder, and salt. Add the wet mixture from the food processor to the bowl with the dry ingredients. Combine and knead the dough with your hands; it will be soft and oily. Divide the dough into 4 even portions and shape each into a ball. Working with one ball at a time, place each on a piece of plastic wrap. Flatten the ball with the palm of your hand, cover it with another piece of plastic, and roll with a rolling pin into a ³⁄₈-inch (1 cm) thick circle. Repeat with the rest of the dough. The dough will be very soft, so carefully transfer all 4 pieces into the freezer placing them on a flat surface. Chill the dough for 1 hour.

4. Prepare a cutting board or another flat surface that fits in your freezer and cover it with parchment paper. If your freezer is big enough to accommodate your baking sheet, you may cover it with parchment and place your cookies directly on it. You may need 2 of them depending on the size.

5. Working with one piece of dough at a time, unwrap it and cut out as many cookies as you can with your cookie cutters. Place them on the board or a baking sheet. Reshape, reroll, and recut the dough until all of it is used up. Try cutting the leftover dough into small triangles when there is not enough left for a whole cookie. Freeze for another 30 minutes.

6. Preheat the oven to 350°F (180°C).

7. Bake for 10 to 12 minutes, until the bottom is lightly browned. Remove the cookies from the oven and let cool on the baking sheet for at least 10 minutes. The cookies are very soft when still hot and will hold their shape only when cooled. They are best eaten the day they are made, but will keep in an airtight container for up to 3 days.

Note: Carob powder is a great alternative to cocoa. It comes from the dried pods of the carob tree, is mildly sweet, and doesn't contain caffeine. Carob is a good source of calcium, iron, and various antioxidants. It can be found in most health food stores, some supermarkets, and through many online sources.

Whole-Grain Crust Mini Pizzas

with sweet potato, tomato, and kale

Makes four 6-inch (15 cm) pizzas

All I have to do is say the magic word, *pizza*, and Paloma will be by my side, ready to cook and eat. She loves to roll the crust and enjoys playing with the toppings in this recipe. This crust is made of cooked brown rice or millet and other nutritious ingredients and doesn't resemble traditional pizza dough. Nevertheless, the trick works every time: if Paloma participates in the cooking, she will gladly eat it. As with all pizzas, you can customize the amount of spices, herbs, and toppings to your liking.

For the crust

⅔ cup uncooked brown rice or ½ cup uncooked millet

1½ cups (360 ml) purified water

1 teaspoon sea salt, divided

¼ teaspoon ground coriander

¼ teaspoon dried oregano (optional)

¼ cup (32 g) flax or chia meal

½ cup (70 g) buckwheat flour

2 tablespoons minced fresh parsley (optional)

2 tablespoons olive oil

½ cup (120 ml) unsweetened full-fat canned coconut milk

¼ cup (60 ml) purified water

For the topping

1 medium sweet potato, peeled and thinly sliced

2 medium tomatoes, thinly sliced

1 teaspoon olive oil

Sea salt and freshly ground black pepper

2 to 3 kale leaves, stems removed, minced (about 1 cup loosely packed)

2 ounces (60 g) soft feta cheese, preferably goat's milk and/or sheep's milk feta, or other cheese of choice

TO PREPARE THE CRUST

1. In a colander, rinse the rice or millet and put it in a medium saucepan. Cover with water and add ½ teaspoon of the salt and all the coriander and oregano, if using. Bring to a boil, lower the heat, and cook for 45 minutes for the rice or 12 to 15 minutes for the millet, until the grain is soft. Fluff with a fork and let sit, covered, for another 10 minutes. Let cool. You should have about 2 cups of rice or millet.

2. Preheat the oven to 365°F (185°C).

3. In a large bowl, combine the flax meal, buckwheat flour, the remaining ½ teaspoon salt, and the parsley, if using. Add the olive oil, coconut milk, and water and mix to incorporate. Then add the cooked rice or millet and mix into a wet dough.

4. Cover a large, flat baking sheet with parchment paper. With a wet spoon, ladle one-quarter of the batter at a time onto the sheet to form 4 small (6-inch [15 cm]) pizza crusts.

TO ASSEMBLE AND BAKE THE PIZZAS

1. Place the sweet potato and tomato slices on top of the crusts, alternating them, or arrange the sweet potato and tomato slices in layers. Lightly brush the vegetables with olive oil and sprinkle with salt and pepper. Bake for 30 minutes. Remove the pizzas from the oven and increase the oven temperature to 400°F (200°C).

2. Top the pizzas with the kale and cheese, return them to the oven, and bake for an additional 10 minutes. Let cool slightly before slicing and serving.

Sweet Potato and Apple Doughnuts

Makes about 12 small doughnuts

These doughnuts are so good-looking that people often have a hard time believing they are full of nutritious ingredients. Sweet potato is often baked first before using in desserts and other baked goods, but in this recipe, I add raw shredded sweet potato directly into the batter. That eliminates an extra step and adds more flavor and moisture to the doughnuts. For the glazes, you can use the recipe below or use the glaze recipe from the Rum and Raisin Bundt Cakes (page 209), then sprinkle dried coconut flakes, cacao nibs, or chopped dried fruits on top.

For the doughnuts

1 small sweet potato, peeled and finely grated

1 medium Granny Smith apple, peeled and coarsely grated

1 large egg

¼ cup (35 g) coconut sugar

3 tablespoons ghee (page 27)

½ cup (90 g) plus 2 tablespoons brown rice flour

½ cup (50 g) almond flour

¼ cup (30 g) coconut flour

¼ cup (30 g) plus 2 tablespoons tapioca starch

1 teaspoon baking powder

½ teaspoon baking soda

¼ teaspoon sea salt

For glazing

Coconut glaze

1½ tablespoons coconut butter (see Note), melted

½ teaspoon honey

Chocolate glaze

1½ tablespoons coconut butter (see Note), melted

½ teaspoon honey

1½ teaspoon unsweetened (preferably raw) cocoa powder

Strawberry glaze

1½ tablespoons coconut butter (see Note), melted

½ teaspoon honey

1 teaspoon strawberry powder or ground freeze-dried strawberries (see Resources, page 319), plus more to taste

Apricot glaze

1½ tablespoons coconut butter (see Note), melted

1 teaspoon apricot puree (see page 235)

½ teaspoon honey

For the toppings

Dried coconut flakes

Ground cacao nibs or chocolate

Chopped unsweetened dried papaya

Chopped dried pineapple

Chopped dried apricots

Chopped dried or freeze-dried cherries

Chopped and/or ground dried or freeze-dried strawberries

TO PREPARE THE DOUGHNUTS

1. Measure 1 cup packed shredded sweet potato and place it in a food processor; add the shredded apple. Add the egg and coconut sugar and process until well combined. Add the remaining ingredients and mix into a smooth, soft, and wet batter. Transfer to a medium bowl.

2. Preheat the oven to 350°F (180°C).

3. Cover a baking sheet with parchment paper. Gather a small ice cream scoop and a pastry bag tip. Have a small bowl with water ready for dipping in the ice cream scoop and pastry tip.

4. Dip the ice cream scoop into the water, then into the batter. Place scoops of doughnut batter onto the parchment paper, about 2 inches (5 cm) apart. Dip the scoop into the water between every scoop of batter, tapping it at the edge of the bowl to shake off the excess. With wet fingers or a spoon, slightly flatten the center of each scoop. You can bake the doughnuts as is or make doughnut holes:

To make doughnut holes: Wet the pastry tip and cut a hole (about 1 inch [2½ cm] wide) in the center of each doughnut with the wide end of the tip. Remove it carefully and scoop out the batter from the inside of the tip with a narrow knife. Make sure to wet the tip between each doughnut. You may want to dry your fingers occasionally as you're working, as the tip may become slippery and sometimes stubborn when removing it from a doughnut. The batter should be very soft, wet, and tender. You can collect all the scooped-out batter and reshape it into a small doughnut at the end.

5. Bake the doughnuts for 20 to 25 minutes, until slightly golden and a toothpick comes out dry. Let cool before glazing.

TO PREPARE THE GLAZES AND FINISH THE DOUGHNUTS

In separate bowls, combine all the ingredients for the glazes of your choice and stir. Spoon over the doughnuts and decorate with toppings.

Note: Coconut butter is a wonderfully delicious product in which the contents of a whole coconut are blended together to make a rich butter, with no additives. It can be found in most health food stores.

Chocolate Milkshake

2 large handfuls green leafy vegetables, such as spinach, Swiss chard, or kale (use softer greens like spinach and Swiss chard if you don't have a high-speed blender)

1½ (375 ml) cup almond milk (page 30)

3 to 4 tablespoons unsweetened cocoa powder, preferably raw

1 large ripe banana

1 cup diced ripe papaya

½ cup frozen or fresh strawberries (see Note)

1 tablespoon pea protein or other vegetable protein powder (optional)

Serves 2 to 3

I've made a habit of including green leafy vegetables in most of my meals. For adults it's a manageable commitment, as most of us are willing to eat salads, but it tends to get tricky for little ones. That is when quick, tasty shakes like this one come in handy. Your child will be too distracted by the sweet, choco-laty flavors and smooth creaminess to ever suspect the presence of greens.

If you are using greens with hard stems such as kale or chard, remove and discard the stems. Then combine all the ingredients in a blender and blend until smooth.

Note: If using fresh strawberries, add several ice cubes to the blender to make the smoothie cold. You could also use a frozen banana. Add a sweetener (honey, agave syrup, maple syrup, or rice syrup) if your child is used to very sweet drinks, but try to use less and less of it over time. Gradually your child will adjust to just the sweetness of the ripe fruits.

Flower Vegetable Tartlets

Makes 18 small tartlets

Paloma is much more inclined to eat food she has helped prepare. She will at least try it and give it a chance, instead of saying no right away as she tends to do with some dishes—she *is* a four-year-old, after all. She loves to roll the dough and cut out the flowers, tucking them into the muffin pan holes. The different shapes and bright colors attract her and get her eating foods like beets, which she normally would have a hard time trying.

I give you two options for filling your tartlet shells: honey-roasted sweet potatoes and balsamic-glazed roasted beets; other filling options include steamed edamame, a simple bean and radish salad, hummus (page 101), or fresh ricotta (page 26).

This tartlet shell is one of only two recipes in this book that contain gluten (the other is Quick Spelt Bread, page 315).

For the tartlet shells
1½ cups (250 g) whole spelt flour, preferably sprouted
½ teaspoon sea salt
1 teaspoon baking powder
2 tablespoons olive oil, plus more for greasing the muffin holes
About ½ cup (120 ml) leftover whey from making ricotta cheese (page 26) or purified water, plus more for brushing the shells

For the fillings (your choice from below)

Honey-roasted sweet potatoes
3 tablespoons olive oil
2 tablespoons balsamic vinegar
1 teaspoon honey
½ teaspoon sea salt

2 medium sweet potatoes (about 450 g), peeled and cut into bite-size pieces
1 medium shallot, finely chopped
3 large kale leaves, stems removed, finely chopped
½ lemon
½ cup chopped pecans (optional)

Balsamic-glazed roasted beets
5 baby beets (about 450 g), peeled and cut into bite-size cubes
½ tablespoon olive oil, divided
Sea salt
1 tablespoon melted ghee (page 27) or olive oil
1 tablespoon honey
1 tablespoon balsamic vinegar
½ tablespoon minced fresh ginger (optional)

TO PREPARE THE TARTLET SHELLS

1. Preheat the oven to 390°F (200°C).

2. In a large bowl, combine the flour, salt, and baking powder. Add the olive oil and rub it in with your hands. Start adding water a little at a time, kneading the dough as you go, until it is soft and no longer sticky. You may need more of the liquid depending on the flour you are using.

3. Roll the dough into a thick log and cut it in half. Wrap one of the portions into a piece of plastic wrap to keep it from drying. Roll the other half out ⅛-inch (3 mm) thick and cut out as many flowers as you can with a 3¾-inch (9½ cm) cookie cutter. Reroll and recut the dough until all is used up. Repeat with the second portion.

4. Lightly oil 18 muffin pan holes (or use smaller pan and work in 2 batches) or use silicone muffin liners. Tuck each flower into the muffin holes, lightly brush with whey, and prick each shell with a fork several times. Bake for 13 to 15 minutes, until golden brown. The shells will keep in an airtight container for up to 3 days.

TO PREPARE THE HONEY-ROASTED SWEET POTATOES

1. Preheat the oven to 400°F (200°C).

2. In a small bowl, whisk together the olive oil, vinegar, honey, and salt and set aside. In a large bowl, combine the sweet potatoes and shallot, pour the dressing over, and mix to coat.

3. Spread out on an aluminum foil–covered baking sheet and roast for 20 minutes. Take the sheet out of the oven, add the kale, and mix to incorporate. Roast for another 20 minutes, or until the sweet potatoes are fully cooked. Transfer the vegetables to a medium bowl, squeeze some lemon juice over it, and add the pecans, if using. Gently stir to coat.

TO PREPARE THE BALSAMIC-GLAZED ROASTED BEETS

1. Preheat the oven to 450°F (230°C).

2. In a medium bowl, combine the beets with ½ tablespoon of the olive oil, season with salt, and mix to coat. Transfer the beets to a medium baking dish and cover with aluminum foil. Roast for 15 minutes or until beets are soft when pricked with a knife.

3. In a small bowl, whisk together the ghee, honey, vinegar, and ginger, if using. Take the dish out of the oven and pour the glaze over the beets. Cover again and bake for another 5 minutes.

TO ASSEMBLE

Fill the flower shells with your choice of filling.

Pink Lemon Coconut Bonbons

2 cups (245 g) macadamia nuts

3½ cups (310 g) unsweetened shredded coconut, divided

⅓ cup honey

¼ cup (60 ml) coconut oil, melted

Zest of 1 lemon

3 tablespoons freshly squeezed lemon juice, from about ½ lemon

1 teaspoon vanilla extract

Small pinch of sea salt

About ½ teaspoon freshly squeezed beet juice, or more for a more intense color

Makes 40 bonbons

These bonbons are another kid-friendly kitchen project. They are super-cute and fun to roll, not to mention that lemon and coconut seem to be made for each other. I use fresh beet juice to color the coconut pink. You can use carrot or spinach juice to play with different colored bonbons. Berry or vegetable powders are other food coloring options; look for them at online retailers.

1. Place the macadamia nuts in the freezer for 15 minutes or longer. This helps to prevent the bonbon mixture from becoming too oily.

2. In a food processor, combine the macadamia nuts, 2 cups of the shredded coconut, the honey, coconut oil, lemon zest and juice, vanilla, and salt. Process until everything comes together in a sticky mixture. Take care to not overmix; the mixture can be a bit chunky. Take about half of it and place it into a medium bowl. Refrigerate for 1 hour.

3. Add the beet juice to the rest of the mixture and mix to incorporate the juice and give it an even color. You can also play with making different shades of light pink to a deeper purple if you divide your mixture into several portions and add different amounts of the juice. Transfer the pink mixture to a medium bowl and refrigerate for 1 hour.

4. Put the remaining 1½ cups of shredded coconut into a medium bowl. Take the macadamia mixture (one color a time) out of the refrigerator and begin to form the bonbons. Scoop out 1 tablespoon of the mixture at a time and roll into a ball between the palms of your hands. Then roll in the shredded coconut to coat the surface well. Place inside a parchment paper–covered dish (such as a large glass Pyrex dish) and keep refrigerated and covered until ready to serve. The bonbons can also be kept in the freezer, as they never become completely frozen. If you freeze them, let them sit at room temperature for 5 to 10 minutes before eating them, or eat them right away if you'd prefer an ice cream–like texture.

Note: It's easy to make a small amount of beet juice without a juicer. For this recipe, you will need just about one-eighth of a small beet. Shred it finely and place on a double layer of cheesecloth. Over a bowl, twist the shredded beets inside the cheesecloth to extract the juice. Discard the pulp. Beet juice is a very potent coloring liquid, so make sure to protect your clothes and hands so they don't stain a bright magenta color.

Apple and Kale Chips

For the apple chips

Makes about 4 cups

¼ cup (35 g) coconut sugar

1 teaspoon ground cinnamon

3 medium apples (about 15 oz [430 g])

For the kale chips

Makes about 14 cups

2 bunches (about 6 leaves or 6½ oz [185 g] each bunch) curly kale, stems removed

¾ cup (165 g) sesame tahini (page 32)

½ cup (120 ml) apple cider vinegar

½ cup (120 ml) purified water, plus more if needed

¼ cup packed torn fresh cilantro leaves and stems

¼ cup (60 ml) nama shoyu or tamari or Bragg Liquid Aminos (see Note)

2 scallions, chopped (optional)

1 garlic clove

Juice of 1 lemon (about ⅓ cup)

Note: Nama shoyu is considered raw, unpasteurized soy sauce, which is more appropriate for raw kale chips, but tamari is also a good, gluten-free choice.

Although I like to play around with making all sorts of fruit and vegetable chips, apple and kale chips are my (and Paloma's) favorite. Most children love chips, and these kale and apple chips are a great alternative to classic potato chips. Apple chips stay crisp after they have cooled and are perfect for a quick snack or a lunch box treat.

You can find plenty of recipes for baked kale chips, but none of them compares with this incredibly flavorful and perfectly crunchy dehydrated version.

FOR THE APPLE CHIPS

1. Preheat the oven to 225°F (105°C).

2. In a coffee grinder, grind the coconut sugar into a powder. Pour into a medium bowl and mix with the cinnamon. Set aside. Slice the apples thinly (about 2 mm thick) on mandoline. Line 2 baking sheets with parchment paper, arrange the apple slices on them without overlapping, and sprinkle with the cinnamon sugar.

3. Bake for 2 hours, rotating the sheets and flipping the apple slices after 1 hour. Remove from the oven. The chips will become crisper as they cool down. Keep refrigerated in an airtight glass container for up to 1 week.

FOR THE KALE CHIPS

1. Dry the kale leaves thoroughly using a salad spinner or paper towels. Tear or cut them into medium pieces (about 16 cups total). Place into a large bowl and set aside.

2. Combine the remaining ingredients in a blender and blend until smooth. Pour it over the kale and mix thoroughly with your hands to coat each piece on both sides. Spread on 4 mesh screen–lined dehydrator trays, making sure not to crowd the chips. Dehydrate at 110°F (43°C) for 4 to 6 hours, rotating and flipping the chips occasionally, until completely dry and crisp. The chips will keep in an airtight container in the refrigerator for 3 to 4 days.

Beet and Chocolate Pudding

Requires a high-speed blender

1 small beet

¼ cup (50 g) good-quality chopped dark chocolate or chocolate chips

¼ cup (57 g) sesame tahini or almond butter

1 cup (240 ml) plus 1 tablespoon unsweetened full-fat canned coconut milk

2 tablespoons chia seeds

2 tablespoons pistachio butter or almond butter

3 tablespoons coconut sugar

2 tablespoons unsweetened cocoa powder

1 tablespoon hemp protein (optional)

Makes five 4-ounce ramekins

When I plan our family meals, I look for ways to pack in nourishing ingredients whenever possible. Some vegetables effortlessly incorporate into desserts, and I never hesitate to take advantage of that. This pudding is incredibly rich but much lighter and healthier than traditional chocolate pudding. Once the beet is cooked, it is simple and quick to make, which makes it easy for children to observe and participate.

Blending different nut butters such as tahini and pistachio butter gives more dimension to the flavor, and each contributes its own nutritional value, but you can use just one type if you prefer.

1. Cook the beet any way you prefer—roasted, boiled, or steamed. Cool it completely, peel, and puree in a food processor or shred it finely. Reserve ½ cup of the beet puree and refrigerate or freeze the rest for another use. Alternatively, leave the beet raw, finely shred it to make ½ cup, and use it instead of the cooked beet puree.

2. Preheat the oven to 425°F (220°C).

3. Combine the chocolate and tahini in the top of a double boiler over low heat. Let it melt slowly, mixing with a spoon until smooth.

4. In a high-speed blender, combine the coconut milk, chia seeds, pistachio butter, coconut sugar, cocoa powder, hemp protein, if using, and the reserved ½ cup beet puree. Blend until very smooth, scraping the sides of the blender. Add the chocolate mixture and blend more to combine thoroughly.

5. Divide the batter among five 4-ounce ramekins. Bake for 10 minutes, or until the tops feel firm to the touch. Remove from the oven and let cool slightly before serving. Or cool completely, cover the ramekins with plastic, refrigerate, and serve cold.

Note: Pistachio butter is one of my favorite nut butters, beautifully green in color and wonderful in taste. We love to snack on it and add it to dressings and baked goods. Like any nut butter, it is very easy to make: Grind 1½ cups (200 g) pistachios into flour in a food processor, add 2 tablespoons of your choice of nut oil and a small pinch of sea salt and continue to process until creamy, adding more oil if needed. Keep refrigerated and use in pesto or baked goods, as a spread on bread and crackers, or a base for ice cream.

Quick Spelt Bread with Concord Grape Jelly

My friend Irina has a degree in Ayurvedic medicine, and at a Vedic retreat she was impressed by the quick bread that was served at some of the meals. Curious, I researched the Vedic approach to bread and came up with this simple recipe. This bread is easy to prepare and requires no yeast; just spelt flour and kefir, yogurt, or whey.

For children, you can serve this bread with the raw Concord grape jelly included with the recipe, or spread it with nut butter dotted with banana slices for a healthier alternative to the classic PB&J lunch or snack. Try making the raw jelly with other fruit or berries—strawberries, raspberries, and persimmon are among my favorites. Of course, adults will love it too!

This bread is also delicious with pumpkin seed pesto (see page 186) and Roasted Kala Chana Hummus (page 101).

This bread is one of only two recipes in this book that contain gluten (the other is Flower Vegetable Tartlets, page 305).

For the quick spelt bread
Makes two 7-inch (18 cm) rounds

2 cups (7 oz [200 g]) sprouted spelt flour or regular whole spelt flour
¼ cup (25 g) oat bran (optional)
Handful of rolled oats (optional)
1 teaspoon sea salt
1 teaspoon baking powder
½ teaspoon baking soda
1 teaspoon freshly squeezed lemon juice
½ cup (4½ oz [130 ml]) plain or coconut yogurt, kefir, or whey from making ricotta cheese (page 26)
2 tablespoons olive oil

½ tablespoon sesame seeds for garnish (optional)
½ tablespoon sunflower seeds for garnish (optional)
½ tablespoon pumpkin seeds for garnish (optional)

For the raw Concord grape jelly
Makes 3 cups

Requires a high-speed blender
3 cups Concord grapes
6 tablespoons honey or agave syrup
Juice of 1 lemon
1½ cup Irish moss gel (see Note)

TO PREPARE THE QUICK BREAD

1. In a large bowl, combine the flour, oat bran, rolled oats, salt, and baking powder.

2. In a medium bowl, pour the lemon juice over the baking soda; it will turn foamy. Add the yogurt and olive oil and whisk until well combined. Add the wet ingredients into the dry mixture. Briefly mix with a spoon to combine, then knead with your hands into a soft dough. Divide the dough into 2 equal balls. Place each on a piece of plastic wrap and slightly flatten it with the palm of your hand. Cover each piece with more plastic and flatten again to form a disk. Refrigerate for 30 minutes.

3. Preheat the oven to 390°F (200°C).

4. Take the dough out of the refrigerator, one disk at a time. Unwrap and place on a piece of parchment paper big enough to accommodate both breads. Roll each disk ¼ inch (6 mm) thick. Sprinkle with the seeds, if using, and roll the rolling pin over them a couple of times to lightly press them into the dough. Cut each bread into 8 segments.

5. Place in the oven and bake for 20 to 25 minutes, until golden. Alternatively, you can shape and roll all of the dough into a large rectangle and cut it into 8 to 10 smaller rectangles to make a more convenient sandwich shape. Keep in an airtight container at room temperature. The bread is best eaten within 2 days.

TO PREPARE THE CONCORD GRAPE JELLY

Blend the grapes in a high-speed blender until smooth. Strain through a fine-mesh strainer and discard the solids. Rinse out the blender, return the grape puree to the machine, and add the honey, lemon juice, and Irish moss gel. Blend again until smooth. The jelly will keep refrigerated for up to 1 week.

Note: To make Irish moss gel, start out with about ¼ cup packed dried Irish moss (you don't need to weigh an exact amount of it). Rinse it under cool water to remove as much salt and debris as you can. Place into a large bowl and cover with hot water for at least 10 minutes. The Irish moss will expand significantly as it soaks, so make sure that it is covered with water completely. Drain and rinse under warm water one more time, making sure the Irish moss is completely clean. Place into a high-speed blender and add about ½ cup purified water to start with. Begin blending. Stop and add more water, ¼ cup at a time, until you have a very smooth, gel-like consistency. It is important not to leave any hard seaweed pieces in the gel. The gel will keep refrigerated in an airtight glass jar for about 2 weeks.

RESOURCES

Unique Ingredients

SPROUTED FLOURS

Sprouted flours are becoming more common in stores and online. My favorite brand is To Your Health Sprouted Flour Co., because they grind sprouted grains to order to assure freshness. The fact that they grind to order, before shipping, sets them apart from other producers of sprouted flours. I buy their sprouted brown rice and spelt flour.

POWDERS AND OTHER SUPERFOODS

Nutsonline.com has a long list of powders, which consists of everything from very exotic leaves to roots, fruits, and vegetables.

IRISH MOSS

Amazon.com sells whole-leaf wild-crafted Irish moss.

Where I Shop

GREEN MARKETS

Local seasonal produce, artisanal cheese, buffalo yogurt, farm eggs, goat's milk products, honey, teas

WHOLE FOODS AND LOCAL HEALTH FOOD STORES

Produce, bulk grains, beans, nuts, spices, sweeteners, oils, vinegar, bulk olives, unpasteurized cheeses, chocolate, dried fruits, vegan white chocolate, vegan gelatin, sea vegetables

AMAZON.COM

Cocoa powder, cacao nibs, coconut sugar, coconut oil and butter, vanilla beans, vegetable protein, hemp hearts, maca powder, mesquite powder, goji berries, flours, Irish moss, vegan white chocolate, vegan gelatin

NUTSONLINE.COM

Chia seeds, nuts (particularly pistachio nuts), seeds, quinoa flakes and puffs, powders, cocoa products, dried fruits

ETHNIC MARKETS

Asian
Herbs, "exotic" fruits and vegetables, noodles, sauces, young Thai coconuts, rice paper

Italian
Unpasteurized cheeses, olives, produce, chestnut flour, oils

Indian
Spices, ghee

Eastern European
Less common frozen berries: huckleberries, sour cherries

Preferred Brands

Nutiva for coconut oil
Navitas Naturals for raw cacao products
To Your Health Sprouted Flour Co. for sprouted flours
Natural Desserts for vegan gelatin
King David Gourmet for vegan white chocolate chips
Explore Asian for black bean spaghetti
Artisana for coconut butter
Sambazon for frozen açai puree

ACKNOWLEDGMENTS

To Masha, my daughter, coauthor, photographer, editor, stylist, and creative force behind both the book and our blog, *Golubka*. You are my inspiration, source of wisdom and balance, and the main reason this book is seeing light.

To Paloma, my little girl, for inspiring the many healthy dishes in this book, for putting up with my long hours in the kitchen, and for always being so eager to help and taste away.

To Ernie, my husband, for your endless optimism, patience, and open mind. For taking on so much while helping me work through this project and your amazing grocery shopping skills.

To my mother, Elena, for instilling in me a love for beautiful food and for showing such unbelievable strength of mind and body I never knew a human being could have.

Thank you to our friend Elena Bensonoff, for your incredible generosity and welcoming us into your home while we worked on the book. To my dear friend Zhenya, for your willingness to always taste and test my dishes, for all your trips to my house and to the market, for your warm encouragement and support. To Cathy Sue Kurant, for the wonderful supply of amazing props. To my friend Masha Lipovaya, for being in my life. To Irina Grissom, for the constant inspiration and a flow of fresh, healthy ideas. To Lena Blake and Dr. Blake, for your hospitality.

To our editor, Rochelle Bourgault, and everyone at Roost Books for finding us and helping us realize this book. To our agent, Alison Fargis, for being so encouraging, patient, and truthful with us throughout the whole process.

To our recipe testers: special thanks to Ashley Schleeper, Shelley Chase, and Lisa Hörnqvist, as well as Sally Russell, Yulia Palenova, Debbie McQueen, Nicole Carrillo, Penni Shelton, Susanna Eduini, Debra Ginsberg, Florence Arnaud, Eriko Hayashi, Alisha Warren, Skyé Nicole Lee, Géraldine Olivo, Zita Naggy, and Megan Young.

To all the readers of *Golubka*, for your devotion, comments, ideas, and support.

INDEX

ABOUT THE PHOTOGRAPHER

Masha Davydova, Anya Kassoff's older daughter, grew up sampling her mother's homemade delicacies. Recognizing Anya's unique culinary style, Masha encouraged her to start *Golubka* and has taken on the role of self-taught food photographer and art director for her mother's blog. Masha is a graduate of the Rhode Island School of Design and lives in New York City.

ABOUT THE AUTHOR

Anya Kassoff was born in Russia and grew up in a family of passionate home cooks. While following several career paths, one passion remained steady: she ended every day in the kitchen, perfecting her cooking intuition and gaining strong interest in holistic, whole foods–focused recipes. In 2010 Anya started sharing her healthy culinary discoveries on her blog, *Golubka*, which has since gained a worldwide following. Her recipes have appeared on Oprah .com and in the Life & Style section of the Guardian.com. *Golubka* has been a finalist for *Saveur* magazine's Best Food Blog awards and was cited by *Bon Appétit* magazine as one of the best vegan and gluten-free blogs. Anya lives in St. Petersburg, Florida, with her husband and younger daughter.

Visit her at golubkakitchen.com.